OLD APOLOGETICS FOR A NEW AGE

Volume Two:

THE INSPIRATION OF THE BIBLE

MARK TABATA
(Evangelist)

Charleston, AR:
COBB PUBLISHING
2023

All Scripture references (unless otherwise noted) are from the New King James Version (NKJV).

Published in the United States of America by

Cobb Publishing
www.CobbPublishing.com
Editor@CobbPublishing.com
479.747.8372

ISBN: 978-1-960858-07-8

TABLE OF CONTENTS

This is book two in the series on the subject of "Old Apologetics For A New Age." I welcome you to our study and discussion, and am thankful that you have taken an interest in this subject.

As a Gospel preacher and evangelist in the great state of Kentucky, I am blessed to work with people from a variety of backgrounds (atheist, agnostic, pagan, Satanist, Druid, Catholic, Protestant, Muslim, Pentecostal, etc.). One of the reasons I am thankful to be in this area is because I am charged with the defense of the Gospel of Jesus (Philippians 1:17). As a minister with the Couchtown church of Christ, I am entrusted with the charge to preach the truth of God in love (Ephesians 4:15). What you will find in the church of Christ is a group of redeemed but imperfect and struggling sinners, following Jesus and His Word to the best of our ability.

The first book in this series was about some of the evidences which document there is an eternal God Who created the universe, and that the God Who has revealed Himself in nature is identical with the God described in the Bible. This book follows up on that subject by examining some of the evidences which show the Bible is the inspired Word of God, as it claims to be (2 Timothy 3:16-17).[1]

Now, in this book (like in the last one of this series), I will be recounting conversations I have had with people spanning twenty years of ministry. However, I will change names and details to honor anonymity. I believe you will find in these conversations people you can identify with. Please consider these things carefully! Not only will they help strengthen your faith in God's Word, but will help you reach out and share this faith with others as well (1 Peter 3:15; Colossians 4:5-6).

Father God,

I thank You for the one who is reading this book. Please bless him or her and help them as they study and consider these things. Heal their spirit and let them see Your love and grace through Your Word. We praise You and thank You!

In the name of Jesus we pray,

Amen.

CHAPTER ONE:
THE SUPERNATURAL UNITY OF THE BIBLE AS EVIDENCE OF ITS DIVINE INSPIRATION

His name was Jeffrey.

Jeffrey had moved from a large city to a small town and had decided to become a monk in a local pagan monestary. He had been a student of several religions throughout his life, and was still trying to decide about a path to follow. Sadly, his exposure to Christianity had been nominal. His parents were lapsed Catholics, and he had not found much within Catholicism to satisfy his soul's yearning (or his mind's questions and objections).

I was on vacation. Being single, I did not often go on vacation. Jeffrey and I had an instant connection, and we sat at a picnic table and talked about matters of truth carefully.

Jeffrey: Mark, I like you—but I don't see a lot about Jesus that makes me want to follow Him.

Mark: Jeff, I really like you too, buddy. And your honesty is refreshing! Tell me, is there anything in particular about Jesus that offends you?

Jeffrey: Well, I don't like any religion that says we should accept truth on blind faith.

Mark: Me neither.

Jeffrey: Then why are you a Christian?

Mark: Jeff, I am a Christian because Christianity is the only religion which honors the Law of Rationality.

Jeffrey: What's the Law of Rationality?

Mark: It's a law which states we should only accept those conclusions which are warranted by the evidence. Jeff, Christianity is
the only religion which does this! The Apostle Paul said the words
of Christianity are words of truth and reason (Acts 26:25). The fact
is, it is the other religions which demand blind faith: Christianity
is the only one which provides proof that its claims are true.

Jeffrey: Man, I hadn't heard that before. I thought the Bible
teaches we aren't supposed to think and ask questions.

At that point, Jeff and I had a thorough discussion about one of
the strongest evidences that the Bible is the Word of God: the supernatural unity of the Bible.

The Rationality of Christianity

Jeffrey and I spoke about the Law of Rationality.

Christianity is the only religion which truly honors the law of
rationality. This basic and irrefutable principle simply points out
we should only draw conclusions which are warranted by the evidence; or, stated another way, we must justify our conclusions with
adequate evidence. Of all the religions, Christianity is unique in
honoring this law.

> *Acts 26:25—But he said, "I am not mad, most*
> *noble Festus, but speak the words of truth and*
> *reason.*

The words "truth and reason" suggest the idea of logic and rationality.[2]

> "Paul has not lost his mind but speaks "true and prudent
> words" (ἀληθείας καὶ σωφροσύνης ῥήματα , alētheias kai
> sōphrosynēs rhēmata), or "the sober truth." The combina-
> tion of "true" and "prudent" is common in Greek, as is a
> contrast between "prudent" and "mad" (Lucian, Timon 55;
> Xenophon, Memorabilia 1.1.16; P.Oxy. 1.33; Plato, Phae-
> drus 244D; Barrett 1998: 1168). In this context, where Paul
> has been accused of being crazy, his reply is that his words
> are truth. He has not lost control of his thoughts; they are

quite sober and thought through. "The metaphor of things not being done in a corner refers to no hidden events tucked away somewhere in the corner out of public sight (BAGD 168; BDAG 209; Malherbe 1985–86; Epictetus, Discourses 2.12.17; Plutarch, Moralia 777B; Fitzmyer 1998: 764). The idiom means not doing one's philosophical reflection in a way that is disengaged from the public. Paul can speak boldly and say that these events were public enough that anyone paying attention could appreciate them. Paul asks the king if he believes the prophets, who declare that such things are possible and a part of God's plan. The issue Paul wants to focus on is God's teaching as set forth in the prophets. "Paul is a model witness and evangelist here. Agrippa is capable of understanding and appreciating what Paul claims (Acts 26:2–3)." (Darrell L. Bock, Acts: Baker Exegetical Commentary On The New Testament,17597-17611 (Kindle Edition); Grand Rapids, Michigan; Baker Academic)

In this series of lessons, we will investigate some of the evidences which demonstrate that the Bible is the Word of God. We will proceed with a simple argument demonstrating that the Bible is the Word of God.

Our Argument

1. If the Bible contains traits which may only be explained by Divine inspiration, then the Bible is the Word of God.
2. 2. The Bible contains traits which may only be explained by Divine inspiration.
3. 3. Therefore, the Bible is the Word of God. Please notice that this argument is set forth in valid format; as such, if the propositions are proven to be sound, then the truthfulness of the conclusion MUST follow.

Understanding the Circumstances of the Bible's Writing

The Psalmist wrote:

> Psalm *119:105—Your word is a lamp to my feet And a light to my path.*

One evidence that the Bible is the Word of God comes from its supernatural unity.

To understand what we are talking about clearly when we study the supernatural unity of the Bible, we must understand the various circumstances of the formation of the Bible. The Bible is actually a Book of 66 Books. It was written by forty different men over a period of some sixteen hundred years. It was written in three languages (Hebrew, Greek, and parts in Aramaic), and its writers lived during different eras of history. Some lived in times of peace and prosperity; some in times of war and despair. Some lived under monarchies, enjoying freedom as citizens of the kingdoms of Israel and Judah; some lived as captives to various nations (Egypt, Assyria, Babylon, Persia, and Rome). Some received no formal education, while some were scholars; some were fishermen, and some stood as advisors to kings. Some lived during times of famine, others during times of abundance. Some were poor, some were rich; some were married, and some were single. Some lived during times when the people were faithful to God, and others during times of great national apostasy.

You would think that when you join these Books together, they would be one huge mass of contradictions that would make no sense whatsoever. However, what you find instead is that these Books go together and manifest a unity of thought, theme, and character that may only be explained by Divine inspiration! This supernatural unity is manifested from the beginning of Genesis all the way to the end of Revelation.

Now, we are not saying that because a book manifests unity, that it must be supernatural. Not at all! If that were the case, then many Steven King books could be called "inspired." No, what we are saying is that the unity found in the Bible, despite its many diverse characteristics of formation, may only rightly be explained by a Guiding Hand that was involved in its creation and completion.

Illustrations of the Supernatural Unity of the Bible

Over the years, there have been many illustrations to demonstrate this supernatural unity of the Bible. Examples include noticing the diverse background of the Bible writers, [3] and others compare it to amazing illustrations of archery and artwork.[4]

"Man Appointed To Mortal Sorrow But The Blessed God Shall Come Down Teaching (And) His Death Shall Bring The Broken-Hearted Peace"

I was preaching and teaching at a drug rehab. One thing that I have learned about addicts: these folks are warriors! Quite often, they have seen the worst of life. Some are blessed to have family and friends that love them, yet many come from a background of abuse and suffering. As a result, from a young age they learn to begin asking questions as they look for hope and try to make sense out of their suffering.

On this day, I had written ten words on the board and told them that within these words was a Message that could change their lives. The words were: Adam, Seth, Enosh, Cainan, Mahalalel, Jared, Enoch, Methuselah, Lamech, and Noah. These were the names of the men listened in Genesis 5 from Adam to Noah. (One of Moses' purposes' in writing Genesis was to document the Bloodline through whom the Messiah of God would eventually arrive.)

I asked them what they thought about these names, and we spent a good deal of time considering. Then, I showed them the meaning of these names in Hebrew.

Check it out: [5]

The Patriarchs Of Genesis 5

Name	Meaning
Adam	Man
Seth	Appointed
Enosh	Mortal
Cainan	Sorrow
Mahalalel	The Blessed God
Jared	Shall Come Down
Enoch	Teaching
Methuselah	His Death Shall Bring
Lamech	The Broken-hearted
Noah	Peace

"Man Is Appointed To Mortal Sorrow (But)
The Blessed God Shall Come Down Teaching
And His Death Will Bring The Broken-hearted
Peace"

We see here, my friends, the Gospel of Jesus Christ, "hidden in plain sight" in the names of these men. The grand theme of the entire Bible is Jesus Christ. [6] This was written at least fifteen hundred years before Jesus Christ was born!

What About Contradictions?

Many object to the Bible, claiming that there are contradictions within it which show that it is not the Word of God. Indeed, I would say in my experience, this is one of the most often heard charges against the Bible.

Many do not realize what a contradiction actually is.[7] A contradiction is more than just a difficulty. A contradiction involves a conflict between two (or more) passages of Scripture which are unresolvable. As such, the Bible apologist needs only to show that the passages which form the alleged contradiction may actually be harmonized. When that is accomplished, the alleged contradiction vanishes.[8] Because people do not understand the difference between a difficulty and a contradiction, they are unaware that true contradictions within the Bible text have not been found. [9]

Unintentional Witness Corroboration

Jay Warner Wallace was a committed atheist who investigated cold-case homicides as a Los Angeles detective. He had, like many people, been taught that the Bible isn't real and that there are contradictions in the text. However, he quickly learned that in fact many of the alleged contradictions are actually examples of something called "unintentional witness corroboration" which logically explain many of the alleged contradictions. [10]

Following is a chart based upon some examples of unintentional eyewitness corroboration. Notice how questions raised by one text of Scripture are answered by the observations or statements of another text of Scripture, both written from different points of view. This again argues for the authenticity and veracity of the Bible text. Others through the years have also noted how alleged discrepancies in the Bible are cleared away by further study.[11]

Puzzling Passage	Questions Raised by the Text	Unintentional Witness Corroboration Text	Answer Provided To Questions
Matthew 8:16	Why wait till evening to bring sick people to Jesus?	Mark 1:21; Luke 4:31	Because it was the Sabbath.
Matthew 14:1-2	Why did Herod tell many of his servants that he believed Jesus was John the Baptist raised from the dead?	Luke 8:3; Acts 13:1	Many of Jesus' followers were from Herod's household.
Luke 23:1-4	Why couldn't Pilate find a charge against Jesus, even though He claimed to be King?	John 18:33-38	Jesus told Pilate that His kingdom was not of this world.
Matthew 4:18-22	Why would Peter and Andrew and James and John drop everything to follow Jesus just because He said "follow Me?"	Luke 5:1-11	The Apostles witnessed the miracle of the fish (which also explains why James and John were "mending (fixing/repairing) their news" in Matthew's account.

Matthew 26:67-68	Why would the men who were hitting Jesus say, "Who hit You?" They were standing right in front of Him! Why would that be called "prophesying?"	Luke 22:63-65	Luke provides the detail that Jesus was blindfolded while He was being punched.
Matthew 26:71	Why did the maid notice Peter?	John 18:16	John pointed out Peter to her.
Mark 15:43	Why did Mark say that Joseph of Arimathea acted boldly?	John 19:38	Joseph was secretly a believer in Jesus.
Mark 6:30-44	Why was there a crowd gathered together before Jesus and the Apostles arrived?	John 6:1-13	Because they had heard of Jesus' miracles, and it was Passover
John 6:1-13	Why did Jesus single out Philip and Andrew?	Luke 9:10-17 & John 1:44	They are both from Bethesda.

Keys to Deal with Alleged Contradictions

Key # 1: Language

The Bible was originally written in three languages: Hebrew, Aramaic, and Greek.

Often alleged contradictions are cleared up by studying the original languages of the Bible.

Wine Or No Wine?

Many claim that the Bible contradicts itself because it teaches that Christians should abstain from alcohol and other intoxicating substances (Proverbs 23:29-35; Titus 2:11-14; Ephesians 5:18). Yet we are also told that Jesus Himself made wine from water at the wedding feast (John 2:1-11)! How could Jesus make alcoholic wine when the Bible clearly indicated that such was condemned by God?

The answer, of course, lies in realizing that the word "wine" in the Bible often had reference to simple grape-juice and not fermented drink. For example:

> *Isaiah 16:10—Gladness is taken away, And joy from the plentiful field; In the vineyards there will be no singing, Nor will there be shouting; No treaders will tread out wine in the presses; I have made their shouting cease.*

> *Isaiah 65:8—Thus says the LORD: "As the new wine is found in the cluster, And one says, 'Do not destroy it, For a blessing is in it,' So will I do for My servants' sake, That I may not destroy them all.*

> *Jeremiah 40:10—As for me, I will indeed dwell at Mizpah and serve the Chaldeans who come to us. But you, gather wine and summer fruit and oil, put them in your vessels, and dwell in your cities that you have taken."*

*Jeremiah 48:33—Joy and gladness are taken
From the plentiful field and from the land of
Moab; I have caused wine to fail from the
winepresses; No one will tread with joyous
shouting—Not joyous shouting!*

Even more revealing is the fact that there were several words in the Hebrew and Greek which are translated by our English word "wine." These words can have reference to either fermented or unfermented wine, depending on the context in which the word is found.[12]

Saved By Works Or Not?

Consider another example of how studying the original languages of the Bible can clear up alleged contradictions, regarding the subject of faith and works.

Repeatedly we are told in the Bible that we are not saved by faith and not by works (Ephesians 2:8-9; Titus 3:3-8; Romans 4:1-4), yet a host of other Scripture make it clear that we are saved by faith and by works (Matthew 7:21-23; Luke 6:46; Acts 10:34-35; Romans 1:5; 2:3-12; James 2:14-26; Hebrews 5:8-9).

So, which is it? Are we saved by faith, or by works?

Is there a contradiction here?

Not at all!

When we go back and study the original languages of the Bible, we quickly learn that the entire concept of "belief" and "faith" in Scripture carried the idea of obedience.

We are saved by works of faith, but not by works of merit. Studying the original languages of the Bible helps us to understand this.

Did They Hear Or Not?

Finally, consider one final example of how studying the original languages of the Bible can help to dismantle supposed Bible contradictions, i.e., in the conversion of Saul of Tarsus.

In one account of his conversion, we are told:

> *Acts 9:7—And the men who journeyed with him stood speechless, hearing a voice but seeing no one.*

Yet later we are told:

> *Acts 22:9-9—"And those who were with me indeed saw the light and were afraid, but they did not hear the voice of Him who spoke to me.*

How can the people who were with Saul have "heard" and yet "not heard" the voice that spoke to him?

The answer lies in studying the original languages of the Bible. The text in Acts 22:9 has the men hearing a sound but not understanding what it was communicating. They "heard" in one sense, but not in another (i.e., they did not understand what they were hearing).[13]

Key # 2: Look At The Timeframe
Another important key in studying alleged Bible contradictions is in keeping the timeframes of different passages in mind.

Staff Or No Staff?
For example, one alleged contradiction that is often hinted at is found in Jesus' instructions to His disciples regarding the Limited Commission. In Mark 6:8, we are told that Jesus tells His disciples to take nothing for their journey, except for a staff; yet in the parallel account in Matthew 10:9-10, we see Jesus telling His disciples not to "provide" a staff for themselves.

Is there a contradiction?

Not at all.

Jesus' meaning is very simply that the disciples are to take a staff if they have one with them; but that they are not to procure another one in the future. Instead, they are to trust completely in God to provide for their needs. The text is speaking of events from two different time-frames.

Another good example in this regard comes from the fact that when Cain was banished from his home after slaying his brother Abel, we are told that he went to the land of Nod and married a woman (Genesis 4:16). Many claim that this must be a contradiction, since the Bible records that the only people present were Adam, Eve, and Cain and Abel.

However, the Bible tells us quite differently, and answers this alleged contradiction:

> *Genesis 4:3—And in the process of time it came to pass that Cain brought an offering of the fruit of the ground to the LORD.*

Notice that phrase "in the process of time." Moses is honing in on the fact that there has been a great deal of time to elapse between the Fall in the Garden and the time of these events. As a result, there were no doubt many people living in the world by the time that Cain went to Nod!

Remembering the timeframe of passages is an important key in overcoming alleged Bible contradictions.

Key # 3: Remember The Context Of The Passage

What Time Was Christ Crucified?

One Gospel writer tells us that Christ was crucified at the third hour of the day, another at the sixth hour:

> *Mark 15:25—Now it was the third hour, and they crucified Him.*

> *John 19:14—Now it was the Preparation Day of the Passover, and about the sixth hour. And he said to the Jews, "Behold your King!"*

Is this a contradiction?

Not at all.

When we realize that Mark and John are referencing two different cultural ways of reckoning time, the difficulty is cleared up.

Basically, John is following the Roman method of telling time while Mark is using the Jewish system.[14]

All Women Have To Wear Veils?

Consider another example. Many people proclaim that Christian women are obligated by God to wear veils in the church assembly, based on what the Apostle Paul wrote in 1 Corinthians 11:1-16. Yet studying the language of this passage, and the cultural background of it, we see that Paul was dealing with a local phenomenon involving the church at Corinth. The languages of the passage makes this clear.[15] The cultural situation in Corinth was such that the women in the church needed to wear their veils, lest they be identified in that city as the temple prostitutes (who advertised their sexual services by removing their veils).[16]

Understanding the cultural context of a passage can certainly help in establishing the overall unity of Scripture.

Key # 4: Consider Whether A Passage Is Using Figurative Or Literal Language

A vast majority of Bible contradictions are suggested based on the failure of some to remember that the Bible uses both figurative and literal language.[17]

Do People See God?

Some have suggested that the Bible contradicts itself in regards to whether or not people can actually see God. For example, we are told that man absolutely cannot see God:

> *Exodus 33:20—But He said, "You cannot see My face; for no man shall see Me, and live."*

> *John 1:18—No one has seen God at any time. The only begotten Son, who is in the bosom of the Father, He has declared Him.*

Yet we are then told that some in the Bible saw God:

Genesis 32:30—So Jacob called the name of the place Peniel: "For I have seen God face to face, and my life is preserved."

Exodus 3:1-6—Now Moses was tending the flock of Jethro his father-in-law, the priest of Midian. And he led the flock to the back of the desert, and came to Horeb, the mountain of God. And the Angel of the LORD appeared to him in a flame of fire from the midst of a bush. So he looked, and behold, the bush was burning with fire, but the bush was not consumed. Then Moses said, "I will now turn aside and see this great sight, why the bush does not burn." So when the LORD saw that he turned aside to look, God called to him from the midst of the bush and said, "Moses, Moses!" And he said, "Here I am." Then He said, "Do not draw near this place. Take your sandals off your feet, for the place where you stand is holy ground." Moreover He said, "I am the God of your father—the God of Abraham, the God of Isaac, and the God of Jacob." And Moses hid his face, for he was afraid to look upon God.

Exodus 33:11—So the LORD spoke to Moses face to face, as a man speaks to his friend. And he would return to the camp, but his servant Joshua the son of Nun, a young man, did not depart from the tabernacle.

Many would claim that these are contradictions; yet a study of the context of these passages reveals that when man "saw" God, he was not looking upon Him directly, but in a figurative sense.

Again, in the story of Jacob wrestling with God, we are assured that figurative language is in play, for the text identifies "God" as a "man" (Genesis 32:24). Further, the Prophet Hosea identifies this as being an encounter with an 'angel' of the Lord

*Hosea 12:3-5—He took his brother by the heel
in the womb, And in his strength he struggled
with God. Yes, he struggled with the Angel and
prevailed; He wept, and sought favor from
Him. He found Him in Bethel, And there He
spoke to us—That is, the LORD God of hosts.
The LORD is His memorable name.*

In the same way, did Moses actually "see" God in Exodus 3? The text itself shows that he did not LITERALLY see God, but instead saw a burning bush (Exodus 3:2). This was an example of a theophany-God appearing in another form to His people.

What of the fact that Moses spoke to God "face to face," as friends speak? The text itself shows that this was not Moses and God LITERALLY speaking face to face, for observe:

*Exodus 33:20—But He said, "You cannot see
My face; for no man shall see Me, and live."*

The very text that tells us of God and Moses speaking 'face to face' makes it clear that this was not a literal example of Moses seeing God! The phrase "speaking face to face" carried with it the idea of an intimate relationship or friendship.[18]

The Testimony of a Lifelong Student
of Alleged Bible Contradictions

Gleason Archer spent his entire career studying alleged discrepancies within the Bible text.

What did Archer learn about these alleged contradictions in the Bible?

"As I have dealt with one apparent discrepancy after another and have studied the alleged contradictions between the biblical record and the evidence of linguistics, archaeology, or science, my confidence in the trustworthiness of Scripture has been repeatedly verified and strengthened by the discovery that almost every problem in Scripture that has ever been discovered by man, from ancient times until now, has been dealt with in a completely satisfactory manner by the biblical text itself—or else by objective archaeological information. The deductions that may be validly drawn from ancient Egyptian, Sumerian, or Akkadian documents all harmonize with the biblical record; and no properly trained evangelical scholar has anything to fear from the hostile arguments and challenges of humanistic rationalists or detractors of any and every persuasion. There is a good and sufficient answer in Scripture itself to refute every charge that has ever been leveled against it. But this is only to be expected from the kind of book the Bible asserts itself to be, the inscripturation of the infallible, inerrant Word of the Living God." (Gleason L. Archer Jr., New International Encyclopedia of Bible Difficulties, 15 (Kindle Edition); Grand Rapids, Michigan; Zondervan)

Conclusion

There are no contradictions in the Bible, which is an amazing aspect of its supernatural unity.

"To what can one attribute this unity running through the whole Bible: unity of vision, structure, message and doctrine-in spite of the long centuries and the many individuals used as instruments for its completion? To this question there can be only one answer: in reality, Scripture has but one Author, the Holy Spirit. To Him, it is but one revelation, since he speaks throughout of the only true and proper Object of worship. There is just one salvation: announced, then effected and consummated by one only Saviour. Human nature is the same through all the ages: its needs, weaknesses and potential will always require this same divine communication. For the ever-living, omniscient God, time is as one instant; in other words, eternity means an eternal present, from the first page of Scripture to the last. Finally, truth itself is "one" and could never be contradictory." (Rene Pasche, *The Inspiration And Authority Of*

Scripture, transcribed by Helen I. Needham, 117; Chicago: Moody Press)

The grace of The Lord Jesus Christ, and the love of God, and the communion of the Holy Spirit be with you all. Amen.

CHAPTER TWO:

PROPHECY AND FULFILLMENT AS PROOF OF THE DIVINE INSPIRATION OF THE BIBLE

Sarah and Jared were both practicing witches

She worshipped the gods of Greece, and he worshipped the gods of Hinduism (although I am not certain which ones). .

They were a kind-hearted couple, and we had some amazing Bible studies. One day, while we were studying, they were telling me about their gods.

Sarah: As a Christian, why do you believe in the Bible?

Mark: That is a great question. Before I answer let me ask you: what do you believe about the Bible?

Jared: The Bible is a propaganda puff piece. It was put out by the Catholic Church to con Christians into believing their (exploitive) about Jesus Christ. Sarah and I spent a lot of time researching this. All the information is there for anyone on YouTube.

Mark: I see! Thanks for letting me know that. Now, here is where I am: I believe the Bible is the Word of God because the evidence backs up that claim.

Sarah and Jared: (Laughing).

Mark: (Smiling)

Sarah: You know Mark, my gods are powerful. I don't mean to be rude, but Jesus Christ was a crucified dog.

Mark: I respect your opinion on that my friend. But let me ask you: how powerful are your gods?

Sarah: VERY powerful.

Mark: Powerful enough to prophesy the future?

Sarah: (Silence).

Mark: If your gods really are Divine, then surely they can prophesy the future, right?

Sarah: Well they can.

Mark: Great! Then I am sure you can show me an example of how they can show the future.

Jared: Actually, we can't. That isn't something our gods do.

Mark: Well, that's interesting. (Laying my Bible on the table). My God...CAN!

One of the greatest evidences that the Bible is the Word of God is through the proof of prophecy and fulfillment.

In this study, we will learn how the evidence from prophecy and fulfillment constitutes further proof that the Bible is the inspired Word of God.

Let's Talk Prophecy

What exactly is prophecy?

The main idea behind the word family of "prophet" is "one who speaks on behalf of another."

> *Exodus 7:1—So the LORD said to Moses: "See, I have made you as God to Pharaoh, and Aaron your brother shall be your prophet.*

Thus the Prophet of God was primarily one who spoke the Word of God to others[19]. This was done by inspiration of the Holy Spirit.

2 Peter 1:20-21-knowing this first, that no prophecy of Scripture is of any private interpretation, **21** for prophecy never came by the will of man, but holy men of God spoke *as they were* moved by the Holy Spirit.

The text here teaches us that God's Spirit so worked on the writers of Scripture that they wrote down words that her their origin with God.[20]

Sometimes God would grant the Prophets detailed knowledge of future events as proof that the Prophets were truly speaking His Word.

We need to remember that there are qualifications for true prophecy that need to be met.[21] The Bible Prophets spoke as they were moved by the Holy Spirit (cf. 2 Peter 1:20-21). In contrast, the "prophets" of the pagans often couched their messages in the jargon of bizarre and easily questionable language. Indeed, they often practiced glossolalia (speaking in gibberish) which is so commonplace in today's religious world.[22] Some researchers have noticed how this aspect of paganism eventually made its way into Christendom via the Pentecostal movement.[23] In fact, the glossolalia of paganism is virtually identical to that of Pentecostalism, which should be very concerning to professing disciples of Christ today. The Bible gift of tongues was the ability to speak fluently in the language of another nation which the speaker had not previously studied (cf. Acts 2:4-13; 1 Corinthians 14:21).

I learned this lesson in a very personal way in jail ministry. A young man who identified as a Satanist and who was afflicted by demons became visibly upset as I spoke to him about Jesus. At one point, he put his hand on my head and began to speak over me in an unintelligible gibberish as is practiced in modern day charismatic churches. When I inquired what he was doing, he explained that he was summoning his demons to come and kill me!

Jesus has my back.

However, let me note: it is concerning that what is often practiced in these churches and mistakenly referred to as the work of the Holy Spirit is identical to what has been practiced by pagans and Satanists for centuries.

Furthermore, the pagan "prophets" would often make use of drugs in order to induce hallucinations for both themselves and those who came to them for answers.[24] Archaeological excavations from Delphi especially have highlighted this aspect of the prophets of ancient paganism.[25] This was a widespread practice among many of the older civilizations of the world.[26] In contrast to this, the Prophets of God spoke by inspiration (2 Timothy 3:16-17). They were not to allow their minds to be intoxicated (Isaiah 28:7; 56:10-12; Micah 2:11).

Nostradamus:
Powerful Example of Pagan "Prophecy"

Michel de Nostredame (i.e., Nostradamus) lived between 1503-1566. He is well known and remembered for being a psychic and astrologer (and many hail him as a "prophet"). Born to Jewish-Christian parents, Nostradamus eventually turned to paganism. He would record his "prophecies" in a form of writing known as "quatrains."

I still remember a Bible study that I had with Jessica as we discussed true versus false prophecy. She had been raised in a pagan home which espoused a great deal of belief in the writings of Nostradamus. She was quite surprised to learn that many of his alleged prophecies were so vague that they did not really constitute prophecy, and even the ones which she had comes to believe were specific (such as his famous "hister" prophecy) had been so distorted that they did not stand the test of scrutiny when carefully examined.[27] Add to this the fact that many of Nostradamus' "prophecies" were vague and easily open to various interpretations and we begin to realize that he was not a true Proophet.[28] Furthermore, Nostradamus used occult methods for deriving his knowledge..[29] There is also considerable evidence from his writings that he was demonically afflicted and possessed.[30] Factors such as this need to be carefully considered when examining Nostradamus, and these things remind us of the need to consider criteria for valid prophecy.

Looking at Criteria
for Valid Bible Prophecy

Deuteronomy 18:21-22—And if you say in your heart, 'How shall we know the word which the LORD has not spoken?'—when a prophet speaks in the name of the LORD, if the thing does not happen or come to pass, that IS the thing which the LORD has not spoken; the prophet has spoken it presumptuously; you shall not be afraid of him.

Here are some general guidelines for genuine prophecy.

First, valid prophecy generally needs to be specific in language. This is, of course, unless the prophecy is conditional. For example, the Prophet Jonah told the people of Nineveh that they would be destroyed:

Jonah 3:4—And Jonah began to enter the city on the first day's walk. Then he cried out and said, "Yet forty days, and Nineveh shall be overthrown!"

However, the people repented of their sins and so God relented concerning His judgment:

Jonah 3:10—Then God saw their works, that they turned from their evil way; and God relented from the disaster that He had said He would bring upon them, and He did not do it.

Earlier in the Book of Jeremiah, God promised that He would relent of His judgments against nations if they repented and turned to Him:

Jeremiah 18:7-10—The instant I speak concerning a nation and concerning a kingdom, to pluck up, to pull down, and to destroy IT, if that nation against whom I have spoken turns from

> *its evil, I will relent of the disaster that I*
> *thought to bring upon it. And the instant I*
> *speak concerning a nation and concerning a*
> *kingdom, to build and to plant it, if it does evil*
> *in My sight so that it does not obey My voice,*
> *then I will relent concerning the good with*
> *which I said I would benefit it.*

Furthermore, we must remember that sometimes prophecies may appear vague but later are seen to foreshadow very specific events. We are speaking here of types and antitypes.[31] Examples of this type of prophecy will be examined in detail further in this section.

Second, the details need to be beyond the ability of a person to "guess" from everyday events.

Third, the prophecy needs to be shown to have been in advance of the actual event prophesied. It is important to demonstrate that the Bible Prophets actually foretold the future before the events happened, and not that they recorded history after the events had occurred! Fortunately (as we will see) the evidence for the Bible prophecies being written well in advance of their fulfillment is considerable and demonstrated in numerous ways (especially through the findings of archaeology like in the case of the Dead Sea Scrolls).[32]

When valid prophecy is truly demonstrated, it provides powerful and undeniable evidence that the Bible truly is the Word of God, that Yahweh is the one true God, and that Jesus Christ is the Son of God.

We see some good examples in Scripture of this principle at work.

Consider:

> *Isaiah 41:21-24— "Present your case," says*
> *the LORD. "Bring forth your strong reasons,"*
> *says the King of Jacob. "Let them bring forth*
> *and show us what will happen; Let them show*
> *the former things, what they were, That we may*

consider them, And know the latter end of them; Or declare to us things to come. Show the things that are to come hereafter, That we may know that you are gods; Yes, do good or do evil, That we may be dismayed and see it together. Indeed you are nothing, And your work is nothing; He who chooses you is an abomination.

Isaiah 42:9—Behold, the former things have come to pass, And new things I declare; Before they spring forth I tell you of them."

Isaiah 44:6-7— "Thus says the LORD, the King of Israel, And his Redeemer, the LORD of hosts: 'I am the First and I am the Last; Besides Me there is no God. And who can proclaim as I do? Then let him declare it and set it in order for Me, Since I appointed the ancient people. And the things that are coming and shall come, Let them show these to them.

In these passages, God calls upon the pagan gods to demonstrate that they are truly Divine by demonstrating prophecy of the future. They are unable to do so! Yet Yahweh IS able to demonstrate the future accurately, providing undeniable proof that He is the true God.

Again, consider this example from Jeremiah the Prophet:

Jeremiah 32:6-8—And Jeremiah said, "The word of the LORD came to me, saying, 'Behold, Hanamel the son of Shallum your uncle will come to you, saying, "Buy my field which is in Anathoth, for the right of redemption is yours to buy it." ' Then Hanamel my uncle's son came to me in the court of the prison according to the word of the LORD, and said to me, 'Please buy my field that is in Anathoth, which is in the

> *country of Benjamin; for the right of inher-*
> *itance IS yours, and the redemption yours; buy*
> *IT for yourself.' Then I knew that this was the*
> *word of the LORD.*

Notice that Jeremiah was told of a specific incident which would occur. It was random enough that Jeremiah could not have "predicted" such, and yet it was specific enough that its fulfillment was proof positive that the prophecy came from the Lord.[33]

Later, Jesus told His disciples:

> *John 14:29—And now I have told you before it*
> *comes, that when it does come to pass, you may*
> *believe.*

Let's notice some examples of Bible prophecy and then move on to investigate some very specific Messianic prophecies.

Daniel's Prophecy of God's Kingdom

The Book of Daniel contains some truly amazing prophecies. Because of the specificity of the prophecies and their fulfillment, many have tried to claim that the Book of Daniel was written after the events happened. However, their objections have been ably met and both linguistic[34] and archaeological[35] evidence from a wide field of sources confirm that this Book was indeed written by the Prophet Daniel some five to six hundred years before the time of Christ (and hence long before the prophecies therein were fulfilled).

In the second chapter of the Book of Daniel, we read an amazing prophecy of the kingdom that God would establish:

> *Daniel 2:36-44—This is the dream. Now we*
> *will tell the interpretation of it before the king.*
> *You, O king, are a king of kings. For the God of*
> *heaven has given you a kingdom, power,*
> *strength, and glory; and wherever the children*
> *of men dwell, or the beasts of the field and the*
> *birds of the heaven, He has given them into*

your hand, and has made you ruler over them all—you are this head of gold. But after you shall arise another kingdom inferior to yours; then another, a third kingdom of bronze, which shall rule over all the earth. And the fourth kingdom shall be as strong as iron, inasmuch as iron breaks in pieces and shatters everything; and like iron that crushes, that kingdom will break in pieces and crush all the others. Whereas you saw the feet and toes, partly of potter's clay and partly of iron, the kingdom shall be divided; yet the strength of the iron shall be in it, just as you saw the iron mixed with ceramic clay. And as the toes of the feet were partly of iron and partly of clay, so the kingdom shall be partly strong and partly fragile. As you saw iron mixed with ceramic clay, they will mingle with the seed of men; but they will not adhere to one another, just as iron does not mix with clay. And in the days of these kings the God of heaven will set up a kingdom which shall never be destroyed; and the kingdom shall not be left to other people; it shall break in pieces and consume all these kingdoms, and it shall stand forever.

Daniel is told that the dream of king Nebuchadnezzar represented four great world empires which would arise (the first one being Babylon itself, represented by Nebuchadnezzar, according to Daniel 2:37). Three kingdoms would follow, each weaker than Babylon itself yet they would be able to take dominance one after the other. History reveals that these kingdoms arose, just as the Prophet declared would happen. The four kingdoms are: Babylon, the Medes-Persians, Greece, and finally Rome.

It is was during the days of the Roman Empire that Jesus promised to establish the kingdom of God.

During the lifetime of Jesus, the Roman Empire was the dominant power in the world. Jesus Christ declared:

> *Mark 9:1—And He said to them, "Assuredly, I say to you that there are some standing here who will not taste death till they see the kingdom of God present with power."*

Jesus established the kingdom of God, just as it was prophesied that He would. He identifies the kingdom for us in His conversation with His Apostles:

> *Matthew 16:18-19—And I also say to you that you are Peter, and on this rock I will build My church, and the gates of Hades shall not prevail against it. And I will give you the keys of the kingdom of heaven, and whatever you bind on earth will be bound in heaven, and whatever you loose on earth will be loosed in heaven."*

Jesus uses the phrase "kingdom of Heaven" interchangeably with the church. The reason why is because the kingdoms IS the church. Many believe that the kingdom was not established. This is because they believe that the kingdom of God would be an earthly political kingdom with a military power. This was actually a teaching of Judaism which some heretics in the early church embraced, but which was soundly refuted.[36] however, the Scripture is clear that it was. When Paul wrote Colossians, he identifies the brethren there as being in the kingdom:

> *Colossians 1:13—He has delivered us from the power of darkness and conveyed us into the kingdom of the Son of His love,*

When the Apostle John wrote his Book of Revelation, he identified the Christians as already being in the kingdom of God as well:

> *Revelation 1:9—I, John, both your brother and companion in the tribulation and kingdom and*

patience of Jesus Christ, was on the island that is called Patmos for the word of God and for the testimony of Jesus Christ.

Daniel the Prophet foretold the establishing of God's kingdom, at the time that he said it would be established.

The "Little Horn" Prophecy

In Daniel chapter seven, we read another remarkable prophecy that Daniel makes:

Daniel 7:1-8—In the first year of Belshazzar king of Babylon, Daniel had a dream and visions of his head while on his bed. Then he wrote down the dream, telling the main facts. Daniel spoke, saying, "I saw in my vision by night, and behold, the four winds of heaven were stirring up the Great Sea. And four great beasts came up from the sea, each different from the other. The first was like a lion, and had eagle's wings. I watched till its wings were plucked off; and it was lifted up from the earth and made to stand on two feet like a man, and a man's heart was given to it. "And suddenly another beast, a second, like a bear. It was raised up on one side, and had three ribs in its mouth between its teeth. And they said thus to it: 'Arise, devour much flesh!' "After this I looked, and there was another, like a leopard, which had on its back four wings of a bird. The beast also had four heads, and dominion was given to it. "After this I saw in the night visions, and behold, a fourth beast, dreadful and terrible, exceedingly strong. It had huge iron teeth; it was devouring, breaking in pieces, and trampling the residue with its feet. It was different from all the beasts that were before it, and it had ten horns. I was considering the horns, and there

was another horn, a little one, coming up
among them, before whom three of the first
horns were plucked out by the roots. And there,
in this horn, were eyes like the eyes of a man,
and a mouth speaking pompous words.

When we look at the specifics of this prophecy, we see some truly amazing things.

First, there are three clears that Daniel is told to interpret this vision.

First, the "beasts" in the vision represent "kings" that would arise.

Daniel 7:17—Those great beasts, which are
four, are four kings which arise out of the
earth.

Second, these "kings" would stand for "kingdoms" over which they would reign.

Daniel 7:23—Thus he said: 'The fourth beast
shall be A fourth kingdom on earth, Which
shall be different from all other kingdoms, And
shall devour the whole earth, Trample it and
break it in pieces.

Third, the "horns" actually stand for "kings," which in this context is the same as "kingdoms."

Daniel 7:24—The ten horns are ten kings Who
shall arise from this kingdom. And another
shall rise after them; He shall be different from
the first ones, And shall subdue three kings.

With these things in mind, we can begin to piece together this prophecy that Daniel has.

First, the first three kingdoms are easy to identify. The first one (the lion with eagle's wings) is a clear description of Babylon. The imagery of a an eagle and a lion were used by the Prophets to describe Babylon.[37] In fact, archaeologists who have excavated Babylon have discovered several statues of winged lions, suggesting that this may have been the symbol for ancient Babylon.[38] Historically, the next kingdom is the Medo-Persian Alliance, followed by the Greeks.[39]

Second, the fourth kingdom historically in this prophecy is Rome. Notice that Daniel says the fourth kingdom would be broken up into ten smaller kingdoms:

> *Daniel 7:24—The ten horns are ten kings Who*
> *shall arise from this kingdom. And another*
> *shall rise after them; He shall be different from*
> *the first ones, And shall subdue three kings.*

Historically, the nation of Rome divided up into ten smaller nations, just as Daniel prophesied would happen nearly a thousand years earlier.[40]

Third, Daniel also describes a religious power which would arise from the ten-fold division of the Roman Empire:

> *Daniel 7:25—He shall speak pompous words*
> *against the Most High, Shall persecute the*
> *saints of the Most High, And shall intend to*
> *change times and law. Then the saints shall be*
> *given into his hand For a time and times and*
> *half a time.*

That this is a religious power is clear from the description that it would attempt to change "times and law." This was a reference in the Old Testament for Divine Law.[41] Further, notice the identification of this "little horn" with a "lamb" in the Book of Revelation:

> *Revelation 13:11-13—Then I saw another beast*
> *coming up out of the earth, and he had two*
> *horns like a lamb and spoke like a dragon. And*
> *he exercises all the authority of the first beast*
> *in his presence, and causes the earth and those*

> *who dwell in it to worship the first beast, whose*
> *deadly wound was healed. He performs great*
> *signs, so that he even makes fire come down*
> *from heaven on the earth in the sight of men.*

Throughout the Book of Revelation, the "Lamb" is usually a reference to Jesus (cf. Revelation 5:6, 8, 12, 13; 6:1, 16; 7:9, 10, 14, 17; 12:11; 13:8; 14:1, 4, 10; 15:3; 17:14; 19:7, 9; 21:9, 14, 22, 23, 27; 22:1, 3). In fact, the only other time that a "lamb" is mentioned is in reference to the "little horn" of Revelation 13:11! The implication is that this "little horn" would appear to be a religious power that is in some way connected with Jesus Christ, likely trying to take His authority or stand-in His place.[42] There has only been one institution which completely fulfills this prophecy: the papacy of the Roman Catholic church. That this interpretation is correct is seen not only in the previous comments, but in the destruction of the three fragments which Daniel said would oppose the "little horn."

> *Daniel 7:8, 24—I was considering the horns,*
> *and there was another horn, a little one, com-*
> *ing up among them, before whom three of the*
> *first horns were plucked out by the roots. And*
> *there, in this horn, were eyes like the eyes of a*
> *man, and a mouth speaking pompous*
> *words. ...The ten horns are ten kings Who shall*
> *arise from this kingdom. And another shall rise*
> *after them; He shall be different from the first*
> *ones, And shall subdue three kings.*

Three of the ten remnants of the Roman Empire (the Heruli, the Vandals, and the Ostrogoths) opposed the papacy, and were destroyed. [43]

Please observe the amazing specificity and accuracy of the Prophet, and see how these prophecies have come to pass!

The 430 Year Prophecy

In the Book of Ezekiel, God told the Prophet to prophesy to the people of Judah in a very unusual way.

We are told:

> *Ezekiel 4:4-6—Lie also on your left side, and lay the iniquity of the house of Israel upon it. According to the number of the days that you lie on it, you shall bear their iniquity. For I have laid on you the years of their iniquity, according to the number of the days, three hundred and ninety days; so you shall bear the iniquity of the house of Israel. And when you have completed them, lie again on your right side; then you shall bear the iniquity of the house of Judah forty days. I have laid on you a day for each year.*

God instructed Ezekiel to lie on his left side for 390 days, following by lying on his right side for 40 days. This made a combined total of 430 days. Each day stood for one year of captivity the people of Israel were to endure for their wicked rebellion against God. However, the people were only in captivity for 70 years in Babylon (cf. Jeremiah 29:10). With the commission of Cyrus,[44] a few relatively small groups of Jews returned to the desolate remains of Jerusalem to rebuild it. The first group that went back was led by Zerubbabel, beginning in the year 536 B.C.

However, the prophecy of Ezekiel listed 430 years. Taking into account the 70 year captivity in Babylon, that should leave 360 years of captivity. So that raises the question: what happened to the 360 remaining years?

The answer lies in noticing the response of the people of Israel when God commanded them to return to Israel. It was only a very small percentage that obeyed God and returned. Indeed, we can say that the majority of the people of Israel continued in their rebellion against God's Word.

Long before these events took place, God had told the people of Israel what would happen if they ever refused to obey Him even after going into captivity for their sins. In the Book of Leviticus, God had said:

> *Leviticus 26:18—And after all this, if you do not obey Me, then I will punish you seven times more for your sins.*

Again:

> *Leviticus 26:21—Then, if you walk contrary to Me, and are not willing to obey Me, I will bring on you seven times more plagues, according to your sins.*

> *Leviticus 26:23-24—And if by these things you are not reformed by Me, but walk contrary to Me, then I also will walk contrary to you, and I will punish you yet seven times for your sins.*

Again:

> *Leviticus 26:27-28—'And after all this, if you do not obey Me, but walk contrary to Me, then I also will walk contrary to you in fury; and I, even I, will chastise you seven times for your sins.*

In all of these passages, God declared that He would multiply the captivity of Israel seven times if they refused to repent after being disciplined by Him.

So, taking the remaining number 360 years of captivity, we multiply it by 7, bringing the number of years in captivity to 2,520 years. Taking into account that these are biblical years of 360 days and that there are leap years (and no year zero), we add 2,520 years to the year 536 B.C which is when the 70 year captivity ended.

What does this add up to?

May 14, 1948—the year that the nation of Israel became a nation again![45]

The Prophet Ezekiel described the very DAY the Jewish people would be returned to the land of Israel and be established as a sovereign nation again.

And he did it 2500 years before it happened!!!!

Messianic Prophecy

Throughout the Old Testament Scriptures, there are many prophecies made of the Messiah ("Chosen One"). This Messiah would be the Savior of mankind (Genesis 3:15). Many in our day and age would have us believe that there really was no Messiah prophesied in the Old Testament Scriptures, yet the facts tell a different story. A personal Messiah was understood to be prophesied by the Jewish rabbis.[46] This fact is historically undeniable.[47] Throughout the Old Testament, there are hundreds of prophecies made of this Messiah.[48] Indeed, the reason why many rabbis after the time of Jesus began to come up with a denial of Messianic prophecy in the Old Testament is because the evidence was so clear that Jesus was the Messiah! As a result, Jewish rabbis long after the time of Christ came up with this denial of Messianic prophecy in the Old Testament Scriptures.[49] Furthermore, the obvious expectation in the first century world was that there would be a Messiah sent by God to redeem the world.[50] Following is a chart of some of these Messianic prophecies, along with passages from the New Testament Scriptures which demonstrate their fulfillment in Jesus Christ.

Event Fore-told	Messianic Prophecy	Messianic Fulfillment
Seed Of Woman	Genesis 3:15—I will make you and the woman enemies to each other. Your children and	Galatians 4:4—But when the fullness of the time had come, God sent forth His

	her children will be enemies. You will bite her child's foot, but he will crush your head."	Son, born of a woman, born under the law,
Seed Of Abraham	Genesis 18:18—Abraham will become a great and powerful nation, and all the nations on earth will be blessed because of him.	Acts 3:25—You are sons of the prophets, and of the covenant which God made with our fathers, saying to Abraham, 'AND IN YOUR SEED ALL THE FAMILIES OF THE EARTH SHALL BE BLESSED.'
Seed Of Isaac	Genesis 17:19—God said, "No, I said that your wife Sarah will have a son. You will name him Isaac. I will make my agreement with him that will continue forever with all his descendants.	Matthew 1:2—Abraham begot Isaac, Isaac begot Jacob, and Jacob begot Judah and his brothers.
Promised Seed Of Jacob	Numbers 24:17—"I see him coming, but not now. I see him coming, but not soon. A star will come from the family of Jacob. A new ruler will come from the Israelites. He will smash the heads of the Moabites and crush the heads of all the sons of Sheth.	Luke 3:34—The son of Jacob, *the son* of Isaac, *the son* of Abraham, *the son* of Terah, *the son* of Nahor,

Heir To David's Throne	Isaiah 9:7—His power will continue to grow, and there will be peace without end. This will establish him as the king sitting on David's throne and ruling his kingdom. He will rule with goodness and justice forever and ever. The strong love that the LORD All-Powerful has for his people will make this happen!	Matthew 1:1—The book of the genealogy of Jesus Christ, the Son of David, the Son of Abraham:
Place Of Birth	Micah 5:2—But you, Bethlehem Ephrathah, are the smallest town in Judah. Your family is almost too small to count, but the "Ruler of Israel" will come from you to rule for me. His beginnings are from ancient times, from long, long ago.	Matthew 2:4-6—And when he had gathered all the chief priests and scribes of the people together, he inquired of them where the Christ was to be born. So they said to him, "In Bethlehem of Judea, for thus it is written by the prophet: 'BUT YOU, BETHLEHEM, IN THE LAND OF JUDAH, ARE NOT THE LEAST AMONG THE RULERS OF JUDAH; FOR OUT OF YOU SHALL COME A RULER WHO WILL

		SHEPHERD MY PEOPLE ISRAEL.' "
Born Of A Virgin	Isaiah 7:14—But the Lord will still show you this sign: The virgin is pregnant and will give birth to a son. She will name him Immanuel.	Matthew 1:18—Now the birth of Jesus Christ was as follows: After His mother Mary was betrothed to Joseph, before they came together, she was found with child of the Holy Spirit.
Prophet Like Moses	Deuteronomy 18:15—The LORD your God will send to you a prophet. This prophet will come from among your own people, and he will be like me. You must listen to him.	John 6:14—Then those men, when they had seen the sign that Jesus did, said, "This is truly the Prophet who is to come into the world."
Rejected By Jewish People	Isaiah 53:3—People made fun of him, and even his friends left him. He was a man who suffered a lot of pain and sickness. We treated him like someone of no importance, like someone people will not even look at but turn away from in disgust.	John 1:11—He came to His own, and His own did not receive Him.

Spirit Of Wisdom Upon Him	Isaiah 11:2—The Spirit of the LORD shall rest upon Him, The Spirit of wisdom and understanding, The Spirit of counsel and might, The Spirit of knowledge and of the fear of the LORD.	Luke 2:52—And Jesus increased in wisdom and stature, and in favor with God and men.
Triumphant Entry	Zechariah 9:9—People of Zion, rejoice! People of Jerusalem, shout with joy! Look, your king is coming to you! He is the good king who won the victory, but he is humble. He is riding on a donkey, on a young donkey born from a work animal.	John 12:13-15—took branches of palm trees and went out to meet Him, and cried out: "Hosanna! 'BLESSED IS HE WHO COMES IN THE NAME OF THE LORD!' The King of Israel. Then Jesus, when He had found a young donkey, sat on it; as it is written: "FEAR NOT, DAUGHTER OF ZION; BEHOLD, YOUR KING IS COMING, SITTING ON A DONKEY'S COLT."
Betrayed By A Friend	Psalm 41:9—My best friend, the one I trusted, the one who ate with me—even he has turned against me.	Mark 14:10—Then Judas Iscariot, one of the twelve, went to the chief priests to betray Him to them.

Sold For Thirty Pieces Of Silver	Zechariah 11:12—Then I said, "If you want to pay me, pay me. If not, don't!" So they paid me 30 pieces of silver.	Matthew 26:15-and said, "What are you willing to give me if I deliver Him to you?" And they counted out to him thirty pieces of silver.
False Witnesses Accuse Him	Psalm 27:12—My enemies have attacked me. They have told lies about me and have tried to hurt me.	Matthew 26:60-61-but found none. Even though many false witnesses came forward, they found none. But at last two false witnesses came forward. and said, "This *fellow* said, 'I am able to destroy the temple of God and to build it in three days.' "
Silent When Accused	Isaiah 53:7—He was treated badly, but he never protested. He said nothing, like a lamb being led away to be killed. He was like a sheep that makes no sound as its wool is being cut off. He never opened his mouth to defend himself.	Matthew 26:62-63— And the high priest arose and said to Him, "Do You answer nothing? What *is it* these men testify against You?" But Jesus kept silent. And the high priest answered and said to Him, "I put You under oath by the living God: Tell us if You are the Christ, the Son of God!"

Beat And Spit Upon	Isaiah 50:6—I will let those people beat me and pull the hair from my beard. I will not hide my face when they say bad things to me and spit at me.	Mark 14:65—Then some began to spit on Him, and to blindfold Him, and to beat Him, and to say to Him, "Prophesy!" And the officers struck Him with the palms of their hands.
Crucified	Psalm 22:16—The "dogs" are all around me— a pack of evil people has trapped me. They have pierced my hands and feet.	John 20:27—Then He said to Thomas, "Reach your finger here, and look at My hands; and reach your hand *here,* and put *it* into My side. Do not be unbelieving, but believing."
Side Pierced	Zechariah 12:10—I will fill David's family and the people living in Jerusalem with a spirit of kindness and mercy. They will look to me, the one they stabbed, and they will be very sad. They will be as sad as someone crying over the death of their only son, as sad as someone crying over the death of their firstborn son.	John 19:34—But one of the soldiers pierced His side with a spear, and immediately blood and water came out.

Guards Cast Lots For His Clothes	Psalm 22:18—They divide my clothes among themselves, and they throw lots for what I am wearing.	Mark 15:24—And when they crucified Him, they divided His garments, casting lots for them to determine what every man should take.
Miracles To Prove Claims	Isaiah 35:4-6—People are afraid and confused. Say to them, "Be strong! Don't be afraid!" Look, your God will come and punish your enemies. He will come and give you your reward. He will save you.Then the eyes of the blind will be opened so that they can see, and the ears of the deaf will be opened so that they can hear.Crippled people will dance like deer, and those who cannot speak now will use their voices to sing happy songs. This will happen when springs of water begin to flow in the dry desert.	Matthew 11:4-5—Jesus answered and said to them, "Go and tell John the things which you hear and see: <u>5</u> *The* blind see and *the* lame walk; *the* lepers are cleansed and *the* deaf hear; *the* dead are raised up and *the* poor have the gospel preached to them.

Would Suffer For Others	Isaiah 53:4-5—The fact is, it was our suffering he took on himself; he bore our pain. But we thought that God was punishing him, that God was beating him for something he did. But he was being punished for what we did. He was crushed because of our guilt. He took the punishment we deserved, and this brought us peace. We were healed because of his pain.	Matthew 8:16-17—When evening had come, they brought to Him many who were demon-possessed. And He cast out the spirits with a word, and healed all who were sick, that it might be fulfilled which was spoken by Isaiah the prophet, saying: "HE HIMSELF TOOK OUR INFIRMITIES AND BORE OUR SICKNESSES."
Would Be Divine	Isaiah 9:6—This will happen when the special child is born. God will give us a son who will be responsible for leading the people. His name will be "Wonderful Counselor, Powerful God, Father Who Lives Forever, Prince of Peace."	John 5:18—Therefore the Jews sought all the more to kill Him, because He not only broke the Sabbath, but also said that God was His Father, making Himself equal with God.
No Bones Broken	Psalm 34:20—He guards all his bones; Not one of them is broken.	John 19:33—But when they came to Jesus and saw that He was already dead, they did not break His legs.

Buried With The Rich	Isaiah 53:9—He had done no wrong to anyone. He had never even told a lie. But he was buried among the wicked. His tomb was with the rich.	Matthew 27:57-60—Now when evening had come, there came a rich man from Arimathea, named Joseph, who himself had also become a disciple of Jesus. This man went to Pilate and asked for the body of Jesus. Then Pilate commanded the body to be given to him. When Joseph had taken the body, he wrapped it in a clean linen cloth, and laid it in his new tomb which he had hewn out of the rock; and he rolled a large stone against the door of the tomb, and departed.
To Be Resurrected	Psalm 16:10—For You will not leave my soul in Sheol, Nor will You allow Your Holy One to see corruption.	Luke 24:34—saying, "The Lord is risen indeed, and has appeared to Simon!"

Ascension To Heaven After Descent To Hades	Psalm 68:18—You went up to your high place, leading a parade of captives. You received gifts from people, even those who turned against you. The LORD God went up there to live.	Ephesians 4:8-10— Therefore He says: "WHEN HE ASCENDED ON HIGH, HE LED CAPTIVITY CAPTIVE, AND GAVE GIFTS TO MEN." (Now this, "HE ASCENDED"—what does it mean but that He also first descended into the lower parts of the earth? He who descended is also the One who ascended far above all the heavens, that He might fill all things.)
Establish New Testament	Ezekiel 37:26—Moreover I will make a covenant of peace with them, and it shall be an everlasting covenant with them; I will establish them and multiply them, and I will set My sanctuary in their midst forevermore.	Matthew 26:28—For this is My blood of the new covenant, which is shed for many for the remission of sins.

Let's notice some of the Messianic prophecies in greater detail.

Bereshit

One of the first prophecies worth noting comes from the very first word of the Bible!

Genesis 1:1—In the beginning God created the heavens and the earth.

Many are not aware that the letters of the Hebrew alphabet are much more than just phonetic symbols. Each Hebrew letter represents not only a letter in the alphabet, but also a number, a music note, a color, and an idea![51] Indeed, the Hebrew language is absolutely astonishing![52]

As an example, consider that first word in the Bible. It is the word *bereshit,* and is translated as "in the beginning." What is astonishing is that when you carefully examine the word, you find out that it actually means, "The Son Of God Pressed By His Own Hand To A Cross."[53]

Here we have a remarkable prophecy of the Son of God (Jesus Christ) encoded within the Hebrew text of the very first word of the Bible, written at least fifteen hundred years before Jesus Christ even entered into the world.

Astonishing!

The Protoevangelum
In the Garden of Eden, God told the serpent:

> *Genesis 3:15—And I will put enmity Between*
> *you and the woman, And between your seed*
> *and her Seed; He shall bruise your head, And*
> *you shall bruise His heel."*

At least two things about this prophecy point to Jesus Christ.

First, notice that the promised Seed is specifically identified as "the Seed of woman." This would be a Descendant of humanity that would somehow uniquely be identified with woman. Since often in the Old Testament humans are referred to as the "seed of man," there as something uniquely said here about the Seed and His connection to the woman. There is strong suggestion in this passage that the promised Messiah would be born of a woman without the intervention of man, i.e., the hint of the virgin birth of Christ.[54]

Second, the text specifies that the serpent would bruise the heel of the Messiah. Many believe that this is a specific reference to the death of Jesus by crucifixion-a mode of execution that would not have been invented for several thousand years![55]

The Scepter

Genesis 49:10—The scepter shall not depart from Judah, Nor a lawgiver from between his feet, Until Shiloh comes; And to Him shall be the obedience of the people.

In this passage, Jacob tells his children a very specific detail about when the Messiah would come into the world.

Let's notice several things about it.

First, there is no doubt that this passage is Messianic in scope. The Jewish rabbis clearly understood this to be the case.[56]

Second, the word "Shiloh" means "Peacemaker." [57] This Messiah would be One Who made peace between God and mankind, and between man and his fellow neighbor.

Third, this Messiah would arrive before the "scepter" departed from Judah. This word carried with it the idea of the right of a people to exercise capital punishment.[58] During their various captivities, the Jewish people retained the right of capital punishment. But then, it was taken away by the Roman Empire in the year 7 A.D.. When this happened, the Jewish Sanhedrin mourned because they believed that this prophecy had failed.[59] Yet unknown to them, the Messiah had been born into the world a few years earlier!

The Messianic King Of Psalm 22

Psalm 22 is one of the most powerful and profound Messianic prophecies.

Psalm 22:1-31—To the Chief Musician. Set to "The Deer of the Dawn." a Psalm of David. My God, My God, why have You forsaken Me? Why are You so far from helping Me, And from the words of My groaning? O My God, I cry in

*the daytime, but You do not hear; And in the
night season, and am not silent. But You are
holy, Enthroned in the praises of Israel. Our fathers trusted in You; They trusted, and You delivered them. They cried to You, and were delivered; They trusted in You, and were not
ashamed. But I am a worm, and no man; A re-
proach of men, and despised by the people. All
those who see Me ridicule Me; They shoot out
the lip, they shake the head, saying, "He trusted
in the LORD, let Him rescue Him; Let Him deliver Him, since He delights in Him!" But You
are He who took Me out of the womb; You
made Me trust while on My mother's breasts. I
was cast upon You from birth. From My mother's womb You have been My God. Be not far
from Me, For trouble is near; For there is none
to help. Many bulls have surrounded Me;
Strong bulls of Bashan have encircled Me.
They gape at Me with their mouths, Like a raging and roaring lion. I am poured out like water, And all My bones are out of joint; My heart
is like wax; It has melted within Me. My
strength is dried up like a potsherd, And My
tongue clings to My jaws; You have brought
Me to the dust of death. For dogs have surrounded Me; The congregation of the wicked
has enclosed Me. They pierced My hands and
My feet; I can count all My bones. They look
and stare at Me. They divide My garments
among them, And for My clothing they cast
lots. But You, O LORD, do not be far from Me;
O My Strength, hasten to help Me! Deliver Me
from the sword, My precious life from the
power of the dog. Save Me from the lion's
mouth And from the horns of the wild oxen!
You have answered Me. I will declare Your*

name to My brethren; In the midst of the assembly I will praise You. You who fear the LORD, praise Him! All you descendants of Jacob, glorify Him, And fear Him, all you offspring of Israel! For He has not despised nor abhorred the affliction of the afflicted; Nor has He hidden His face from Him; But when He cried to Him, He heard. My praise shall be of You in the great assembly; I will pay My vows before those who fear Him. The poor shall eat and be satisfied; Those who seek Him will praise the LORD. Let your heart live forever! All the ends of the world Shall remember and turn to the LORD, And all the families of the nations Shall worship before You. For the kingdom is the LORD's, And He rules over the nations. All the prosperous of the earth Shall eat and worship; All those who go down to the dust Shall bow before Him, Even he who cannot keep himself alive. A posterity shall serve Him. It will be recounted of the Lord to the next generation, They will come and declare His righteousness to a people who will be born, That He has done this.

There are several things we need to unpack from this passage of Scripture.

First, Psalm 22 was understood from earliest times to be a Messianic prophecy, as well as a description of king David.[60] One reason that this passage was understood Messianically is because of the amazing work of the Person in this text. His suffering and death bring about the redemption of the world-something which looks far beyond king David![61] There is, in fact, a Messianic theme running throughout many of the Psalms—and this theme runs directly through Psalm 22![62] This theme is found in several Psalms.[63]

As an example of this theme, notice the wording in this verse:

Psalm 22:27—All the ends of the world Shall remember and turn to the LORD, And all the families of the nations Shall worship before You.

This harkens back to the wording of Genesis 12, where God promised to send the Savior into the world through whom all the families of the Earth would be blessed![64] Clearly, Psalm 22 is Messianic in scope![65]

Second, notice there are several prophecies made about the Messiah in this Psalm that find their direct fulfillment in Jesus Christ, nearly fifteen hundred years after they were written!

Psalm 22:1—My God, My God, why have You forsaken Me? *Why are You so* far from helping Me, *And from* the words of My groaning?	Matthew 27:46—And about the ninth hour Jesus cried out with a loud voice, saying, "Eli, Eli, lama sabachthani?" that is, "MY GOD, MY GOD, WHY HAVE YOU FORSAKEN ME?"
Psalm 22:7-8—All those who see Me ridicule Me; They shoot out the lip, they shake the head, *saying,* "He trusted in the LORD, let Him rescue Him; Let Him deliver Him, since He delights in Him!"	Luke 23:35-37—And the people stood looking on. But even the rulers with them sneered, saying, "He saved others; let Him save Himself if He is the Christ, the chosen of God." The soldiers also mocked Him, coming and offering Him sour wine, and saying, "If You are the King of the Jews, save Yourself."
Psalm 22:14—I am poured out like water; all My bones are out of joint; My heart is like wax; It has melted within Me.	John 19:34—But one of the soldiers pierced His side with a spear, and immediately blood and water came out.

Psalm 22:15—My strength is dried up like a potsherd, And My tongue clings to My jaws; You have brought Me to the dust of death.	Matthew 27:31—And when they had mocked Him, they took the robe off Him, put His *own* clothes on Him, and led Him away to be crucified.
Psalm 22:16—For dogs have surrounded Me; The congregation of the wicked has enclosed Me. They pierced My hands and My feet;	John 18:31-32—Then Pilate said to them, "You take Him and judge Him according to your law." Therefore the Jews said to him, "It is not lawful for us to put anyone to death," that the saying of Jesus might be fulfilled which He spoke, signifying by what death He would die.
Psalm 22:16—For dogs have surrounded Me; The congregation of the wicked has enclosed Me. They pierced My hands and My feet;	John 20:25—The other disciples therefore said to him, "We have seen the Lord." So he said to them, "Unless I see in His hands the print of the nails, and put my finger into the print of the nails, and put my hand into His side, I will not believe."
Psalm 22:18—They divide My garments among them, And for My clothing they cast lots.	John 19:23-24—Then the soldiers, when they had crucified Jesus, took His garments and made four parts, to each soldier a part, and also the tunic. Now the tunic was without seam, woven from the top in one piece. They said therefore among themselves, "Let us not tear it, but cast lots for it,

	whose it shall be," that the Scripture might be fulfilled which says: "THEY DIVIDED MY GARMENTS AMONG THEM, AND FOR MY CLOTHING THEY CAST LOTS." Therefore the soldiers did these things.
Psalm 22:21—Save Me from the lion's mouth And from the horns of the wild oxen! You have answered Me.	Luke 23:46—And when Jesus had cried out with a loud voice, He said, "Father, 'INTO YOUR HANDS I COMMIT MY SPIRIT.' " Having said this, He breathed His last.
Psalm 22:22—I will declare Your name to My brethren; In the midst of the assembly I will praise You.	Mark 16:6—But he said to them, "Do not be alarmed. You seek Jesus of Nazareth, who was crucified. He is risen! He is not here. See the place where they laid Him.
Psalm 22:24—For He has not despised nor abhorred the affliction of the afflicted; Nor has He hidden His face from Him; But when He cried to Him, He heard.	Luke 23:46—And when Jesus had cried out with a loud voice, He said, "Father, 'INTO YOUR HANDS I COMMIT MY SPIRIT.' " Having said this, He breathed His last.

Psalm 22:27—All the ends of the world Shall remember and turn to the LORD, And all the families of the nations Shall worship before You.	Matthew 28:19-20—Go therefore and make disciples of all the nations, baptizing them in the name of the Father and of the Son and of the Holy Spirit, teaching them to observe all things that I have commanded you; and lo, I am with you always, *even* to the end of the age." Amen.
Psalm 22:28—For the kingdom *is* the LORD's, And He rules over the nations.	Revelation 1:5-and from Jesus Christ, the faithful witness, the firstborn from the dead, and the ruler over the kings of the earth. To Him who loved us and washed us from our sins in His own blood,
Psalm 22:29—All the prosperous of the earth Shall eat and worship; All those who go down to the dust Shall bow before Him, Even he who cannot keep himself alive.	1 Peter 3:18-19—For Christ also suffered once for sins, the just for the unjust, that He might bring us to God, being put to death in the flesh but made alive by the Spirit, by whom also He went and preached to the spirits in prison,

Let's take a closer look at some of these prophecies.

Prophecy: The Anguished Cry
The psalmist cries out:

> *Psalm 22:1—My God, My God, why have You*
> *forsaken Me? Why are You so far from helping*
> *Me, And from the words of My groaning?*

This prophecy was literally fulfilled by Jesus. However, it raises all kinds of troubling questions.

Did God literally forsake Jesus on the Cross?

If so, will God forsake us in our darkest hour?

If not, then what is going on here?

The passage in Psalms contains what is known as a remez- a deeper meaning behind the text.[66] The passage itself shows us that God did not forsake Jesus on the Cross (Psalm 22:24).[67] Jesus-by the Cross-has descended into all of our suffering. He has allowed Himself to endure everything that we ever can-the worst the world has to offer. By His death, He is able to fully embrace everything that you and I can face.[68] This is why we can boldly proclaim:

> *Romans 8:37-39—Yet in all these things we are*
> *more than conquerors through Him who loved*
> *us. For I am persuaded that neither death nor*
> *life, nor angels nor principalities nor powers,*
> *nor things present nor things to come, nor*
> *height nor depth, nor any other created thing,*
> *shall be able to separate us from the love of*
> *God which is in Christ Jesus our Lord.*

There will be times in life when we "feel" forsaken-just like Jesus "felt" forsaken on the Cross. Yet we can endure because-as we see with Jesus-we are not forsaken! God will act in our lives in the same way that He acted at Calvary, and at the Tomb when He raised His Son from the grave. Beloved, our victory is assured: we only need to wait for God to work!

> *1 Peter 5:6-7—Therefore humble yourselves*
> *under the mighty hand of God, that He may ex-*
> *alt you in due time, casting all your care upon*
> *Him, for He cares for you.*

Prophecy: The Dogs

The Bible says that the Messiah would be crucified by the "dogs."

Amazingly, this was a Jewish description of Gentiles.[69] Amazingly, by the time Jesus was crucified, the Jews were not allowed to carry out capital punishment-they had to go to the Romans-the "dogs" (i.e., Gentiles).

Prophecy: Crucifixion

Several of the passages in Psalm 22 depict crucifixion. This is astonishing for a number of reasons.

First, by the time Psalm 22 was written, crucifixion had not yet been invented. Indeed, it was several hundred years from the time of the writing of Psalm 22 that crucified was invented![70]

Second, Psalm 22:14-15 powerfully describes the horrible and quenching thirst that accompanied the brutality of crucifixion. The anguished and brutal thirst that those condemned to crucifixion had to endure is beyond imagining.[71] We are told about how just prior to His death, a Roman soldier gave Jesus vinegar.

> *John 19:28-29—After this, Jesus, knowing that all things were now accomplished, that the Scripture might be fulfilled, said, "I thirst!" Now a vessel full of sour wine was sitting there; and they filled a sponge with sour wine, put it on hyssop, and put it to His mouth.*

Many believe that this was a compassionate act of the Romans, but the opposite is true. Indeed, this was not her horrible act of attempting to inflict pain on the condemned.[72] This act was fulfillment of another prophetic Scripture (please notice John makes this clear by telling us "that the Scripture might be fulfilled"). Reference here is to another text in the Psalms:

> *Psalm 69:21 (CEV)—Enemies poisoned my food, and when I was thirsty, they gave me vinegar.*

Notice the parallel thought in this passage between the first and second parts of the verse: the "vinegar" given corresponds to the "poison" of the substance ingested.

Third, the very act of crucifixion is vividly described in this passage. The cross itself was composed of two parts: a vertical beam and a horizontal beam.[73] During crucifixion, various body parts were impaled in order to maximize pain.[74] However, it was especially the hands (including the wrists[75]) and feet that were impaled. Again, notice verse 16 in this regard:

> *Psalm 22:16—For dogs have surrounded Me;*
> *The congregation of the wicked has enclosed*
> *Me. They pierced My hands and My feet;*

The psalmist perfectly describes the action of crucified, long before it was invented. Some have tried to claim that the phrase "pierced My hands and My feet" is a mistranslation perpetrated by Christians: but the Hebrew and Greek Old Testament back up the standard wording of the text.[76] A great deal of research confirms this fact.[77]

Fourth, the death of crucifixion is vividly described here.

> *Psalm 22:14—I am poured out like water, And*
> *all My bones are out of joint; My heart is like*
> *wax; It has melted within Me.*

During crucifixion, asphyxiation would become the leading cause of death as the condemned would eventually be unable to hoist themselves up on the cross to breathe.[78] Eventually, the heart itself would fail as a result.[79]

Prophecy: The Onlookers And The Soldiers

The psalmist describes the onlookers who mocked him (Psalm 22:7-8) which were again fulfilled exactly in the death of the Messiah. We are also told about the dividing of the clothes by gambling, which was again fulfilled quite literally.[80] The torture-both prior to[81] and during the execution-were normally carried out while the condemned was naked.[82]

It is important to mention a troubling aspect of crucifixion just here-one that we often shy away from in our day and age. The soldiers who crucified their victims in the ancient world would often induce the most horrible tortures imaginable. They even had a board game which they played together! Depending on where the dice landed and they moved on the board, they would inflict this torture on the condemned.[83] It was commonplace in ancient societies for the soldiers to sexually abuse the condemned[84]-and scholars have noted that the Gospels may indicate that such happened with Jesus.[85]

Jesus fully relates to those who suffer-as well as to those who are guilty. Isn't it amazing that Jesus-while suffering from these horrible forms of abuse-still prayed for His abusers?

> *Luke 23:34—Then Jesus said, "Father, forgive them, for they do not know what they do." And they divided His garments and cast lots.*

Prophecy: The Death And Resurrection Of The Messiah In Psalm 22

The psalmist vividly describes for us the fact that the sufferer of this Psalm died.

> *Psalm 22:15—My strength is dried up like a potsherd, And My tongue clings to My jaws; You have brought Me to the dust of death.*

In this verse, being brought down to the "dust of death" is further explained later as being unable for one to "keep himself alive:"

> *Psalm 22:29—All the prosperous of the earth Shall eat and worship; All those who go down to the dust Shall bow before Him, Even he who cannot keep himself alive.*

These passages clearly show us that the sufferer prophesies of the death of the Messiah, which is also very interesting considering the conclusive medical and scientific evidence which demonstrates that death is the result of crucifixion.[86] This makes sense when we consider what John says regarding the crucifixion of Jesus:

> *John 19:34—But one of the soldiers pierced His side with a spear, and immediately blood and water came out.*

This passage of Scripture confirms an interesting medical fact that actually demonstrates that Jesus was already dead by the time the soldier pierced His side.[87] We have seen several indicators already in Psalm 22 of the death of the Messiah that would take place when He was crucified.

Yet what is also interesting to notice here is that the Messiah's resurrection from the dead is clearly prophesied as well!

Notice:

> *Psalm 22:22—"I will declare Your name to My brethren; In the midst of the assembly I will praise You."*

In the midst of His suffering and death, the Psalmist prophesied that He would still bring praises to God. He had certainly died.[88] How, then, would He be able to sing praises to God among His brethren?

Because He had been resurrected from the dead![89]

Throughout Psalm 22-24, there are several subtle clues which foreshadow the resurrection of the Messiah. Furthermore, there is considerable evidence that Psalm 22, 23, and 24 were understood to form one unit.[90] Psalm 22 describes the suffering of the Messiah; Psalm 23 described the death of the Messiah; and Psalm 24 described in detail the resurrection and ascension of the Messiah.[91]

Conclusion

We have barely scratched the surface regarding the prophetic evidence of the Bible. However, this is more than sufficient to demonstrate that the Bible is the Word of God. The mathematical odds of these prophecies and their fulfillment are powerful proof that the Bible is indeed the Word of God.[92] Indeed, the science of mathematics weighs heavily on these matters in confirming the Divine origin of the Bible![93]

Mary and Martha were escorted out to my jail ministry. Mary had spent several years of her young life incarcerated, and she was very eager to go into the jail church services at every opportunity. As they sat down opposite me, we had an interesting start to our discussion.

Mary: You ain't gonna like me honey!

Mark: Well, I hate to tell you, but you are mistaken. I already like you! Why are you so convinced that I won't like you?

Mary: Baby, me and Martha are witches. I worship the Norse gods and goddesses, and I think that Bible you are holding is a bunch of (exploitive).

Mark: That's an awesome place to start! Which Norse gods do you worship currently?

Mary: What's it matter? You don't believe they are real.

Mark: Actually, I KNOW they are real.

Martha: You can't believe in our gods, you're a Christian!

Mark: Actually, because I am a Christian and because I know that this Book is the Word of God, I know that your gods exist.

Mary and Martha: Silence.

Mark: So, which gods do you worship?

Mary: Oden and Frigg.

Mark: Well, let's start there.

From that point on, we spent four hours studying the Word of God. I spent a great deal of time with my new friends on the subject matter discussed in this chapter. Near the end of our study, Mary started crying. She had been coming to the jail chapel for years, and had never heard any evidence of Christianity. She looked at

Martha while we were going over a Keynote lesson I had made on Prophecy And The Bible and said, "Martha, I am feeling faith! I am believing!"

I explained to her that faith was the result of hearing God's Word in Creation and Scripture (Romans 1:18-20; 10:17), and we spent time discussing the Son of God Who had arranged for her to hear His Word.

What a blessing it was to baptize both of these ladies into Christ that evening.

> *Acts 2:41—Then those who gladly received his word were baptized; and that day about three thousand souls were added to them.*

> *Acts 8:12—But when they believed Philip as he preached the things concerning the kingdom of God and the name of Jesus Christ, both men and women were baptized.*

Christians, let's arm ourselves with knowledge of these evidences and take them to a lost and dying world. There are souls out there who need to know these things, and God has entrusted us with that responsibility.

So we add here another powerful evidence in the Christian arsenal that the Bible is the Word of God.

The grace of the Lord Jesus Christ, and the love of God, and the communion of the Holy Spirit, be with you all. Amen.

CHAPTER THREE

ARCHAEOLOGY AS PROOF THAT THE BIBLE IS THE INSPIRED WORD OF GOD

Archaeology is the study of ancient events, persons, peoples, and civilizations.[94] There has been amazing evidence from archaeology in the last several decades which demonstrate and document that the Bible is historically accurate.[95] In this chapter, we will notice some of these amazing discoveries.

Let's start at the beginning: with the Book of Genesis!

Genesis Authorship and Archaeology

The first five Books of the Bible (Genesis, Exodus, Leviticus, Numbers, and Deuteronomy) are often referred to as the Pentateuch (literally, "Five Books"). They form the basic core of the Law of Moses. Indeed, several Scriptures indicate that Moses wrote these Books:

> *Exodus 17:14—Then the LORD said to Moses, "Write this for a memorial in the book and recount it in the hearing of Joshua, that I will utterly blot out the remembrance of Amalek from under heaven."*

> *Exodus 24:4—And Moses wrote all the words of the LORD. And he rose early in the morning, and built an altar at the foot of the mountain, and twelve pillars according to the twelve tribes of Israel.*

> *Exodus 34:27—Then the LORD said to Moses, "Write these words, for according to the tenor of these words I have made a covenant with you and with Israel."*

Numbers 33:2—Now Moses wrote down the starting points of their journeys at the command of the LORD. And these are their journeys according to their starting points:

Deuteronomy 31:9—So Moses wrote this law and delivered it to the priests, the sons of Levi, who bore the ark of the covenant of the LORD, and to all the elders of Israel.

Deuteronomy 31:24-26— So it was, when Moses had completed writing the words of this law in a book, when they were finished, that Moses commanded the Levites, who bore the ark of the covenant of the LORD, saying: "Take this Book of the Law, and put it beside the ark of the covenant of the LORD your God, that it may be there as a witness against you;

There is considerable evidence from the Bible and the ancient rabbis[96] that Moses wrote the Pentateuch.[97] However, within the last few centuries, there have been those who have raised their voices and claimed that Moses could not have written the Books of the Pentateuch. The early arguments were that no one in the time when the Pentateuch was written knew how to write.[98] However, that argument went out the window when it was discovered that people were not only writing during Moses' day, but long before![99] Indeed, the writing analysis of the Pentateuch shows that it indeed belongs to the time frame of 1500 B.C.[100] Later, the argument switched to try and claim that the Pentateuch was actually based on Babylonian legends. Yet numerous evidences have demonstrated that the Book of Genesis especially predates these Babylonian documents.[101]

The Fall In The Garden

Brad was a nice guy, when he wasn't trying to get his coven to come kill me.

We had met when he saw my former book, "I'm Back Again." Raising his hands in a gesture of worship to a demon known as Baphomet, Brad told me he was a pagan. However, his roots went much deeper than that. He did not realize he was actually serving Satan.

After cursing a friend of mine with a Satanic bible, Brad decided to get on someone's phone and texted his coven with specific instructions. He gave them my name, my phone number, my address, and said, "His church does food boxes: use that and lure him out." One of Brad's group members said, "What do you want us to do?"

Brad responded (and I quote): "I want him dead. I want his family dead. I want his house burnt to the ground lol."

(He did not realize I was given a copy of all the text messages).

What happened with Brad is something that the Bible describes in detail: there is a spiritual war going on, and we are all involved in it. In fact, we have all chosen our sides—and are choosing sides every day we live.

> *James 4:7—Therefore submit to God. Resist the devil and he will flee from you.*

> *Ephesians 6:12—For we do not wrestle against flesh and blood, but against principalities, against powers, against the rulers of the darkness of this age, against spiritual hosts of wickedness in the heavenly places.*

The Bible tells us this war goes back to the Fall in the Garden of Eden:

> *Genesis 3:1-6—Now the serpent was more cunning than any beast of the field which the LORD God had made. And he said to the woman, "Has God indeed said, 'You shall not eat of every tree of the garden'?" And the woman said to the serpent, "We may eat the*

> *fruit of the trees of the garden; but of the fruit*
> *of the tree which IS in the midst of the garden,*
> *God has said, 'You shall not eat it, nor shall*
> *you touch it, lest you die.' " Then the serpent*
> *said to the woman, "You will not surely die.*
> *For God knows that in the day you eat of it*
> *your eyes will be opened, and you will be like*
> *God, knowing good and evil." So when the*
> *woman saw that the tree WAS good for food,*
> *that it WAS pleasant to the eyes, and a tree de-*
> *sirable to make ONE wise, she took of its fruit*
> *and ate. She also gave to her husband with her,*
> *and he ate.*

The account of the Fall was well-known in the ancient world, as demonstrated by the archaeological record. Examples include evidences from Babylon[102] and China.[103] Others could be cited.

Nephilim Giants

The Bible tells us about the nephilim (the offspring of the fallen angels and humanity).

> *Genesis 6:1-4—Now it came to pass, when men*
> *began to multiply on the face of the earth, and*
> *daughters were born to them, that the sons of*
> *God saw the daughters of men, that they were*
> *beautiful; and they took wives for themselves of*
> *all whom they chose. And the LORD said, "My*
> *Spirit shall not strive with man forever, for he*
> *is indeed flesh; yet his days shall be one hun-*
> *dred and twenty years." There were giants on*
> *the earth in those days, and also afterward,*
> *when the sons of God came in to the daughters*
> *of men and they bore children to them. Those*
> *were the mighty men who were of old, men of*
> *renown.*

The word translated as "giants" is the Hebrew word "nephilim." This word includes two ideas, both related together in the ancient languages. First, the word Nephilim means "fallen ones."[104] Second, it carries with it the idea of a "giant."[105]

According to the Bible, these giants were the descendants of the "sons of God" and the "daughters of men." The phrase "sons of God" had specific reference during the time Genesis was written to fallen angels:

> *Job 1:6—Now there was a day when the sons of God came to present themselves before the LORD, and Satan also came among them.*

> *Job 2:1—Again there was a day when the sons of God came to present themselves before the LORD, and Satan came also among them to present himself before the LORD.*

> *Job 38:4-7—Where were you when I laid the foundations of the earth? Tell Me, if you have understanding. Who determined its measurements? Surely you know! Or who stretched the line upon it? To what were its foundations fastened? Or who laid its cornerstone, When the morning stars sang together, And all the sons of God shouted for joy?*

Many are offended by the Bible identification of the "sons of God" with "angels." However, the Bible testimony is clear on the matter. Furthermore, the most ancient Jewish and Christian sources[106] document that the "angel" view was the most ancient.[107]

Now, the giants are also mentioned in numerous other passages throughout the Old Testament.

For example:

Numbers 13:28—Nevertheless the people who dwell in the land are strong; the cities are fortified and very large; moreover we saw the descendants of Anak there.

Numbers 13:32-33—And they gave the children of Israel a bad report of the land which they had spied out, saying, "The land through which we have gone as spies is a land that devours its inhabitants, and all the people whom we saw in it are men of great stature. There we saw the giants (the descendants of Anak came from the giants); and we were like grasshoppers in our own sight, and so we were in their sight."

Deuteronomy 2:9-11- Then the LORD said to me, 'Do not harass Moab, nor contend with them in battle, for I will not give you any of their land as a possession, because I have given Ar to the descendants of Lot as a possession.' ". (The Emim had dwelt there in times past, a people as great and numerous and tall as the Anakim. They were also regarded as giants, like the Anakim, but the Moabites call them Emim.

Deuteronomy 2:20-23—(That was also regarded as a land of giants; giants formerly dwelt there. But the Ammonites call them Zamzummim, a people as great and numerous and tall as the Anakim. But the LORD destroyed them before them, and they dispossessed them and dwelt in their place, just as He had done for the descendants of Esau, who dwelt in Seir, when He destroyed the Horites from before them. They dispossessed them and dwelt in their place, even to this day. And the Avim, who dwelt in villages as far as Gaza—the Caphto-rim, who came from Caphtor, destroyed them and dwelt in their place.)

Deuteronomy 3:11—For only Og king of Ba-shan remained of the remnant of the giants. In-deed his bedstead was an iron bedstead. (Is it not in Rabbah of the people of Ammon?) Nine cubits is its length and four cubits its width, ac-cording to the standard cubit.

1 Chronicles 20:6—Yet again there was war at Gath, where there was a man of great stature, with twenty-four fingers and toes, six on each hand and six on each foot; and he also was born to the giant.

Many reject the Bible teaching regarding the existence of the nephilim giants. However, the nephilim (giants) are mentioned not only throughout the Bible, but by other historians as well. Indeed, such historians as Pliny the Elder, [108] Josephus, [109] the ancient Egyptians,[110] and Herodotus[111] all bear testament to the ancient giants. Indeed, Cooper has documented other examples from numerous ancient sources which document the existence and prevalence of the giants.[112]

Furthermore, there is a great deal of evidence from our day and age regarding the existence of giants. Chief Joseph RiverWind was commissioned by his Native American tribe to document and chronicle their ancient traditions. Many of these share amazing similarities with the Bible, which is very interesting since many of these legends predate their exposure to the Bible! In this regard, there are many legends among the Native Americans regarding gi-ants.[113] There are numerous accounts of newspaper headlines from America which document giant graves and skeletons being found.[114] Some researchers believe that the giant bones are being destroyed by those in positions of power since they are proof that the Bible is true and that Darwinian evolution is false.[115] Never-theless, there is evidence-even from the ancient archives of the

Smithsonian Institute-which confirms the existence and excavation of giant skeletons and accessories from America.[116]

The giants were killed during the Flood and their spirits were left in the world to become demons;[117] yet we know through ancient sources they were brought back through sorcery[118] and twisted science.[119] Indeed, an interesting passage of Scripture from the Book of Ezekiel may shed some light on this subject:

> *Ezekiel 13:17-18—Likewise, son of man, set*
> *your face against the daughters of your people,*
> *who prophesy out of their own heart; prophesy*
> *against them, and say, 'Thus says the Lord*
> *GOD: "Woe to the women who sew magic*
> *charms on their sleeves and make veils for the*
> *heads of people of every height to hunt souls!*
> *Will you hunt the souls of My people, and keep*
> *yourselves alive?"*

Delving into this text reveals some disturbing facts. Notice the phrase "magic charms," "sleeves," and "veils," and their connection to "hunting souls." These terms were used in the ancient world for occult rituals which were designed to try and bring back the spirits of the nephilim into the world of the living.[120]

In numerous ways, we see how the findings of archaeology again confirm the Bible narrative.

The Flood

The Bible teaches that there was a worldwide Deluge (Flood) that God brought upon the Earth because of the wickedness of humankind and mankind (Genesis 6:1-6). While the canon of the Old Testament Scripture was closed at 408 B.C. With our 39 Book Library, the Bible references non-inspired books.

For example, notice these quotations of the New Testament from non-inspired books:

Chart Of Non-Biblical Citations From The New Testament Scriptures

Bible Reference And Quotation	Non-Biblical Source Referred To
1 Corinthians 15:33—Do not be deceived: "Evil company corrupts good habits."	"Paul now moves from a biblical text with an anti-Epicurean thrust (vs. 32 b) to a quotation from the third-to-fourth century Athenian dramatist Meander: 'Do no be misled; bad company corrupts good character.' ...The epigram from Meander's Thais was a popular one in Paul's day and would probably have been known to any educated Corinthian." (Roy E. Ciampa & Brian S. Rosner, The First Letter To The Corinthians: The Pillar New Testament Commentary, 791-792 (Kindle Edition); Grand Rapids, Michigan; William B. Eerdmans Publishing Company)

Matthew 5:21- "You have heard that it was said to those of old, 'YOU SHALL NOT MURDER, and whoever murders will be in danger of the judgment.' (Cf. Matthew 5:31, 33, 38, 43)	"Jesus used the phrase 'You have heard that the ancients were told,' or a similar one, to introduce each of the six corrective illustrations He gives in this part of His sermon (see vv. 21, 27, 31, 33, 38, 43). The phrase has reference to rabbinical, traditional teaching, and in each illustration Jesus contrasts that human teaching with the divine Word of God. The examples show ways in which God's righteousness surpasses that of the scribes and Pharisees (see v. 20)...Jesus is not modifying the law of Moses, the teaching of the Psalms, the standards of the prophets, or any other part of Scripture. The essence of what He has just said in verses 17-20 is (1) that His teaching stands firmly in agreement with every truth, even every word, of the Old Testament, and (2) that the Jewish religious traditions did not...The rabbis of past generations were often called the 'fathers of antiquity,' or 'the men of long ago,' and it is to them that 'the ancients' (vv. 21, 33) refers. Jesus was contrasting His teaching0and the true teaching of the Old Testament Scriptures themselves-with the Jewish written and oral traditions that had accumulated over the previous several hundred years and that had so terribly perverted God's revelation." (John MacArthur, The MacArthur New Testament Commentary: Matthew 1-7, 7025-7066 (Kindle Edition); Chicago, Illinois; Moody Press)

Acts 17:26-28—And He has made from one blood every nation of men to dwell on all the face of the earth, and has determined their preappointed times and the boundaries of their dwellings, 27 so that they should seek the Lord, in the hope that they might grope for Him and find Him, though He is not far from each one of us; 28 for in Him we live and move and have our being, as also some of your own poets have said, 'For we are also His offspring.'

"The precise expression is found in the writings of Aratus (270 B.C.); and though not the exact words still the idea is found in the writings of Cleanthes (300-220 B.C.). Cleanthes was a Stoic philosopher, and the sentiment here quoted was directly at variance with the Epicureans' beliefs. Aratus was a native of Cilcia, the same country Paul was from. This quotation of the heathen poets would at once quicken the attention of the hearers. This was not an illiterate Jew, but a man of culture, acquainted with the thoughts of their own great poets." (Gareth Reese, Acts: New Testament History, 632; Joplin, Missouri; College Press)

Titus 1:12-13—One of them, a prophet of their own, said, "Cretans *are* always liars, evil beasts, lazy gluttons." 13 This testimony is true. Therefore rebuke them sharply, that they may be sound in the faith,	"This phrase is found in the Minos of the Cretan poet Epimenides, a sixth-century B.C. poet of Knossos, Crete, quoted by Callimachus (ca. 300-240 B.C.). Epimenides joked of his own people that the absence of wild beasts on the island was supplied by its human inhabitants...Paul occasionally quoted Ancient Greek poets (Acts 17:28)." (Thomas C. Oden, First And Second Timothy And Titus: INTERPRETATION: A Bible Commentary For Teaching And Preaching, 65-66 (Kindle Edition); Louisville, KY; Westminster John Knox Press)
Jude 1:9—Yet Michael the archangel, in contending with the devil, when he disputed about the body of Moses, dared not bring against him a reviling accusation, but said, "The Lord rebuke you!"	"This phrase is found in the Minos of the Cretan poet Epimenides, a sixth-century B.C. poet of Knossos, Crete, quoted by Callimachus (ca. 300-240 B.C.). Epimenides joked of his own people that the absence of wild beasts on the island was supplied by its human inhabitants...Paul occasionally quoted Ancient Greek poets (Acts 17:28)." (Thomas C. Oden, First And Second Timothy And Titus: INTERPRETATION: A Bible Commentary For Teaching And Preaching, 65-66 (Kindle Edition); Louisville, KY; Westminster John Knox Press)

Jude 1:14-15—Now Enoch, the seventh from Adam, prophesied about these men also, saying, "Behold, the Lord comes with ten thousands of His saints, 15 to execute judgment on all, to convict all who are ungodly among them of all their ungodly deeds which they have committed in an ungodly way, and of all the harsh things which ungodly sinners have spoken against Him."	First Enoch 1:9-"Behold! He comes with ten thousands of His holy ones to execute judgment upon all, to destroy all the ungodly, to convict all flesh of all the works of their ungodliness which they have ungodly committed, and of all the harsh things which ungodly sinners have spoken against Him." Quoted in Jude 14-15

Again, notice how the Book of Revelation references many non-inspired works:[121]

The Book Of Revelation	Non-Canonical Books Referenced
Revelation 1:1-20; 9:1-21; 20:1-15	1 Enoch
Revelation 2:1-3:22; 18:1-24	The Epistle Of Enoch
Revelation 4:1-11	The Testament Of Levi
Revelation 5:1-14; 11:1-19; 13:1-18; 21:1-22:5	4 Ezra (Also Known As 2 Esdras)
Revelation 6:1-17	2 Maccabees

Revelation 7:1-17; 19:1-21	Psalms Of Solomon
Revelation 8:1-13	The Testament Of Adam
Revelation 10:1-11	Book Of Jubilees
Revelation 12:1-17	The Life Of Adam And Eve
Revelation 14:1-20	The Damascus Document
Revelation 15:1-16:21	Words Of The Luminaries
Revelation 17:1-18	Joseph And Aseneth
Revelation 22:6-21	The Apocalypse Of Zechariah

According to the Bible and extra-biblical documents (such as 1 Enoch, Jasher, etc.), there were many reasons for the Flood. God gave people time to repent, but they refused to do so.

Reason For Flood	Biblical And Extra-Biblical References
Sexual Sin Between Angelkind And Mankind	Genesis 6:1-4; 2 Peter 2:4-6; Jude 6-7
Acceptance/Practice Of Homosexual Marriage And Bestiality	Genesis Rabbah 26:4-5; Leviticus Rabbah 23:9
Wickedness	Genesis 6:5
Sorcery And Various Forms Of Occultism/Astrology	Enoch 7:1-6; 8:1-4

Sexual Sin	Enoch 7:1-6; 8:1-4
Cannibalism And Vampirism	Enoch 7:1-6
Genetic Experimentation Mixing Different Species With Mankind	Enoch 7:1-6; Jasher 4:18
Warfare/Violence	Enoch 8:1-6; 69:69:4-6
Abortion	Enoch 69:12

In the time leading up to the Flood, God apparently allowed the righteous people in the world to die.[122] This was so that the people would not see the devastation of the Flood. However, God saved Noah and his family in the Ark along with the animals (Genesis 6-9). Scripture affirms that the Ark landed on Mount Ararat (Genesis 8:4). There is, indeed, many evidence from around the globe which document the historical accuracy of the Flood.

Eyewitness Testimony Of The Ark

There have been many eyewitnesses of Noah's ark on Mount Ararat. Here is a partial list:[123]

Berosus (a historian who lived in Babylon, who wrote three books between 350-290 B.C.) wrote:

> "It is said there is still some part of this ship in Armenia, at the mountain of the Cordyaeans; and that some people carry off pieces of the bitumen, which they take away, and use chiefly as amulets for the averting of mischiefs."

Nicolas Of Damascus:

> "There is a great mountain in Armenia, over Minyas, called Baris, upon which it is reported that many many who fled at the time of the Deluge were saved; and that one who was

caried in an ark came on shore upon the top of it; and that the remains of the timber were a great while preserved. This might be the man about whom Moses the legislator of the Jews wrote."

Josephus:

"However, the Armenians call this place, The Place of Descent; for the ark being saved in that place, its remains are shown there by the inhabitants to this day."

Bishop Theophilus:

"And of the Ark, the remains are to this day to be seen in the Arabian mountains."

Bishop Epiphianus (a Christian who was defending the truthfulness of the Bible against skeptics around the year 380 A.D.)-

"Do you seriously suppose that we are unable to prove our point, when even to this day the remains of Noah's Ark are shown in the country of the Kurds?"

Isidore Of Seville (560-636 A.D.)-

"Ararat is a mountain in Armenia, where the historians testify that the Ark came to rest after the Flood. So even to this day, wood remains of it are to be seen there."

William of Rubruck (a Franciscan monk who was sent by King Louis IX of France to the Mongolian Emperor, wrote the following when he travelled near Mount Ararat):

"Near this city (Naxua) there is a mountain of which it is said, 'Here lies Noah's Ark.' The one (is) larger than the others, and Araxes (River) flows at the foot of them; there is a city they call Cemanum, which, when translated, means 'eight,' and they say that it is named after the eight people that came out of the Ark and who built it on the great mountain.'

Sir John Madeville:

"...and there beside is another mountain called Ararat, but the Jews call it Taneez, where Noah's ship rested, and still is upon that mountain; and men may see it afar in clear weather. That mountain is a full seven miles high; and some men say that they have seen and touched the ship, and put their fingers in the parts where the devil went out, when Noah said 'Benedicte.' "But they that say so speak without knowledge; for no one can go up the mountain for the great abundance of snow which is always on the mountain, both summer and winter, so that no man ever went up since the time of Noah, except a monk, who, by God's grace, brought one of the planks down, which is yet in the monastery at the foot of the mountain."

Jan Janszoon Struys (a slave who was near Ararat travelled from 1647-1672.). Writing of a monk who was suffering from a hernia, he was encouraged by other monks to help him. After rendering service, he recorded:

"The brave hermit thanked me so profusely that I was embarrassed. He added that his sacred vows prevented him from giving me rich presents and that he had nothing more precious than a cross attached to a little silver chain. He removed it from his neck and gave it to me. It consisted of a little fragment of reddish- brown wood, and with it he gave me a piece of the rock on which the Ark came to rest. Such a high value did he attribute to these pieces of wood and rock that, in his judgment, I would be too rich if I retained them. If, on the other hand, I was willing to take them to St. Peter's Church in Rome, he assured me a recompense that would make my fortune. He had been born at Rome, and he said that his name was Domingo Alessandro, and he was the son of one of the richest and most influential families of Rome… When I was ready to depart, I thought that it might not be a bad idea to obtain from him an attestation as to my experience on Mt. Ararat. He willingly gave it to me in the following terms: 4 I have thought it unreasonable to refuse the request of Jan Janszoon (Struys) who besought me to testify in writing that he was in my cell on the holy Mt. Ararat, subsequent to his climb of some thirty-five miles. This man cured me of a serious hernia, and I am therefore greatly in his debt for the conscientious treatment he gave me. In return for his benevolence, I have presented to him a cross made of a piece of wood from the true Ark of Noah. I myself entered that Ark and with my own hands cut from the wood of one of its compartments the fragment from which that cross is made. I informed the same Jan Janszoon in considerable detail as to the actual construction of the Ark and also gave him a piece of stone which I had personally chipped from the rock on which the Ark rests. All this I testify to be true – as true as I am in fact, alive here in my sacred hermitage. Dated the 22nd of July, 1670, on Mt. Ararat."

Haji Yearam. Haji Yearam is a man who grew up near Greater Mount Ararat. His family would take specially chosen individuals to see the remains of Noah's Ark. Once they were approached by a group of atheists who wanted to disprove the story of Noah and the worldwide Deluge. Years later, Haji reported the event to a close friend, Harold Williams, in 1952:

"When Haji was a large boy, but not yet a man fully grown, there came to his home some strangers. If I remember correctly there were three vile men who did not believe the Bible and did not believe in the existence of a personal God. They were scientists and evolutionists. They were on this expedition specifically to prove the legend of Noah's Ark to be a fraud and a fake. They hired the father of young Haji Yearam as their official guide...."It was an unusually hot summer, so the snow and glaciers had melted more than usual. The Armenians were very reticent to undertake any expeditions to the Ark because they feared God's displeasure, but the father of Haji thought that possibly the time had come when God wanted the world to know the Ark was still there and he wanted to prove to these atheists that the Bible story of the Flood and the Ark is true. "After extreme hardship and peril the party came to the little valley way up on Greater Ararat, not on the very top, but a little down from the top. This little valley is surrounded by a number of small peaks. There the Ark came to rest in a little lake, and the peaks protected it from the tidal waves that rushed back forth as the Flood subsided. "On one side of the valley the water from the melting snow and glacier spills over in a little river the rims deep mountain as they reach the spot there they found the crown of a mighty ship protruding out of the ice. They went inside the Ark and did considerable exploring. It was divided up into many floors and stages and compartments and had bars like animal cages of today. The whole structure was covered with a varnish or lacquer that was very thick and strong both outside and inside the ship. "The ship was built more like a great and mighty house on the whole of the ship without any windows there was a great doorway of immense size but the door was missing. The scientists were appalled and dumbfounded and went into a Satanic rage at finding with they hoped to prove nonexistent." They were so angry and mad that they said they would destroy the ship but the wood was more like stone than any wood we have now. They did not have tools or means to wreck so mighty a ship and had to give up. They did tear out some timbers and tried to burn the wood but it was so hard it was almost impossible to burn it. They held a council and then took a solemn and fearful death oath. Any man present who would ever breathe a word about what they found would be tortured and murdered. They told their guide and his son that they would keep tabs on them and that if they ever told him anyone and they found it out they would surely be tortured and murdered. For fear of their lives Haji and his father had never told what they found except to their best trusted and closest relatives. "Here Haji was in America, an old man about 75 years old by this time. The scientists were much older and he doubted if any of them were then living. To be sure the record was left he wanted his story recorded before he died. So I recorded it very carefully and he went over it again and again to make sure no mistakes had been made. He felt quite sure that the men who had threatened his life if he told were dead and gone by then..."One evening... I sat reading the daily paper in our apartment in Brockton. Suddenly I saw in very small print a short story of a dying man's confession. It was a news item one column wide and, as I remembered it, not more than 2 inches deep. It stated that an elderly scientist on his deathbed in London was afraid to die before making a terrible confession. It gave briefly the very date and facts that Haji Yearam had related to us his story. I got out the composition book containing the story he had me write. It was identical in every detail. "Haji Yearam had died in my parents home in Oakland California about the same time that the old scientist who died in London. We had never for one moment doubted Haji's story, but when this scientist on his deathbed on the other side of the world confessed the same story in every detail, we knew positively that the story was true in every detail." (As reproduced in Tim LaHaye and John Morris, *The Ark On Ararat,* 43-49; (published jointly) Nashville, TN and New York, N.Y.; Thomas Nelson Publishers and Creation Life Publishers)

Flood Legends

There are hundreds of Flood legends from around the world that provide further confirmation of the Bible.

"The story of the Flood permeates nearly every culture of the world in some way, shape, or form. While some of the details vary between the different cultural versions, the same basic plotline occurs in all of them: a god becomes angry and destroys the earth with a flood but preserves the human race by selecting a certain number of people to survive the catastrophe. These people are saved from the flood by a vessel, which carries them throughout the duration of the event. In the stories, it is this same group of people that is then responsible for repopulating the earth." (Charles Martin, Flood Legends: Global Clues Of A Common Event, 83-89 (Kindle Edition); Green Forest, AR; Master Books).

One of the most amazing Flood legends comes from the Hmong:

"In remote times, ca 2000 BC, as the original Chinese settlers entered the country, they were joined by another group travelling up through Indo-China. They were soon dubbed the Miaotsu by the Chinese population, a somewhat derogatory term, the miao-element meaning 'barbarian' or 'outsider.' 5 They are more properly known as the Hmong, and today number some 12 million. They were a brave people. For nigh 4000 years they fought off all attempts by the Chinese to destroy them, but the interesting part of their story for our purpose is that, from the earliest times, they meticulously kept their ancestral records and pedigrees, happily recording the fact that they are descended, not from Ham as the Chinese are, but from Jah-phu, Japheth, the son of Nuah, Noah –no, I'm not making this up, really! The Miaotsu recollect other named patriarchs who appear also in the Book of Genesis: Lama (Lamech, the father of Noah); Cusah (the Cush of the Bible), and Mesay (the Biblical Mizraim), who are both descendants of Lo Han (Ham); Elan (the Elam of the Bible), and Nga-shur (the Biblical Asshur), these being descended from Lo Shen (Shem, exactly as in Genesis); and we have Go-men (Gomer), the son of Jah-phu (Japheth, again exactly as in the Book of Genesis). 6 Six generations after Gomer, the Miaotsu record that eleven tribes were descended from a patriarch named Seageweng. 7 Five of these tribes became the ancestors of the Miaotsu themselves, whilst the other six intermarried with the surrounding Chinese population. Now that is a great deal –more, in fact, than modernism has ever been pleased to tell us about –but it is not all, not by any means. In an ancestral song recited since time immemorial by the Miaotsu at funerals, weddings and like occasions, and in which all the above details are included, we find the following remarkable account enshrined in that song. 8 Of great interest to us is the fact that the song is written in couplets, which not only aids the memory of those who have to recite it, but also ensures that additions and interpolations are impossible to insert. 9 It is also worth bearing in mind that this song was already of great antiquity when Christian missionaries first encountered the Miaotsu, a people so introverted and shut off from the outside world, that they had no idea that the earth was even round. But the writers of this ancient song knew it, and knew it of old. 10 They knew many other things too. Consider the opening lines: " On the day God created the heavens and earth, On that day He opened the gateway of light." 11 Compare this with Genesis 1:3. The two accounts are not a million miles removed from one another, are they? Nor are the other lines of the song removed from Genesis to any great degree. The song goes on to tell of the creation of the land, the plants, the animals and birds, and then lastly of man himself: " On the earth He created a man from the dirt, Of the man thus created, a woman He formed." It goes on to tell how the Miaotsu's Adam (named as in the Bible after the clay from which he was made) measured the earth's weight and the stars of heaven, and pondered the ways of God. The line of his children from Se-teh (Seth, Genesis 5:4) to Lama (Lamech, the father of Noah, Genesis 5:26) is also given (as is the name of Noah's wife, Gaw Bo-lu-en). Their three sons, Lo-Han, Lo-Shen and Jah-phu (Ham, Shem and Japheth) make their appearance at this point, and: " So the earth began filling with tribes and with families. Creation was shared by the clans and the peoples." 12 The song goes on to tell in great but independent detail (no rehash of Genesis this) how things then went between mankind and God: " These did not God's will nor returned His affection, But fought with each other defying the Godhead. But their leaders shook fists in the face of the Mighty..." So, the Miaotsu remembered things just as the Bible describes them (Genesis 6:1-12). The earth was filled with violence. Judgment must come, and judgment did come. The song recalls further that God determined to destroy all flesh from off the face of the earth, save righteous Nuah and his wife and family. They build a boat and come safely through the

Flood, with male and female animals on board and birds mated in pairs. But it is the Miaotsu's graphic depiction of the Flood that is of particular interest to us, largely because of the fact that it radically departs from the commonly found 'seven days of rain 'that most other cultures speak of: " So it poured forty days in sheets and in torrents, Then fifty-five days of misting and drizzle. The waters surmounted the mountains and ranges. The deluge ascending leapt valley and hollow. An earth with no earth upon which to take refuge! A world with no foothold where one might subsist! The people were baffled, impotent and ruined, Despairing, horror-stricken, diminished and finished." 13 Forty days of torrential rain is exactly right and agrees with Genesis 7:4 precisely. But the added detail, which Genesis doesn't give, of a following fifty-five days of drizzle and mist rings true too. After the initial forty-day downpour, the air would have been unimaginably heavy with moisture producing constant drizzle and heavy mist, a detail that the occupants of the Ark were doubtless to pass on to their many hearers. Indeed, it may well account for the notable darkness that seems to have enveloped the earth during the Flood, and which is pointedly remembered in several Flood traditions. This fascinating song of the Miaotsu goes on to tell of Nuah releasing a dove to see if the waters had abated, and the sacrifice which he made after leaving the Ark. God blesses him and there follows the lineage of Nuah's grandsons, Cusah and Mesay (Cush and Mizraim), and Elan and Nga-shur (Elam and Asshur)." (Bill Cooper, The Authenticity Of The Book Of Genesis, 3979-4037 (Kindle Edition))

It is amazing how this account confirms the Book of Genesis in numerous ways!

In fact, Cooper (investigating the numerous Flood legends from around the world) shows how these legends confirm the account in the Book of Genesis:

"Well, we have reached the end of our enquiry. We have noted dozens of Flood traditions that are preserved by nations around the world, making sure that we have noted only those which date to times before any Christian influence could have placed them there. We have listened to witnesses that have often been hostile, or indeed ignorant of the issues involved. Some of the evidence heard, dates from the end of the third millennium BC; some of it to the 20th century CE, a span of 4000 years or more. It has come to us in languages as diverse as the many cultures of the world. But however old the testimony, and no matter where in the world it has come from, it has always proved remarkably consistent and faithful to the known facts as contained in the Book of Genesis. No other subject on earth has ever produced the like....When witnesses are few and their testimonies inconsistent and contradictory, then the court will invariably decide that the case is not proven. But if, in any given case, witnesses, hundreds of them (some of them hostile) from all parts of the world, turn up and give independent and consistent testimony to the fact that such and such took place at such a time, then the laws of probability alone would compel the court to pronounce that the case is indeed proven. Men have been hanged on much less testimony than that of hundreds of witnesses. Would it therefore be reasonable, or just, to declare that the entire world's testimony to a Great Flood is worth nothing, and that it proves nothing? Hardly. To evaluate the quality of the evidence that we have heard, we would do well to consider the work of Dr John Morris in this field. Dr Morris had collected (by 2001) more than 200 Flood traditions from around the world, and dismantling them down to their component parts, he found that 88% of the traditions feature a 'favored 'family; 66% tell of the warning that that family received of the coming Flood; 66% tell how the coming Flood was due to man's wickedness; 95% mention that the Flood alone was responsible for the world's destruction; 95% likewise testify to the universality (global extent) of the Flood; 70% testify to a boat being the means of survival; 67% state that animals were also saved; 73% testify to the participation of animals (birds being sent out, and so on); 57% state that the survivors landed on a mountain; 82% name local places and peoples; 35% testify to the use of birds; 7% hark back to the rainbow; 13% state that the survivors offered a sacrifice; and 9% specifically state that eight persons were saved. It was a brilliant piece of research, and we may assume that the traditions we have looked at would yield a similar indication of evidential quality. Dr. Morris remarks, concerning this data: "Putting them all back together, the story would read something like this: Once there was a worldwide flood, sent by God to judge the wickedness of man. But there was one righteous family which was forewarned of the coming flood. They built a boat on which they survived the flood along with the animals. As the flood ended, their boat landed on a high mountain from which they descended and repopulated the whole earth." 1...(Bill Cooper, The Authenticity Of The Book Of Genesis, 5490-5525 (Kindle Edition))

With these things firmly in mind, Cooper has come to this powerful conviction:

"That is surely reason enough for any man to believe the Book of Genesis. But God Himself, whose Word Genesis is, has gone the extra mile with us. He has given us a whole world of witnesses—a veritable cloud of witnesses—to persuade us of the Eternal Truth of His Word. Consider. That part of His Word that the world has learned to laugh at the most, the Flood, is the very part that has the most witnesses to its Truth." (Bill Cooper, The Authenticity Of The Book Of Genesis, 5557-5562 (Kindle Edition))

Archaeology also confirms many other aspects of the Flood account, including the long lifespans of the patriarchs.[124] It is also amazing how the science of Population Statistics confirms the timeline presented in the Book of Genesis regarding the Flood.[125]

The Table Of Nations

In Genesis 10-11, the Bible tells us about the Table of Nations and the Tower of Babel. The Table of Nations is a list of seventy nations that were descended from Noah's descendants. Bill Cooper spent years studying the Table of Nations to determine if it was accurate or a fabrication.

What did he learn?

"When I first came across this problem some fifty years ago, I found it most perplexing. On the one hand I had the Bible itself claiming to be the very Word of God, and on the other I was presented with numerous commentaries that spoke with one voice in telling me that the Bible was nothing of the kind. It was merely a hotch- potch collection of Middle- Eastern myths and fables that sought to explain the world in primitive terms, whose parts had been patched together by a series of later editors. Modem scientific man need have nothing whatever to do with it. Now, it simply was not possible for both these claims to be valid. Only one of them could be right, and I saw it as my duty, to myself at least, to find out which was the true account and which was the false....Either way, I would discover once and for all whether the Biblical record was worthy of my trust or not. It seemed a little irreverent to treat a book that claimed to be the very Word of God in such a fashion. But if truth has any substance at all, then that Book would surely be able to bear such a test. If Genesis contained any falsehood, error or misleading statement of fact, then a severe testing would reveal it and I would be the first to add my own voice to those of all the other scholars who declared the Book of Genesis to be little more than fable...What I had not expected at the time was the fact that the task was to engage my attention and energies for more than twenty- five years. Nor had I expected the astonishing degree to which Genesis, particularly the tenth and eleventh chapters, was to be vindicated. These chapters are conveniently known to scholars as the Table of Nations, and the sheer breadth and depth of the historical evidence that was available for their study astonished me....Today I can say that the names so far vindicated in the Table of Nations make up over 99% of the list, and I shall make no further comment on that other than to say that no other ancient historical document of purely human authorship could be expected to yield such a level of corroboration as that!" (Bill Cooper, *After The Flood: The Early Post-Flood History Of Europe Traced Back To Noah,* 80-111 (Kindle Edition))

Other archaeological evidences from this period of Genesis include the Ebla tablets (which confirm monotheism and Bible names of that era)[126]and the discovery of the remains of Sodom and Gomorrah.[127]

Joseph

One of the most thrilling and heart-wrenching Bible stories is that of Joseph and his "coat of many colors." Sold into slavery by jealous brothers (who then took his coat of many colors and tore it, dipped it in blood, and told their father he had been killed by a wild beast), Joseph was taken to Egypt where he was then falsely accused of rape and thrown into prison. Near the end of two years, Joseph had developed quite a reputation as an interpreter of dreams. The Lord God warned Pharaoh (through his dreams) that there would be seven years of great abundance in the crops and fields of Egypt, followed by seven years of great famine that would sweep through the entire Earth.

However, Pharaoh could not understand the meaning of the dreams! It was then that he was told about Joseph. When Joseph explained the meaning of the dreams, Pharaoh set him in charge to build and prepare great storehouses to stock with grain and flour so that when the seven years of famine finally hit, people would be able to come to Egypt for food. Indeed, Joseph was made the second most powerful man in Egypt at this time!

Yet the story gets deeper and more tangled. When the seven years of famine finally hit, guess who ends up coming to Egypt looking for food? Joseph's brothers! They don't recognize him, and

the Book of Genesis tells us of the incredible and beautiful recon-
ciliation that took place when Joseph finally forgave them of their
horrible wickedness. So great is his mercy that Joseph allows his
brothers to bring all of their families to the land of Egypt, to settle
in the land of Goshen (Genesis 45:10).

Critics of the Bible, of course, have said for years that the
Egyptians would never make a Hebrew the second most powerful
man in the land. To many, the thought is preposterous, and the Bible is often dismissed out of hand as a reliable document at this
point. Therefore, it is with this thought in mind we will begin studying and learning of the findings of archaeology in regard to these
matters.

Archaeology has recorded ample evidence of the seven years
of abundance and famine.

> "We dwelt at ease in this castle a long tract of time; nor had
> we a desire but for the region-lord of the vineyard. Hun-
> dreds of camels returned to us each day at evening, their
> eye pleasant to behold in their resting-places. And twice
> the number of our camels were our sheep, in comeliness
> like white does, and also the slow moving kine. We dwelt
> in this castle seven years of good life—how difficult for
> memory its description! Then came years barren and burnt
> up: when one evil year had passed away, then came another
> to succeed it. And we became as though we had never seen
> a glimpse of good. They died and neither foot nor hoof re-
> mained. Thus fares it with him who renders not thanks to
> God: His footsteps fail not to be blotted out from his dwell-
> ing." (Charles Forster, *Sinai Photographed* (London:
> Richard Bentley, 1862); quoted in Jeffrey).

Again:

> "In thy name O God, the God of Hamyar, I Tajah, the
> daughter of Dzu Shefar, sent my steward to Joseph, And he
> delaying to return to me, I sent my hand maid With a meas-
> ure of silver, to bring me back a measure of flour: And not
> being able to procure it, I sent her with a measure of gold:
> And not being able to procure it, I sent her with a measure

of pearls: And not being able to procure it, I commanded them to be ground: And finding no profit in them, I am shut up here. Whosoever may hear of it, let him commiserate me; And should any woman adorn herself with an ornament From my ornaments, may she die with no other than my death." (Rule and Anderson, Biblical Monuments, 9; also quoted in Jeffrey).

Another amazing find of archaeology which confirms the Bible narrative regarding Joseph is the Joseph Coins.

""Recent research conducted on previously overlooked Egyptian coins confirms the biblical story of Joseph and his role in government service in ancient Egypt. In 2009, archaeological authorities from the Egyptian National Museum announced that a cache of ancient coins had been "rediscovered." Initially discovered almost a century earlier, the coins had been in storage. They were uncovered in the vast storage vaults of the national museum and the Antiquities Authority. Cairo's Al Ahram newspaper reported that the coins bear the name and image of the biblical Joseph.21 The cache of more than five hundred coins had been set aside decades earlier in the belief that they were miscellaneous objects of worship and likely of no significance. However, scientists re-examined the coins using recently developed technology and discovered that a number of them dated to the time of ancient Egypt. Most of the coins were engraved with the year they were minted and their monetary value and the effigies or images of the pharaohs ruling Egypt when the coins were minted. Researchers concluded that the "Joseph coins" originated in the period when Joseph served as Pharaoh's treasurer—during the seven years of plenty and seven years of famine (see Genesis 41:41–45). Biblical history suggests a date for Joseph's high position in the Egyptian government that coincides with the date of the minting of the coins in the cache (approximately 2000 B.C.). Amazingly, some of the coins bear both Joseph's name and image." (Grant R. Jeffrey, The Signature Of God: Conclusive Proof That Every

Teaching, Every Command, Every Promise In The Bible Is
True, 69-70 (Kindle Edition); Waterbrook Press)

We should also make mention here of the "Joseph Canal."

"And what shall we say of the common assertion amongst
modernists that no Egyptian monument exists which bears
the name of Joseph? Well, we can always point out the fact
that about 80 miles south of Cairo, there lies the still- flour-
ishing town of Medinet-el-Faiyum. It is a lush and fertile
area, famed for its 'gardens, oranges, mandarines, peaches,
olives, pomegranates and grapes.' It has been like this for
well over 3,000 years, and owes its lush fertility to a 200
mile-long canal which still conveys to it the waters of the
Nile in a constant year-round flow. It is an astonishing feat
of engineering which to this day is known throughout
Egypt as the 'Bahr Yusuf'—the Joseph Canal. This has always been its name. Moreover, the people of Egypt are perfectly happy to tell you that it was built by the Joseph of
the Bible who once was Pharaoh's 'Grand Vizier.' 14".
(Bill Cooper, The Authenticity Of The Book Of Genesis,
2040-2046 (Kindle Edition))

Indeed, there is a great deal of evidence that during the time of
Joseph, there was a significant Semitic population in Egypt.

"There is no doubt that there was a significant Semitic population throughout Egypt during the New Kingdom (see
chap. 3).Because of the preponderance of epigraphic evidence for a Syro-Palestinian presence in Egypt from the
mid to late second millennium B.C., even the most skeptical historian cannot dismiss the fact that both the Bible and
Egyptian sources agree on this situation.42 Even as far
south as Thebes there was a significant number of Semitic-
speaking people during the Empire period.43 The names of
Semites have even turned up among the workers of Deir el-
Medineh in western Thebes.44" (James K. Hoffmeier, Israel In Egypt: The Evidence For The Authenticity Of The
Exodus Tradition, 3689-3697 (Kindle Edition); New York,
New York; Oxford University Press)

The Hebrews In Egypt As Slaves

At the end of Genesis, the Hebrews are living in the land of Egypt. At the beginning of Exodus, the people are now enslaved. It is a common claim that the Bible depiction of the Hebrews being slaves in Egypt is a myth invented by the Jewish people. Yet there is strong evidence that the Bible is correct.

"The Brooklyn Papyrus was acquired by the founder of the Brooklyn Museum, Charles Edwin Wilbour, during his winter travels in Egypt during the years 1881-1896. It was first understood in 1938 that this text mentioned "a list of slaves of foreigners." It was a tiresome work to put all the 500-600 fragments in order and interpret the ancient text, which was done in 1952. The total length of the papyrus is 182 cm. Above, an important section is shown representing a part of the list of foreign slaves in Egypt. The dating, based on information in the text, places the papyrus somewhere from the late 12th to the mid 13th dynasty, which is during the period when the Hebrews were enslaved in Egypt. The character of the papyrus is a business document used by Egyptian administrators to keep order in the family structures and duties of the slaves. A typical design of a section with slave names is: "The female Asiatic Siprah." One list contains 79 slaves, with 33 Egyptians and 45 Asiatics (and one unknown). In total 20 were males, 43 were females and the remaining were children. It is stated that the Asians probably were Semites of Syrian and Palestinian background. The Hebrews were Semites and came from areas of Syria and Palestine. A number, at least 30, of the slaves listed have names that are Semitic/ Hebrew to their character. Shiphrah is one slave name identical to the Hebrew midwife mentioned in Ex. 1: 15. Other Hebrew related names are Dodihu, Hayabilu, Hayimmi, Munahhima, Yasaskir, Aduttu, Ahatu, Dodihuat, Sukrapati, Aser, Aqabtu, Abu, etc. Translation of other names clearly indicate foreigners, as the example "I-am-prayed-for-in-a-foreign-land" (102). It is of great interest to find an Egyptian source from the time of the Hebrews in Egypt, that lists slaves with Hebrew names, in particular one name that is identical to a Hebrew name found in the book of Exodus. This is a strong support to the history of the Hebrews." (Lennart Moller, The Exodus Case: New Discoveries Of The Historical Exodus, 2168-2180 (Kindle Edition); Copenhagen NV, Denmark; Scandinavia Publishing House)

The Ten Plagues

The Pharaoh of the Exodus would not let the people of Israel go, so the Lord brought Ten Plagues upon the Egyptians. There is an ancient Egyptian document known as the Ipuwer Papyrus.

Many believe that it is an account of the Ten Plagues.

"Though the evidence for the Exodus has been slow to be gathered, there is good reason to believe that it actually occurred as described in the Bible. This thinking is based on the biblical testimony, Egyptian extrabiblical sources, and archaeological excavation in Egypt and neighboring regions. For example, one of the most well-known documents in Egyptology is the Ipuwer papyrus (officially known as Papyrus Leiden 344), which records an account remarkably similar to the plagues described in the book of Exodus. The papyrus was obtained by Swedish diplomat, Giovanni Anastasi, and sold to the Leiden Museum in Holland in 1828. No one realized the exact significance of the contents of the document until the first full translation was done in 1909 by a British Egyptologist, Alan H. Gardiner, under the title The Admonitions of an Egyptian Sage from a Hieratic Papyrus in Leiden. In addition, there have been many later full translations made, including an Oxford edition (2009). Currently, the document is stored at the National Museum of Antiquities in the Netherlands. Its contents are widely regarded by Egyptologists as a lamentation over the catastrophic conditions in Egypt written by a high Egyptian official named Ipuwer sometime prior to the thirteenth century BC (which is consistent with either an early or late chronology for the Exodus). Ipuwer was known as one of the great wise sages in Egyptian tian history. His astonishing description of the conditions, to the surprise of Egyptologists, appeared remarkably similar to the biblical account of the ten plagues recorded in the book of Exodus. The date of the Ipuwer manuscript approximately fits the Exodus date. The hieratic script style was in use at that time period, the events described are remarkably similar to the plagues, the location of the events (Egypt) matches the setting of the Exodus, and the odds of all these calamities occurring at the same time make them more than coincidental. There is no scientific, linguistic, or historical fact that Egyptologists can point to that would decisively preclude the content of the papyrus being a lament over the Exodus plagues. A simple comparison of the content in both the book of Exodus and the Ipuwer papyrus leaves little doubt to their similarities (see table below)." (Joseph M. Holden & Norman Geisler, The Popular Handbook Of Archaeology And The Bible: Discoveries That Confirm The Reliability of Scripture, 2555-2568 (Kindle Edition); Eugene, Oregon; Harvest House Publishers).

Please note some of the ways in which the Ipuwer Papyrus confirms the biblical narrative:

> *Exodus 4:9—And it shall be, if they do not believe even these two signs, or listen to your voice, that you shall take water from the river and pour it on the dry land. The water which you take from the river will become blood on the dry land."*

> Ipuwer 7:5—Behold, Egypt is fallen to the pouring of water. And he who poured water on the ground seizes the mighty in misery."

> *Exodus 7:20-21—And Moses and Aaron did so, just as the LORD commanded. So he lifted up the rod and struck the waters that were in the*

river, in the sight of Pharaoh and in the sight of his servants. And all the waters that were in the river were turned to blood. The fish that were in the river died, the river stank, and the Egyptians could not drink the water of the river. So there was blood throughout all the land of Egypt.

Ipuwer 2:10—The River is blood. If you drink of it, you lose your humanity, and thirst for water ."

Exodus 9:6, 23, 31—So the LORD did this thing on the next day, and all the livestock of Egypt died; but of the livestock of the children of Israel, not one died....And Moses stretched out his rod toward heaven; and the LORD sent thunder and hail, and fire darted to the ground. And the LORD rained hail on the land of Egypt....Now the flax and the barley were struck, for the barley was in the head and the flax was in bud.

Ipuwer 6:3; 3:3; 7:13—Gone is the barley of abundance . . . . Food supplies are running short. The nobles hunger and suffer . . . . Those who had shelter are in the dark of the storm ."

Exodus 10:15, 7—For they covered the face of the whole earth, so that the land was darkened; and they ate every herb of the land and all the fruit of the trees which the hail had left. So there remained nothing green on the trees or on the plants of the field throughout all the land of Egypt....Then Pharaoh's servants said to him, "How long shall this man be a snare to us? Let the men go, that they may serve the LORD their God. Do you not yet know that Egypt is destroyed?"

Ipuwer 3:13-"What shall we do about it? All is ruin! "

*Exodus 12:29—And it came to pass at midnight
that the LORD struck all the firstborn in the
land of Egypt, from the firstborn of Pharaoh
who sat on his throne to the firstborn of the
captive who was in the dungeon, and all the
firstborn of livestock.*

Ipuwer 2:5, 6, 13; 4:3-"Behold, plague sweeps the land,
blood is everywhere, with no shortage of the dead . . . . He
who buries his brother in the ground is everywhere . . . .
Woe is me for the grief of this time."

*Exodus 12:30—So Pharaoh rose in the night,
he, all his servants, and all the Egyptians; and
there was a great cry in Egypt, for there was
not a house where there was not one dead.*

Ipuwer 3:14—Wailing is throughout the land, mingled
with lamentations."

The Apiru

One of the ancient names for the Hebrews among the Egyptians and Canaanites is the name Apiru.

"(2) The initial reed leaf in the caption of Sinai 115 is consonantal, and thus probably a glottal stop, rather than i. This option accepts as valid that the original spoken-Hebrew word for "Hebrew," whatever its initial consonant must have been, is synonymous with Akkadian ḫa-bi-ru and Egyptian apir(u), which used to be the time-honored view in scholarship. James Hoch (1994: 63), whose treatment of WS foreign words in Egyptian was referred to by Redford (1997a: 59) as the most thorough study on the topic, stated that Egyptian ᶜapiru and Akkadian ḫa-bi-ru is "very likely related to the Biblical term/ name עִבְרִי 'Hebrew'," while Waterhouse (2001: 31) affirmed that "it is now agreed upon that indeed there is a valid etymological relationship between the term 'Habiru 'and the biblical name 'Hebrew ' (ᶜibrî)." The potential validity of this view simply cannot be swept under a rug, even though the full range of meaning for Habiru/ Apiru is a matter that cannot be taken up here. With this second option of a glottal stop, Ḥebeded would have departed from rendering into ME writing the same sound as the initial ḫ consonant of the Akkadian noun ḫa-bi-ru. However, neither was the Akkadian consonant rendered into ME with phonetic precision. Seemingly, no scholar disputes that apir(u) "Apiru" and ḫa-bi-ru "Habiru" are synonymous, that the term and the people originally came from Mesopotamia, or that their appearance in Egypt and Egyptian writings was a later phenomenon. If this is true, the Akkadian form is the earlier one. According to Huehnergard (2011: 2), Caplice (2002), and Marcus (1978: 1), Akkadian ḫ is pronounced ch, as in the Scottish word loch. Yet Hoch (1997: 8) noted that in ME the unvoiced velar x (Aa1, unclassified sign [a circle with horizontal lines interspersed within]) is the consonant pronounced as ch in Scottish loch, not the a (D36, the forearm glyph) of apir(u). Akkadian ḫ is unvoiced, whereas ME a is "produced with a restriction in the pharynx and with voicing" (Hoch 1997: 8). Even in proto-Northwest Semitic, the consonant ḫ is listed as an unvoiced velar fricative, whereas ᶜayin traditionally is considered a voiced pharyngeal fricative. Plus, proto-Northwest-Semitic ḫ merges into ḥ in Hebrew (preserved in Ugaritic and Arabic), and ME ḥ (V28, wick thread or twisted flax: a pharyngeal aspirate) is the unvoiced counterpart of ᶜayin (Hoch 1997: 8). The point is that during the NK, ME's choice of a (ᶜayin) to represent Akkadian ḫ is anything but a phonetic match, yet the connection between the Habiru and the Apiru has gone unchallenged, despite the linguistic incongruity. Evidently, the congruity between the third consonant of each word + the second consonant of each word, if the need for a b $\rightarrow$ p shift can be overcome (Petrovich 2016b: 73–74), has been enough to prevent scholars from contending that the association of the Habiru with the Apiru is invalid or flawed. In like manner, the present writer merely is appealing for the same allowance in this case, namely that the congruity in the final two consonants (i.e., the br of iBr/ jBr in Sinai 115 and the br in ḫa-bi-ru) is enough to establish the validity of the connection. The phonetic incongruity in the first consonant of iBr/ jBr with the ḫ of ḫa-bi-ru is no more objectionable than ME's rendering of the Akkadian unvoiced velar with the voiced pharyngeal. It also must not be forgotten that Sinai 115 dates to 1842 bc, whereas the consistent use of a in apir(u) dates to no earlier than the fifteenth century bc. What was standard and expected in the rendering of foreign words at one time in history cannot be expected to have been exactly the same 400 years earlier. Perhaps the use of ᶜayin in ME and later Hebrew arose (i.e., between 1842 and 1500 bc) for some unknown but intricately-connected reason. This principle, and valid possibility, takes all of the sting out of Schneider's criticism. Kogan (2001: 291) even stated that ḫāpiru is obviously a non-Akkadian term, while CAD (1956: 84) calls it a "foreign (prob. WSem.) word." When discussing the lack of consistent correspondence between Akkadian ḫ and WS consonants, Huehnergard (2003: 112) added that "[w] hen confronted with such a situation, where two co-equal branches of a language family exhibit a large set of cognates in which one of the consonants differs consistently in the two branches, and yet no conditioning factors can be found to account for the difference, the historical linguist is justified in suggesting that the cognates reflect mergers in the two branches of an earlier, now lost, third consonant." Therefore, it seems that a number of consonants can actualize in Akkadian as ḫ, and that the reed leaf on Sinai 115 may preserve some hint of that third, now lost, consonant. Why should one consider as valid that the original spoken-Hebrew word for "Hebrew" is synonymous with Akkadian ḫa-bi-ru and Egyptian apir(u)? Among the texts from southern Mesopotamia of about 1850 bc is one that departs from the typical use of the Sumerian logogram SA.GAZ by supplying the Akkadian cuneiform ḫapiri. According to biblical history/ chronology, Abram ventured from southern Mesopotamia in ca. 2091 bc. Therefore, if Abram was a historical figure, he undoubtedly would have spoken Akkadian as a resident of southern Mesopotamia, in addition to his own native Semitic tongue. If this was the case, why should one expect an initial voiced pharyngeal on the Semitic (Hebrew?) term that he used of his own ancestry (Eberite/ Heberite → Hebrews, Habiru, Hapiru, Hapiri, Apiru, etc.), and before his offspring had been in Egypt for any considerable length of time? This matter is discussed more elsewhere (Petrovich 2016b: 24), but the point to emphasize here is that the second and third Hebrew consonants on Sinai 115's caption match perfectly with the br of ḫa-bi-ru/ ḫa-pi-ru, which should be viewed as no less tolerable than the accepted but linguistically imperfect match between Habiru/ Hapiru and Apiru." (Douglas Petrovich, Origins of the Hebrews: New Evidence of Israelites in Egypt from Joseph to the Exodus, 186-190 (Kindle Edition); Nashville, TN: New Creation)

The Amarna Tablets

The Amarna Tablets are a series of records that were kept by the Canaanites, many of them from the time the Bible says that Joshua lived. Found therein is a very interesting word, Apiru. Cooper points out that this is an Akkadian form of the word "Hebrew," and that the Amarna Tablets tell us a great deal about the Hebrew invasion of Canaan. He writes:

> "It is therefore with considerable surprise that we read about Joshua and his people, not just once in some ambiguous, fragmentary inscription of dubious date and interpretation, but plainly and at least 85 times in that 15th-century BC Canaanite archive known as the Tell El Amarna Tablets. The critics don't like to mention the fact, but Joshua himself is sometimes obliquely referred to in the Tablets. There is one man in particular who is referred to as 'that Hebrew'; 'that Hebrew dog'; at least three times as the 'chief of the Hebrews'; and, it seems, in one inscription he is called 'Ilimilku, 'which name is the Akkadian cognate of the Hebrew name Elimelech, God is my King. It is a nick-

name which would have suggested itself to Canaanite observers after it became clear to them that Joshua was not a king, but that he fought under the God of Israel. Though not a name that the Bible specifically gives him, it is one that the Canaanites seem to have known him by, and they accordingly wrote it down in their correspondence - 'Ilimilku! '1 The Hebrews themselves are referred to in the Amarna Tablets as slaves '–runaway dogs 'in some of the Tablets '–slaves that have become Habiru 'in another -recalling the history of their escape from slavery in Egypt. This again is entirely natural and to be expected....What has been made available is the somewhat inaccurate notion that a couple of the tablets mention some 'Apiru,' a name which, we are asked to believe, *may* be derived from the Assyrian word *habbatu,* meaning robber, and that these occurrences must therefore refer to some troublesome bandits that were roaming the area at that time. Nothing could be more distorted and inaccurate. It is a forced and false derivation which misleads the reader. The Canaanite kings were certainly strong enough and well enough organized to see off any such bands of robbers, whom they would have hunted to extinction. It is what they did, and they were very good at it. Canaan could never have become a land flowing with milk and honey had it been a land in which lawless bands of cutthroats carried the day. Neither do bands of robbers capture whole swathes of territories along with their walled and fortified cities which were protected by regiments of disciplined and armed soldiers. No. The term Apiru, which appears throughout the archive, is merely the Akkadian cognate of the word Hebrew (Habiru), Akkadian being the diplomatic language in which most of the tablets are written." (Bill Cooper, The Authenticity Of The Book Of Joshua, 240-249 (Kindle Edition).

With this knowledge, look at how the Canaanite Amarna Tablets confirm the teachings of the Bible the fact that the Hebrews invaded the land of Canaan.

Cooper (Bill Cooper, The Authenticity Of The Book Of Joshua, 255-294, Kindle Edition) tells us of some of the concern that the Canaanite kings and leaders had about the Jewish people:

> "Now he is like the Hebrew, a runaway dog...' (EA 67:17).

> "The war of the Hebrew hosts against me is most severe...". (EA 68:18).

> "Through the Hebrews his auxiliary force is strong!....Let him not gather together all the Hebrews....". (EA 71:21 & 29).

> "Kill your lord and join the Hebrews...and all the lands will be joined to the Hebrews...." (EA 73:29 & 33).

> "They were won over following his message, and they are like Hebrews....that the entire country be joined to the Hebrews." (EA 74:29 & 36).

> "The war, however, of the Hebrews against me is severe...The Hebrews killed Aduna, the king of Irqata, and so they go on taking territory to themselves." (EA 75:10 & 27).

> "He has just gathered together all the Hebrews against Sigata and Ampi, and he himself has taken these two cities." (EA 76:18).

> "...speak to your lord so that he will send you at the head of the archers to drive off the Hebrews..." (EA 77:24 & 29).

> "....all the Hebrews...have turned against me...If there are no archers, then all lands will be joined to the Hebrews. Listen!" (EA 79:10 & 20).

> "He said to the men of Gubla, 'Kill your lord, and be joined to the Hebrews like Amiya.'" (EA 81:13).

> "All the Hebrews are on his side...he is strong." (EA 82:9).

> "The Hebrews have taken the entire country!" (EA 83:17).

> "...the Hebrews have gone to Yapah-Hadda in Beirut so an alliance might be formed....the lands have been joined to

the Hebrews...lest he gather together all the Hebrews and they seize the city." (EA 85:41, 73 & 78).

"Let an elite force, together with chariots, advance with you, that I may drive the Hebrews from the gate." (EA 87:21).

"But if the king my lord does not give heed to the words of his servant...all the lands of the king as far as Egypt will be joined to the Hebrews." (EA 88:34).

"You yourself have been negligent of your cities, so that the Hebrew dog takes them." (EA 90:25).

"Why have you sat idly by and done nothing, so that the Hebrew dog takes your cities?...I have just heard that he has gathered all the Hebrews to attack me!" (EA 91:5 & 24).

"They would attack me and I would be unable to get out, and Gubla would be joined to the Hebrews. They have gone to Ibirta, and an agreement has been made with the Hebrews." (EA 104:49-54).

"If this year there are no archers, then all lands will be joined to the Hebrews. Behold, members of the (Hebrew) army have entered Akka..." (EA 11:21).

"I paid 13 shekels of silver and a pair of mantles as the hire of the Hebrews..." (EA 112:46).

"...all my towns have been joined to the Hebrews...". (Ea 116:38).

"There is treachery against me...all the lands will belong to the Hebrews...What am I to do? May the king send a garrison and men from Meluhha to guard me. May the city not be joined to the Hebrews!" (EA 117:58 & 94).

"Behold...the Hebrews will seize the city!" (EA 118:38).

"...the sons of Abdi-Asiata have said to the Hebrews and the men who have joined them...". (EA 121:21).

"Should Gubla be joined to the Hebrews..." (EA 127:22).

"They have won the lands for the Hebrews...". (EA 129.94).

"They are like dogs, and there is no one ho wants to serve them. What am I, who live among the Hebrews, to do?" (EA 130:38).

"Now Aziru has gathered all the Hebrews..." (EA 132:21).

"All the cities that the king put in my charge have been joined to the Hebrews...a man that will lead the archers of the king to call to account the cities that have been joined to the Hebrews, so you can restore them to my charge....". (EA 144:26 & 30).

"The king of Hasura has abandoned his house and has aligned himself with the Hebrews...He has taken over the land of the king for the Hebrews." (EA 148:43 & 45).

"He has made Amurru an enemy territory, and has turned over all the men in the cities of the king....to the Hebrews." (EA 179:22).

There are, indeed, many other references that could be cited.

Conclusion:
The Testimony of Titus Kennedy

There are many, many other examples of archaeological evidence which could be cited that confirm the accuracy and authenticity of the Bible. However, I would like to conclude this section by sharing with you the testimony of a Bible archaeologist named Titus Kennedy.

> "Because the Bible contains stories from the ancient world, written in a style different than the method of modern historians and paired with theology, many have assumed that the narratives in the Bible are myth, legend, and propaganda instead of accurate history. In fact, the majority of scholars, most media and educational sources, and many in

the general public regard the Bible as a fairy tale and frequently portray it as unimportant or irrelevant beyond literary and religious studies. For years, the Bible has been routinely attacked and disregarded on the basis of history or archaeology. And yet when people look into what archaeologists have unearthed, a different story comes to light, showing that instead of fiction and fairy tales, archaeology indicates that the Bible preserves an accurate recounting of the history addressed in its pages. Specifically, hundreds of artifacts from the distant past have demonstrated the events, people, and places in the Bible to be historical." (Titus M. Kennedy, Unearthing the Bible: 101 Archaeological Discoveries That Bring the Bible to Life, 9 (Kindle Edition); Eugene, Oregon; Harvest House Publishers)

Indeed, the contributions of archaeology to the veracity of the Bible continue to abound.

"Artifacts related to the Bible specifically have illuminated or confirmed events, chronologies, practices, terminology, locations, and individuals that would otherwise have remained a mystery. As an example, there are currently about 70 individuals mentioned in the Old Testament who have been confirmed by archaeological artifacts, and about 32 individuals in the New Testament so far confirmed by archaeology, with several more people from the Bible tentatively identified by archaeological artifacts. Many artifacts have also illuminated obscure words and practices in the Bible, from times long ago in lands far away, that would be misunderstood or unknown otherwise...."The fallacious arguments claiming that the archaeological data shows the Bible to be unhistorical myth, legend, or propaganda are demonstrated to be sensationalism and falsehood by the artifact evidence presented in this book. Although 101 objects were presented, there might have been around 500 artifacts noted if there were no space restrictions and the scope was more comprehensive! Further, every year new and significant discoveries connected to the Bible are being made, suggesting that the amount of archaeological evidence will increase as time goes on and as ancient sites are found and excavated. Pass on this information to others, visit archaeological sites and museums to see these artifacts with your own eyes, and be on the lookout for these new exciting finds, which are usually announced in press releases, archaeology journals, and documentaries. Only time will tell what else lies buried, and the mysteries that will be revealed as more artifacts of the past are rediscovered." (Titus M. Kennedy, Unearthing the Bible: 101 Archaeological Discoveries That Bring the Bible to Life, 238-239 (Kindle Edition); Eugene, Oregon; Harvest House Publishers)

CHAPTER FOUR:
THE BIBLE CODES

The phenomenon of the Bible Codes are rejected by many believers. I myself was very skeptical of the subject until I set myself to quite a bit of study regarding the matter. Now, I am convinced that the Bible Codes provide a powerful evidence of the inspiration of the Bible.

What are the Bible Codes?

Long ago, Jewish rabbis noticed something incredible while studying the Old Testament Scriptures: there appear to be messages hidden within the text of God's Word! Many of these codes include prophetic texts. These codes are discovered by counting an equal number of spaces between letters. Thanks especially to the advent of the computer age, many of these ELS (Equidistant Letter Skipping/Sequencing) codes are able to be identified much easier than in previous generations.

As an example of the ELS phenomenon, consider these words from Chuck Missler regarding the "Torah" code in the Pentateuch (the first five Books of the Old Testament). Jewish rabbis long ago realized that by counting every 49th letter in the Book of Genesis, the word "Torah" is spelled from beginning to end! (The Hebrew word "Torah" means "Law").

Yet, there is more.

Missler notes:

> "At the age of 13, Rabbi Michael Ber Weissmandl acquired a commentary by a 13th century sage named Rabbenu Bachya ben Asher of Saragossa, in Spain. Young Weissmandl was fascinated by the notes made by this ancient Hebrew sage, because the rabbi kept making cryptic notes about the importance of skipping certain letters. That intrigued Weissmandl. He took the 304,805 letters of the Torah and wrote them out on 10 by 10 cards. For the rest of his life, Weissmandl maintained his certainty that divinely

ordered information was embedded within the Torah. By writing out the letters in a grid, he was able to facilitate the identification of skipped-letter sequences. Thus, he redis-covered what we today call equidistant letter sequences (ELS). It happens that ELS codes are not a very sophisti-cated form of encryption. It's not good at hiding messages because anybody can start counting letters. No, the strength of ELS codes is that they authenticate the identity of the messenger. Rabbi ben Asher had said, "The secrets of the Torah are revealed in the skipping of the letters." Now what does that mean? That's an invitation to spend some time skipping letters. It was Dr. Gerald Schroeder, a world-fa-mous nuclear physicist, who first showed me what I'm about to lay out here. Dr. Schroeder resides in Jerusalem, and I've had the privilege of spending Passover with him. We're good friends, and he was the one that showed me this, but it's common knowledge among serious Hebrew scholars. While dedicated rabbis counted the letters care-fully for years, we now have the number crunching power of computers at our disposal. I am grateful to mathemati-cian Dr. Eliyahu Rips for the work he has done to reveal the words hidden in the Hebrew Scriptures.[41] We find an interesting series of ELS codes from the very beginning of the Bible, starting in the first chapter of Genesis. Re-member that Hebrew reads from right to left. The Hebrew word Torah"–law"–is made up of four letters, תורה, a tau (ת), vav (ו), resh (ר) and a heh (ה). These are the equivalent of our letters T O R H. Beginning in the first verse of Gen-esis in the Hebrew, we can count from the first tau (ת) 49 letters. Doing so brings us to a vav (ו). We then count an-other 49, which brings us to a resh (ר), and then another 49 letters brings us to heh (ה). In other words, counting the product of 7x7 systematically from the first word of Gene-sis spells out the word "Torah" in Hebrew. That might be a coincidence. There are just 22 letters in the Hebrew "alephbet," and it's not statistically inconceivable. We might find any number of words in Genesis by skipping letters. What starts to make us scratch our heads, however, is that we also find the letters T O R H by counting every 49 letters in the first chapter of Exodus. Once is interesting. Twice begs a closer look. In Leviticus, we get a break, and we almost feel a sigh of relief rise inside us. Nor do we find T O R H in Numbers as we did in Genesis or Exodus. Well then, that seems to be the end of the matter—until we look even more closely. If we take a more careful consideration of Numbers, we find something startling. Counting every 49 letters gives us the word from back to front-ת-ו-ר-ה. There's still a 49-letter interval, but it spells T O R H backwards. In Deuteronomy, the same thing happens again! Again it spells Torah backwards (this time starting on the 5th verse, and including the 49th letter in the count). This no longer appears like mere coincidence. The word "Torah" is found spelled forward in Genesis and Exodus—at 49-letter intervals–and backwards in Numbers and Deuteronomy. When we reexamine Leviticus, we find something we didn't notice before. When we count by sevens—the square root of 49—from the beginning of Leviticus, we find the interval of seven letters gives us the Hebrew word Yahweh[42]-יהוה-the I AM of the Burning Bush. These equidistant letter sequences do not just form words. They paint a picture. We see a design here: Genesis and Exodus spell "Torah" forwards, Numbers and Deuteronomy spell "Torah" backwards. In the four books together, the word Torah points to the name of God in the middle. The conclusion is that the Torah always points to יהוה-YHWH-the name of God." (Chuck Missler, The Fulcrum of the Entire Universe: ISAIAH 53: THE PIVOT POINT OF ALL HISTORY, 987-1032 (Kindle Edition); Coeur d'Alene, ID; Koinonia House)

Astonishing!

Trees

Consider another example.

In Genesis 1:29—Genesis 2:9 we have about 635 words in English. The two aforementioned verses (the starting verse of Genesis 1:29 and the ending verse of Genesis 2:9) discuss in detail the seed-bearing trees and plants that God gave to mankind.

By using equidistant letter skipping, the ancient Jewish rabbis were able to identity all seven edible species of seed-bearing fruit and all 25 trees delineated in Old Testament tradition. Chuck Missler provides the list for us: tamarisk, terebinth, thicket, citron, acacia, almond, wheat, date palm, cedar, aloe, grape, boxthorn or bramble, cassia, pomegranate, gopherwood or fir, thornbush, olive, pistachio nut, hazel, fig, willow, oak, vine, barley, chestnut, poplar.

He writes:

> "In addition to the search for words at varying intervals, there is also the critical aspect of clustering : finding related words hidden together, and in relevant places . As an example, beginning with Genesis 1:29, "And God said, Behold, I have given you every herb bearing seed, which is upon the face of all the earth, and every tree, in the which is the fruit of a tree yielding seed; to you it shall be for meat...." ...and ending with "And out of the ground made the Lord God to grow every tree that is pleasant to the sight, and good for food; the tree of life also in the midst of the garden, and the tree of knowledge of good and evil." Genesis 2:9 All seven edible species of seed-bearing fruit in the Land of Israel are found encoded, as well as the 25 trees delineated by Old Testament tradition. 188 The names, (and their intervals) are listed below: ("-" indicates an interval counting backward, from left to right.)...It is the presence of all of these in this chapter (635 words in English), and their clustering around the very verses which introduces them in the Creation, which eludes any traditional statistical analysis. 190" (Dr. Chuck Missler, Cosmic Codes: Hidden Messages From The Edge Of Eternity, 1603-1609 (Kindle Edition); Coeur d'Alene, Idaho; KOINONIA HOUSE)

The names of all of these trees and plants (which happen to be all of the edible varieties within the land of Israel) were found within this text, which described God giving mankind the trees and plants for food!

According to researchers such as Daniel Michelson, the odds of these all occurring in the text by chance alone are well over one hundred thousand to one! (See Daniel Michelson, "Codes in the Torah" B'Or Ha'Torah , No. 6 (1987), Jerusalem: Shamir)

The Isaiah 53 Megacode

Isaiah 53 is one of the most incredible chapters of the Bible.

Isaiah the Prophet lived and prophesied between the eighth and seventh centuries before Jesus lived. While preaching to the inhabitants of Jerusalem, he provided many incredible prophecies of the coming Messiah.

Starting in chapter 40 of Isaiah, there are several passages that refer to the "servant" of the Lord.

At times, this "servant" has reference to the faithful people of Israel who were to be God's servants in the world. For example:

> *Isaiah 41:8-10—"But you, Israel, are My serv-*
> *ant, Jacob whom I have chosen, The descend-*
> *ants of Abraham My friend. You whom I have*
> *taken from the ends of the earth, And called*
> *from its farthest regions, And said to you, 'You*
> *are My servant, I have chosen you and have not*
> *cast you away: Fear not, for I am with you; Be*
> *not dismayed, for I am your God. I will*
> *strengthen you, Yes, I will help you, I will up-*
> *hold you with My righteous right hand.'*

> *Isaiah 43:10-"You are My witnesses," says the*
> *LORD, "And My servant whom I have chosen,*
> *That you may know and believe Me, And under-*
> *stand that I am He. Before Me there was no*
> *God formed, Nor shall there be after Me.*

While sometimes the "servant" refers to the people of Israel collectively, sometimes the "servant" has a reference to a single individual who would come to the world and serve the Lord, as *contrasted* with the people of Israel. One of these passages (Isaiah 53) describes in remarkable detail the life, suffering, death, burial, resurrection, and exaltation of the Servant, I.e., Jesus Christ.

Speaking of the specifics of the "servant" songs (especially Isaiah 53), Michael Brown tells us:

"Isaiah 52:13-53:12 is one of the most important Messianic prophecies in the entire Hebrew Bible, and I would not be exaggerating to say that more Jews have put their faith in Jesus as Messiah after reading this passage of Scripture than after reading any other passage in the Tanakh... Interestingly, the national interpretation is not found once in the Talmuds, the Targums, or the midrashim (in other words, not once in all the classical, foundational, authoritative Jewish writings). In fact, it is not found in any traditional Jewish source until the time of Rashi, who lived in the eleventh century C.E.105 That is saying something! For almost one thousand years after the birth of Yeshua, not one rabbi, not one Talmudic teacher, not one Jewish sage, left us an interpretation showing that Isaiah 53 should be interpreted with reference to the nation of Israel (as opposed to a righteous individual, or righteous individuals, within Israel), despite the fact that these verses from Isaiah are quoted in the New Testament and were often used in Jewish-Christian debate....The servant of the Lord (Hebrew, 'ebed) is mentioned a total of seventeen times in Isaiah 40-51, sometimes with reference to the nation of Israel as a whole (41:8-9; twice in 42:19; 43:10; twice in 44:21; 45:4; 48:20), and sometimes with reference to a righteous individual within the nation (49:3, 5-7; 50:10)....Significantly, the most personal, specific, individual language is found in Isaiah 52:13 and 53:11, roughly the beginning and the end of this glorious prophetic passage. Reviewing the data just presented, we can see something very important: The references to the servant as a people actually end with Isaiah 48:20, while the references to the servant as an individual come into indisputable focus beginning with Isaiah 49 and continuing through the end of chapter 53. Thus, by the time we reach Isaiah 52:13, the spotlight is on a person, not a people. The picture is becoming clearer!...This servant is obedient and righteous, setting captives free, and according to the Targum, this servant is none other than the Messiah. 107 This is confirmed by Rabbi David Kimchi—one of the so-called "big three" medieval Rabbinic commentators—who also interpreted the words "Behold my servant" in Isaiah 42:1 with specific reference to "King Messiah."108 And this image occurs even more plainly in Isaiah 49, where the servant is called Israel and yet is sent on a mission to redeem Israel. The servant is a righteous individual who represents the nation.109 The servant, as in Isaiah 42, is the Messiah!110" (Michael L. Brown, Answering Jewish Objections To Jesus: Volume Three-Messianic Prophecy Objections, 40-43 (Kindle Edition); Grand Rapids, Michigan; Baker Books)

Why did the Jewish people believe that the "Servant" in some of these passages was not a reference to the collective people of Israel?

Actually, there are several reasons why they had this understanding!

There are several places where we see that the Servant is sometimes distinct and separate from the nation of Israel. For example, in Isaiah 52:14, the "Servant" is contrasted with the people of Israel.

More to the point, in Isaiah 53:8, the "Servant" is said to bear the sins of God's people (in context, the nation of Israel).

It is also worth noting that we are told that the Servant is sinless (Isaiah 50:9; 53:9) as opposed to the people of Israel (42:18-25). Even the righteous remnant in Israel were sinners (Isaiah 6:5)!

For these, as well as other reasons, the earliest Rabbis under-stood the Servant Song of Isaiah 53 to be a reference to the Messiah:

> "For more than 1700 years, the Jewish rabbis interpreted this passage almost unanimously as referring to the Messiah. This fact is thoroughly documented in S. R. Driver and Adolf Neubauer's The Fifty-Third Chapter of Isaiah According to the Jewish Interpreters. 19/37-39 They quote numerous rabbis during this period who equated the serv-ant of Isaiah 53 with the Messiah. Not until the twelfth cen-tury A.D., no doubt under the suffering of the Jews at the hand of the Crusaders, did any Jewish interpreter say that Isaiah 52:13-53:12 refers to the whole nation of Israel, the most common interpretation today among Jewish scholars. Even after Rashi (Rabbi Solomon Yazchaki) first proposed this interpretation, however, many other Jewish interpret-ers have held, even to the present, the traditional Talmudic view that Isaiah 53 speaks of the Messiah. One of the most respected Jewish intellectuals of all history, Moses Mai-monides (A.D. 1135 -1204) rejected Rashi's interpretation, and he taught that the passage was messianic. 59/364-65" (Josh McDowell & Bill Wilson, A Ready Defense: The Best Of Josh McDowell, 254 (Kindle Edition); Nashville, TN: Thomas Nelson, Inc.)

With this in mind, let's consider some of the things which we find in Isaiah 53 when we apply the equidistant letter skipping principle.

In Chuck Missler's excellent book, *The Fulcrum of the Entire Universe: Isaiah 53: The Pivot Point of All History*, we find a list of words in the text of Isaiah 53 which have been discovered:

Passover

The Man Herod

Wicked Caesar Perish

The Evil Roman City

Let Him Be Crucified

Moriah

Cross

Pierce

From The Atonement Lamb

Bread

Wine

Obed

Jesse

Seed

Water

Jonah

The Disciples Mourn

Peter

Matthew

John

Andrew

Philip

Thomas

James

James

Simon

Thaddeus

Matthias

Mary

Mary

Mary

Salome

Joseph

Yeshua Is My Name

His Signature

Messiah

Nazarene

Galilee

Shiloh

Pharisee

Levites

Caiphas

Annas

In describing the incredible details of these facts from Isaiah 53, Missler writes:

"Let's focus now on Isaiah 53 itself. We've spent a lot of time covering this amazing prophecy about the sacrificial death of our Lord. Let's take a moment to consider the words coded within the 15 short verses from Isaiah 52:13 to Isaiah 53:12....We find more than 40 words and phrases associated with the crucifixion hidden amongst the letters of the Suffering Servant passage. We find the name of the high priest and the various elements of the Passover feast. We find the names of the disciples coded in Isaiah 52 and 53. It gets even better. "James" isn't listed once, but twice, which is interesting because there were two disciples named James. Both James the son of Zebedee, brother of John, and James the son of Alphaeus would have witnessed the crucifixion of Jesus Christ. The name "Mary" is encoded three times, along the woman Salome. One of the Marys was Jesus 'own mother, but we also find Mary Magdalene and "the other Mary" involved personally in Christ's death. Any one of these names in isolation would not be particularly impressive. For instance, the name "Philip" is found 15 places elsewhere in Isaiah while the name "Thomas" shows up more than 200 times in Isaiah. The isolated appearance of any one name is not so important. We're interested in the ELS codes here because of the clustering of names all in one small location. There are more than 40 words relevant to the crucifixion of Christ densely encrypted in the 15 sentences of this passage. To suggest that this just happened by random chance denies the overwhelming strength of the evidence. There are some interesting things to note. One of the three ELS codes for "Mary" is encrypted in such a way that it interweaves with "John." We find this significant when we recall that, while He was hanging on the cross, Jesus handed responsibility of His mother to His disciple, John. What's more, all three sequences of "Mary" use the same letter yod that encodes the name "Yeshua."" (Dr. Chuck Missler, The Fulcrum of the Entire Universe Isaiah 53: The Pivot Point of All History, 1166-1184 (Kindle Edition); Coeur d'Alene, ID; Koinonia House).

However, there is more. Indeed, there are MANY more codes found within Isaiah 53.

"Fifth is the apparent topical arrangement of portions of this mega-cluster into sub-clusters focused around specific subtopics. The Judas cluster is a clear example of this. Included in this very tight cluster are ELSs for "Judas," "zealot," "thirty (pieces of)," "silver," "shekels," "field of blood," "money" (mammon), "execute," "potter's field," "deceived," "darkness," "whipping," "Caesar," "enemy," and "dreadful day for Mary." If we were able only to say that we had found all of these ELSs in the entire Hebrew Bible, you would yawn. And you should. If we were only able to say that we had found all of these ELSs in only one book of the Bible, you should still yawn, but not quite as deeply. However, when we say that all of these discoveries cross a tiny span of only 18 letters of text in the 13th and

14th verses of chapter 52, you should be astonished. Finding that many thematically-related ELSs in one small space is almost certainly not coincidental. These 18 letters are composed of the last letter of one word, four subsequent complete words, and the first two letters of the sixth word. What does the literal text say? We have put the English equivalents of this 18-letter section in capital letters from the text of verses 13 and 14: "Behold, My servant shall rule wisely; he shall be exalted and lifted up AND BE VERY HIGH. JUST AS MANY WERE ASTONISHED OVER YOU —so much was the disfigurement from man, His appearance and His form from sons of mankind —" The locations of the key letters of these ELSs in the 13th and 14th verses of Isaiah 52 are shown below. We then show the Hebrew letter of the ELS, then the English for the ELS, and then the size and direction of its skips: (13: 6: 4) Resurrected (-144) (13: 7: 1) Execute (-88); Blood (-2); Abraham (-419) (13: 7: 2) Zealot (+ 223) (13: 7: 3) Field (+ 30); Blood (–2); Blood (+ 6); Blood (+ 7). (14: 1: 1) Dreadful day for Mary (-13); Silver (-40); The way (+ 4) (14: 1: 2) Darkness (-186) (14: 1: 3) Thirty [pieces of] (+ 106) (14: 1: 4) (14: 2: 1) Simon (+ 7); Caesar (-89); Enemy (-15) (14: 2: 2) Blood (+ 6); Money [mammon] (+ 13); Deceived (-131) (14: 2: 3) Shekels (-642); Field (+ 135); Blood (+ 7); Lots (+ 93) (14: 2: 4) Foundation (+ 270) (14: 3: 1) Darkness (-63); Seed (-19); Savior (+ 99) (14: 3: 2) Whipping (+ 475), Savior (+ 42) (14: 3: 3) Judas (-531) (14: 3: 4) Silver (-143) (14: 4: 1) Master (-37) (14: 4: 2) Dreadful day for Mary (-13); Archenemy (-29) It seems unusual that only one of the 18 letters has not been crossed by any of the 31 ELSs we located (these 31 ELSs cross this section a total of 35 times). And it is unusual. The probability of that happening by chance is about 7.6%. To find over 30 ELSs that are tightly related thematically and that cross such a short segment of text is, to say the least, extremely unusual. According to our calculations, the odds of such a cluster, or one we would consider to be comparable to it, being this compact, are about 1 in 490 million!" (R. Edwin Sherman with Nathan Jacobi, PH.D, and Dave Swaney, Bible Code Bombshell: Compelling Scientific Evidence That God Authored The Bible, 1231-1270 (Kindle Edition, emphasis added, M.T.); Green Forest, AR; New Leaf Press)

What are the odds of all this being coincidence?

"It should be evident from this comparison that the Isaiah 53 code cluster must largely be intentional in nature. It cannot be the result of chance. One would have to seriously downgrade a large number of these codes before the hypothesis that they were coincidental would even be a very remote possibility. The obvious presence of a very high percentage of extended codes that are related to the content of the literal text is one of the most convincing ones to me as an expert in statistical analysis." (R. Edwin Sherman with Nathan Jacobi, PH.D, and Dave Swaney, Bible Code Bombshell: Compelling Scientific Evidence That God Authored The Bible, 72 (Kindle Edition); Green Forest, AR; New Leaf Press)

Again:

"While many of the shorter ELSs we discovered in Isaiah 53 could reasonably have occurred by chance, the large number of long, topically relevant ELSs regarding Jesus Christ that we found in this text is far beyond the workings of coincidence. We have estimated that the odds of chance occurrence of the collection of long ELSs located in Isaiah 53 are so incredibly remote that the only rational conclusion is that this text was intentionally encoded. In the next chapter, we will describe how we arrived at this conclusion. What we are talking about here is nothing short of a proof of the miraculous that directly challenges the wisdom of our scientific age, a "wisdom" that denies all miracles. While the combined probability of this mega-cluster will vary depending on a few key assumptions, any choice of reasonable assumptions results in odds that are astronomically beyond chance. Most of them had to be intentionally encoded within this prophetic passage of the Old Testament....We have seen that it is a virtual certainty that the transcendent intelligence that authored the Isaiah 53 passage intended to link to prophetic surface text with Jesus Christ...The Christian points of view about the link between the prophecies in these chapters and Jesus Christ is bolstered significantly by the discovery of the great number of codes in this section. There is simply overwhelming evidence of a prophetic concurrence beyond human capability in the huge number of phrases and words straight out of the Gospel's account of Christ's execution that appear in these two chapters of Isaiah. The fact that so many codes in the underlying Hebrew text contain the details of the playing out of the prophecy of Isaiah, Moses and many other Old Testament prophets is totally beyond human comprehension." (R. Edwin Sherman with Nathan Jacobi, PH.D, and Dave Swaney, Bible Code Bombshell: Compelling Scientific Evidence That God Authored The Bible, 87-91 (Kindle Edition, emphasis added, M.T.); Green Forest, AR; New Leaf Press) (R. Edwin Sherman with Nathan Jacobi, PH.D, and Dave Swaney, Bible Code Bombshell: Compelling Scientific Evidence That God Authored The Bible, 87-91 (Kindle Edition, emphasis added, M.T.); Green Forest, AR; New Leaf Press).

Some Additional Examples

Another fascinating thing to consider are some of the many ELS codes found throughout certain sections of the Old Testament that deal specifically with the Messiah. Let's notice some.

The following excerpts (unless otherwise noted) are from R. Edwin Sherman with Nathan Jacobi, PH.D., and Dave Swaney, in their book, Bible Code Bombshell: Compelling Scientific Evidence That God Authored The Bible (Kindle Edition; Green Forest, AR; New Leaf Press).

The authors note:

"What follow is a collection of the most cogent Jesus codes, drawn from only four locations in the Old Testament: (1) Isaiah 53, (2) Psalm 22, (3) the Ten Commandments (Exodus 20), and (4) Proverbs 15. The forcefulness and forthrightness of many of these codes is breathtaking. Within each topic, codes are presented in their descending order of: (1) relevance and appropriateness of content, and (2) length. Twice as much weight was given to relevance as to length in determinism in each ranking." (R. Edwin Sherman with Nathan Jacobi, PH.D, and Dave Swaney, Bible Code Bombshell: Compelling Scientific Evidence That God Authored The Bible, 184-194 (Kindle Edition); Green Forest, AR; New Leaf Press)

Notice some of the codes which their scholars have uncovered through meticulous research.

Table 7A (Top Crucifixion Codes)

"You will cry out for the blood of the Messiah." (Psalm 22)

"The guilt offering, the son of man, humbled himself." (Psalm 22)

"Golgotha, where his reputation came from." (Psalm 22)

"And where are they? The Sanhedrin is finished." (Isaiah 53)

"Dreadful day for Mary." (Isaiah 53)

"And chief cornerstone found guilty." (Psalm 22)

"Piercers of my feet." (Isaiah 53)

"Deer of the Dawn." (Isaiah 53)

"Who crucified Jesus?" (Psalm 22)

"Deer of the Dawn." (Proverbs 15)

"Who is Jesus? The guilt offering." (Psalm 22)

"Those who hated me without cause." (Isaiah 53)

"Three holidays, Mount of Olives is a witness." (Exodus 20)

"Extinguish the light A living sacrifice." (Proverbs 15)

"Final guilt offering." (Psalm 22)

"She wept much." (Isaiah 53)

"Living offering." (Psalm 22)

"She weeps much." (Psalm 22)

"Mt. Moriah." (Psalm 22)

"My God, Why?" (Psalm 22)

"He was oppressed." (Exodus 20)

"It is finished." (Isaiah 53)

"The evil Roman city." (Isaiah 53)

"Yeshu be judged." (Isaiah 53)

"Struck by God." (Psalm 22)

"It is finished." (Proverbs 15)

"His spirit on a tree." (Isaiah 53)

Table 7B

"He offended. The resurrection of Jesus. He is risen indeed." (Isaiah 53)

"And command fleets of resurrection from above to flee with raging excitement." (Isaiah 53)

"Rejoice, he said, with fire from his soul, and he arose." (Proverbs 15)

"And bless her people as in the resurrection." (Proverbs 15)

"It is enough for us. And the resurrection is lofty. And God (Jehovah) died. And God (Elohim), the prophet of the temple is afraid." (Psalm 22)

"He will know the turmoil of resurrection. I will carry this declaration, my mother." (Psalm 22)

"The value of resurrection is thus dear." (Isaiah 53)

"Long live the risen God of action. It is finished. And where is the resurrection of Jesus of blessed memory? For whom are the twelve?" (Psalm 22)

"The ascension of Jesus, and light preserved for them." (Proverbs 15)

"Resurrection, his end will be built up into a humble messenger." (Proverbs 15)

"His word was defeated. The people have turned and nourished the shoot of my womb in the resurrection of last evening." (Proverbs 15)

"The sea in the land of promises, and the head of resurrection, are repeated with me here." (Proverbs 15)

"From my fear of the resurrection he made a monument, or the power of the mouth." (Isaiah 53)

"I will be asleep. Take bread and water. I will console the living by the resurrection of my cedar, the lamb of everybody's daughter." (Proverbs 15)

"Keep resurrection for heaven. You were a man." (Psalm 22)

"The memory of resurrection is in me." (Psalm 22)

"Resurrection, let it be obscure." (Psalm 22)

"God-which God?-is resurrection." (Psalm 22)

Table 7D (Top Divinity Of Jesus Codes)

"Please be merciful, miracle of God, rule gently, the Son soars from on high." (Psalm 22)

"They are for him-God and Jesus are one-and for you." (Proverbs 15)

"God is for them, and long live the exalted flame. God is Jesus." (Isaiah 53)

"Jesus has laid the foundation for existence. Where is the I AM?" (Exodus 20)

"And the Son of God loved you." (Psalm 22)

"Mary is the mother of God." (Isaiah 53)

"Jesus is God Almighty." (Proverbs 15)

"God's Son will count for them." (Psalm 22)

"Jesus (Yeshu) is the living God." (Psalm 22)

"Jesus (Yeshu) is the living God." (Proverbs 15)

"It will be understood. Jesus created." (Isaiah 53)

"Jesus (Yeshu) is man and God." (Proverbs 15)

"Yeshu is Son of the name." (Proverbs 15)

"Jesus created to the Father." (Isaiah 53)

"Jesus created a high gift." (Isaiah 53)

"Son of the name." (Proverbs 15)

"Son of the highest." (Proverbs 15)

'Your God is Jesus" (Proverbs 15)

"God and man." (Psalm 22)

"King of kings." (Psalm 22)

"Man and God." (Proverbs 15)

"Son of God." (Proverbs 15)

"Son of Elohim." (Isaiah 53)

"Son of Elohim." (Exodus 20)

"Living Yahweh." (Proverbs 15)

"The Trinity." (Proverbs 15)

"Immanuel." (Proverbs 15)

"Immanuel." (Proverbs 15)

Table 7E (Top Messiah Codes)

"And only Messiah; dwell in those words that he taught on high as our prince." (Psalm 22)

"You will cry out for the blood of the Messiah." (Psalm 22)

"Give them a Jewish Messiah who will become a priest." (Isaiah 53)

"For the weak ones, the prophesied Messiah is a prevention." (Exodus 20)

"Jesus the Messiah." (Proverbs 15)

"True Messiah, lift up God almighty." (Exodus 20)

"Every eye is looking for a true Messiah." (Exodus 20)

"Hello, the one mentioned above! Where is the rib (i.e, the basis) founded by the convert of Jesus my Messiah?" (Psalm 22)

"Wonderful Counselor." (Proverbs 15)

"Newborn infant is a king." (Proverbs 15)

"Your God Jesus is putting on a crown." (Proverbs 15)

"What is the false messiah?" (Exodus 20)

"Prince of peace." (Exodus 20)

"Jesus reigns." (Isaiah 53)

"Ruler In Israel." (Proverbs 15)

"Prince Who Is Light." (Proverbs 15)

"And father root of Jesse." (Proverbs 15)

"True Messiah." (Isaiah 53)

"My Messiah is Jesus." (Psalm 22)

"Only Messiah." (Psalm 22)

"King Jesus." (Psalm 22)

"Jesus is Messiah." (Proverbs 15)

"Son of David." (Exodus 20)

"Everlasting Father." (Exodus 20)

"The Promised One." (Proverbs 15)

"He will be great." (Proverbs 15)

"The king." (Psalm 22)

"Messianic." (Psalm 22)

Still More Examples

Here are still more examples of the Bible Codes.

"What follow is a collection of the most cogent Jesus codes, drawn from only four locations in the Old Testament: (1) Isaiah 53, (2) Psalm 22, (3) the Ten Commandments (Exodus 20), and (4) Proverbs 15. The forcefulness and forthrightness of many of these codes is breathtaking. Within each topic, codes are presented in their descending order of: (1) relevance and appropriateness of content, and (2) length. Twice as much weight was given to relevance as to length in determinism in each ranking." (R. Edwin Sherman with Nathan Jacobi, PH.D, and Dave Swaney, Bible Code Bombshell: Compelling Scientific Evidence That God Authored The Bible, 184-194 (Kindle Edition); Green Forest, AR; New Leaf Press)

Table 7A

Text	Top Crucifixion Codes (Codes In Descending Order Of Relevance And Length)
Ps. 22	You will cry out for the blood of the Messiah.
Ps. 22	The guilt offering, the son of man, humbled himself.
Ps. 22	Golgotha, where his reputation came from.
Isa. 53	And where are they? The Sanhedrin is finished.
Isa. 53	Dreadful day for Mary.
Ps. 22	And chief cornerstone found guilty.
Isa. 53	Piercers of my feet.
Isa. 53	Deer of the Dawn.
Ps. 22	Who crucified Jesus?
Pro. 15	Deer of the Dawn
Ps. 22	Who is Jesus? The guilt offering.
Isa. 53	Those who hated me without cause.
Ex. 20	Three holidays, Mount of Olives is a witness.
Pr. 15	Extinguish the light. A living sacrifice.

Ps. 22	Final guilt offering.
Isa. 53	She wept much.
Ps. 22	Living offering.
Ps. 22	She weeps much.
Ps. 22	Mt. Moriah.
Ps. 22	My God, Why?
Ps. 22	Jerusalem
Ex. 20	He was oppressed.
Pr. 15	Jerusalem
Ps. 22	Crucified.
Ps. 22	And he will reach about the humble Kidron, as if bearing my robe.
Isa. 53	It is finished.
Isa 53	The evil Roman city.
Isa. 53	Yeshu—be judged.
Ps. 22	Struck by God.
Pr. 15	It is finished.
Pr. 15	Cross.
Isa. 53	His spirit on a tree.

Ex. 20	Pierced
Pr. 15	You will see that they will bear arms.
Ps. 22	The damp Kidron is singing for her.

Table 7B

Text	Top Resurrection Codes
Isa. 53	He offended. The resurrection of Jesus. He is risen indeed.
Isa. 53	And command fleets of resurrection from above to flee with raging excitement.
Pr. 15	Rejoice, he said, with fire from his soul, and he arose.
Pr. 15	And bless her people as in the resurrection.
Ps. 22	It is enough for us. And the resurrection is lofty. And God (Jehovah) died. And God (Elohim), the prophet of the temple is afraid.
Ps. 22	He will know the turmoil of resurrection. I will carry this declaration, my mother.
Isa. 53	The value of resurrection is thus dear.
Ps. 22	Long live the risen God of action. It is finished. And where is the resurrection of Jesus of blessed memory? For whom are the twelve?
Pr. 15	The ascension of Jesus, and light preserved for them.

Pr. 15	Resurrection, his end will be built up into a humble messenger.
Pr. 15	His word was defeated. The people have turned and nourished the shoot of my womb in the resurrection of last evening.
Pr. 15	The sea in the island of promises, and the head of resurrection, are repeated with me here.
Isa. 53	From my fear of resurrection he made a monument, or the power of the mouth.
Pr. 15	I will be asleep. Take bread and water. I will console the living by the resurrection of my cedar, the lamb of everybody's daughter.
Ps. 22	Keep resurrection for heaven. You were a man.
Ps. 22	The memory of resurrection is in me.
Ps. 22	Resurrection, but let it be obscure.
Ps. 22	God-which God?-is resurrection.
Ps. 22	Resurrection

Table 7C

Text	Top Ascension Codes
Isa 53	And commanded that we skip everything but the gem of ascension.

Isa. 53	Long love the ascension coming from God.
Isa. 53	The ascension of Jesus: for the sleeping one will shout. Listen!
Isa. 53	Father, the ascension of Jesus is heavenly.
Isa. 53	Ascension, considering God's hands under me.
Ps. 22	The ascension of Jesus, the lofty one, to him.
Pr. 15	The ascension of Jesu, and light preserved for them.
Ps. 22	He disguised the might. And God is there in the gift of dwellings of ascension. Her daughter will rule the sea.
Isa. 53	Ascension, we will thank God, and they will be near my shelter. Recognize her blood.
Isa 53	Ascension, be a cause for my heart, and render my father transformed. I will be ashamed, and will divide the temple of the messenger.
Isa. 53	Ascension, monument to the saturated. And the hand of the monument is the daughter of the cedar supporter.
Isa. 53	The ascension of Jesus is the death of the witness.

Table 7D

Text	Top Divinity Of Jesus Codes
Ps. 22 Pr. 15	Please be merciful, miracle of God, rule gently, the son soars from on high.
Pr. 15	They are for him-God and Jesus are one-and for you.
Isa. 53	God is for them, and long live the exalted flame. God is Jesus.
Ex. 20	Jesus has laid the foundation for existence. Where is the I AM?
Ps. 22	And the son of God loved you.
Isa. 53	Mary is the mother of God.
Pr. 15	Jesus is God Almighty.
Ps. 22	God's Son will count for them.
Ps. 22	Jesus (Yeshu) is the living God.
Pr. 15	Jesus (Yeshua) is the living God.
Isa. 53	It will be understood. Jesus created.
Pr. 15	Jesus (Yeshu) is man and God.
Pr. 15	Yeshu is son of the name.
Isa. 53	Jesus created to the father.

Isa. 53	Jesus created a high gift.
Pr. 15	Son of the name.
Pr. 15	Son of the highest.
Pr. 15	Your God is Jesus.
Ps. 22	God and man.
Ps. 22	King of kings.
Pro. 15	Man and God.
Pr. 15	Son of God
Isa. 53	Son Of Elohim
Ex. 20	Son of Elohim.
Pr. 15	Living Yahweh
Pr. 15	The Trinity
Pr. 15	Immanuel
Pr. 15	Immanuel

Table 7E

Text	Top Messiah Codes
Ps. 22	And only messiah: dwell in those words that he taught on high as our prince.

Ps. 22	You will cry out for the blood of the Messiah.
Isa. 53	Give them a Jewish messiah who will become a priest.
Ex. 20	For the weak ones, the prophesied messiah is a prevention.
Pr. 15	Jesus the messiah.
Ex. 20	True messiah, lift up God almighty.
Ex. 20	Every eye is looking for a true messiah.
Ps. 22	Hello, the one mentioned above! Where is the rib (i.e., the basis) founded by the convert of Jesus my messiah?
Pr. 15	Wonderful counselor
Pr. 15	Newborn infant is a king.
Pr. 15	Your God Jesus is putting on a crown.
Ex. 20	What is the false messiah?
Ex. 20	Prince of peace
Isa. 53	Jesus reigns.
Pr. 15	Ruler in Israel.
Pr. 15	Prince who is light.
Pr. 15	And father of root of Jesse.

Isa. 53	True messiah.
Ps. 22	My messiah is Jesus.
Ps. 22	Only messiah.
Ps. 22	King Jesus
Pr. 15	Jesus is messiah.
Ex. 20	Son of David.
Ex. 20	Everlasting father.
Pr. 15	The promised one.
Pr. 15	He will be great.
Ps. 22	The king
Ps. 22	Messianic

Table FG

Text	Top "Who Is Jesus" Codes
Ex. 20	Jesus is my name as any ignorant person from among them would have realized.
Ex. 20	Or come down, for the father of destiny will make you rejoice. And who is Yeshua? Our master over death. Prevent my fever for him. And who is God, who, like their nation, has crushed you?

Ps. 22	He attracts a man with the lion of Judah.
Ex. 20	They wished evil to Jesus the king.
Ex. 20	King Jesus, the heart of the nation.
Ps. 22	Who is Jesus? The guilt offering.
Ex. 20	His name is Yeshua. Recognize thus.
Pr. 15	What is he? The gift. Yeshua…
Ex. 20	His name is Jesus (Yeshua).
Ps. 22	His name is Jesus.
Ps. 22	Jesus is the shepherd.
Pr	Jesus the Nazarene.
Ex. 20	The last Adam.
Ex. 20	He is the word.
Pr. 15	Newborn king.
Pr. 15	King is a child.
Pr. 15	Descendant of David.
Pr. 15	Second Adam.
Ps. 22	Second Adam.
Pr. 15	Came in the flesh.

Ps. 22	The Nazarene
Pr. 15	Nazareth
Pr. 15	The Galilee
Pr. 15	Son of man.
Pr. 15	Carpenter
Pr. 15	Galilean
Ps. 22	Nazareth

Table 7H

Text	Top "Who Is The Suffering Servant" Codes
Isa. 53	Gushing from above, Jesus is my strong name, and the clouds rejoiced.
Isa. 53	And thirst for all of him is the faith of Mary the mother.
Isa. 53	Jesus the gift is master and my lord.
Isa. 53	Bemoan the prince, Jesus the king.
Isa. 53	The Rabbi fro meth glory of God.
Isa. 53	My shepherds are among the disciples.
Isa. 53	Who is Jesus? Master.
Isa. 53	True Messiah.

Isa. 53	Second Adam

9-11 Codes

(R. Edwin Sherman with Nathan Jacobi, PH.D, and Dave Swaney, Bible Code Bombshell: Compelling Scientific Evidence That God Authored The Bible, 171-176 (Kindle Edition); Green Forest, AR; New Leaf Press)

Table 6B

Codes 46+ Letters Long From Ezekiel 37 Cluster

Expected: 0.092

Actual: 6

(61) There is quarrel in his speeches. A living brother uttered words to them and to me. And Zubaydah turned to his sea, without then lying for a whole week. Oh, the mountain of her interior will bear a testimonial to her name.

(53). The island was restful, elevated, and it happened. Where is Libya? And you have disrupted the nation. She changed a word. He answered them with combat. Why the navy and the smell of the bottom of the sea?

(52). For where has God consumed from you? And in it are stones of substantial sickness for us. You will indeed delay their diagnosis, because of His own reflection in the one who solves.

(52). The trouble of the newborn one is vigilant and honest because of the ruin. Get out as if Iraq had been sent out. The majority is aware that, Rest In Peace, you will come-the villainy with light. You will understand the heart of granite.

(48). Let the oppressed be congratulated, saturated from Him at 2001. And let them be guarded by the echo of the Father's Son, supported by the U.S. I will see but he has the knowledge.

Bible Codes Related To The September 11, 2001 Terrorist Attack

(The following is from Grant Jeffrey, The Signature of God: Astonishing Bible Codes Reveal September 11 Terror Attacks, 240-242 (Kindle Edition); Colorado Springs, CO; Waterbrook Press-he is referencing the work of the authors of R. Edwin Sherman with Nathan Jacobi, PH.D, and Dave Swaney, Bible Code Bombshell: Compelling Scientific Evidence That God Authored The Bible, (Kindle Edition); Green Forest, AR; New Leaf Press, when they were studying the mega-cluster of Ezekiel 37; the number at the end of the code represents the ELS Skip Distance)

Manhattan 698
World Trade Center 78
Tower Destroyed Toward The Mountain O God 904
Toward The Mountain, Pentagon 65626
Hijackers 29
Ignite The Airliner 267
Terror Hot In Me 430
Where Are They? 37
And let God not strike terror 37

Terror of the sea is there in them 448

Jihad 210

Arafat 904

Philistines 1406

Bin Laden Blood of the poor 93

You will spit at tradition Al Kada 1430

Muhammed Omar 37

Taliban 81

Fire from the heart 267

Saddam Hussein 150684

Saddam 87, 942

Hussein 3714, 3985

This is the king of Babylon 5564

Iraq 195

More Codes From Ezekiel 7:2-8

New York

U.S.

An Unheard of Disaster

In The Morning
September 11
2001
Bin Laden
Afghan
Taliban
Airliner
Firemen
Saddam
Iraq
Conspiracy
Devastation
Cruelty
Terror
Horrible
Death
Destruction
Butchery

Bible Codes Related To Saddam Hussein

"But then, we suddenly came across the "Imagine a picture of terminal illness. The days of Saddam are over" code. That discovery woke us up. A few minutes later came "The rest of my severe illness is spreading, Saddam, like a missile to you, Esau. Where is he? Or, who is the tyrant?" (The next day, Nathan revised his translation of this to "The rest of my severe illness is spreading, Saddam, as if from a missile made for you. Where is he? Or, who is the tyrant?"). Fifteen minutes later we found the "Saddam, terminal illness from everything" ELS. Finding all three was like having panned unsuccessfully for gold all day, and then suddenly looking down into our pan to see three golf-ball-sized nuggets. What is unusual about these three ELSs is that they all use the same word for terminal illness, the Hebrew "da'vai" (). To find three ELSs on one subject in one session, all using the same word, is unheard of. We were nearly dumbstruck by it. Later that day, when we ran the full ELSs through the search software and found that they all appeared within 54 letters of each other, and that the seven-letter ELS with Saddam Hussein's full name touched down in the same area, we suspected that this was almost certainly the result of intentional encoding. Two days later, on the ninth day after the attacks, we posted the news of our latest discoveries on the site. Over the next weeks and months, as the war on terror was announced and got underway, we continued our research into this amazing cluster. It eventually yielded a stunning code that accurately foretold the outcome of the war in Iraq some 15 months before it began. You will crush the guilty Saddam and the month of Iyar will be restful. We found this code in December of 2001 and posted it on our web site within days—long before there was serious discussion about an incursion into Iraq. But its message made perfect sense to us when grouped with all of the Saddam Hussein codes we had found along with so many terrorism ELSs in the cluster. As it turned out, coalition forces did crush the Saddam

Hussein government, and the month of Iyar (within the month of May in 2003) was restful. In June, of course, insurgent sneak attacks began to undo the restful atmosphere for occupying forces in Iraq. This code is not the only case we have seen of an ELS issuing a declaration about the outcome of a future event that was borne out by subsequent actions. One such code is legendary among code researchers. Jeffrey Satinover's book, Cracking the Bible Code, told an unverified story about the use of Bible codes by the Mossad, Israel's intelligence agency, to foretell future events. This instance also involved Saddam Hussein. During the first Gulf War in 1991, the Mossad knew that Iraq planned to fire Scud missiles at Israel. But the Israeli government couldn't very well order citizens and tourists into bomb shelters for days on end. Such an action would cripple the nation's economy. The Mossad needed to know exactly when the Scud attacks would come. Satinover states that he has seen a document noting that the date that the first scuds were launched and fell on Israel was found before the war started. He further notes that the contents were confirmed in an audiotaped interview with one of the principal individuals involved. 25 The Mossad is not talking and probably never will, but rumors persist that they had the help of Israeli Bible code researchers in determining the date. They may be keeping this intelligence under wraps in case they have to use it again. We may never know for sure." (R. Edwin Sherman with Nathan Jacobi, PH.D, and Dave Swaney, Bible Code Bombshell: Compelling Scientific Evidence That God Authored The Bible, 136139 (Kindle Edition); Green Forest, AR; New Leaf Press)

There are many other codes which may be considered.

Let's Look At The Numbers

Someone may ask, "Well, what are the odds that these are just random coincidences in the text, and not actually codes?"

Our authors respond to this question in great detail.

Let's look at numbers.

"In this book, we will examine two clusters of codes that are so extensive and complex that it is hard to see how anyone who truly comprehended them could think that they were simply the product of chance. Each cluster includes dozens of lengthy ELSs, all crossing a fairly short portion of the Hebrew Bible that are topically related to one another and to the subject matter of the surface text. In chapter 4, we arrive at the conclusion that the odds that a cluster as extensive as that found in Isaiah 53 could be due to chance are less than 1 in 2,189,000,000,000,000,000, 000,000,000,000,000,000,000,000,000,000,000,0 00,000,000,000,000,000,000,000,000,000,000,000,00 0,000,000,000,000,000,000,000,000,000,000,000,000 ,000,000,000,000,000,000,000,000,000,000,000,000, 000,000,000,000,000,000. Odds so remote are virtually impossible for the human mind to comprehend. It is truly staggering. Something as improbable as the Isaiah 53 cluster has about the same odds as someone buying only one lottery ticket in each of 33 different states and winning the one-in-a-million jackpot in every state. In other words, the chances are about as zero as you can get. In chapter 6, we arrive at the conclusion that the odds that a cluster as extensive as that found in Ezekiel 37 could be due to chance are less than 1 in 640,000,000,000,000,000,000,000,000, 000,000,000,000,000,000,000,000,000,000,000,000,0 00,000,000,000,000,000,000,000,000,000,000,000,00 0,000,000,000,000,000,000,000,000. Such odds, though less remote than those for the Isaiah 53 cluster, are nevertheless far beyond the range of what chance can produce.

Real or Coincidental? The code clusters we have researched and verified in the past five years, taken altogether, present strong evidence that the phenomenon of Bible codes cannot be coincidental. This begs us to somehow reckon with it. If the phenomenon is not coincidental, is not the alternative that they are intentional? If that is indeed true, then a new chapter in the saga of the long struggle between science and religion is now being written. I believe that it must be true and that there can only be one creative mind behind the phenomenon—the same Intelligence that created the cosmos, God himself. There is a growing contingency of mathematicians and intellectuals who have closely examined this phenomenon and are of the opinion that the evidence strongly supports the hypothesis that it is real. They may stop short of claiming publicly that God wrote the Bible, but some have had their lives radically changed by what they have seen in Bible codes. The three authors of the paper, "Equidistant Letter Sequences in the Book of Genesis," published in the August 1994 issue of the journal, Statistical Science (Dr. Eliyahu Rips, Associate Professor of Mathematics, Hebrew University of Jerusalem; and Doron Witztum and Yoav Rosenberg, researchers at Jerusalem College of Technology—the WRR mentioned earlier). Professor Rips is a top-ranked mathematician who was able to leave Lithuania following the fall of communism. After immigrating to Israel, he became interested in Torah codes. His work with them influenced his decision to transition from atheism to orthodox Judaism. 12 Professor Robert Haralick, mentioned earlier, has written an academic paper, "Testing the Torah Code Hypothesis: The Torah Code Effect is Real," showing how the primary skeptic publication refuting the WRR paper in Statistical Science used "cooked" data. Harold Gans, a senior code-breaker at the National Security Agency, 13 and Robert J. Aumann, considered to be Israel's most famous mathematician, one of the world's experts in game theory, and a member of both the Israeli and the U.S. National Academy of Science. 14 Second are three other authors who have published on the subject: Dr. Jeffrey Satinover, author of the excellent Cracking the Bible Code, which was published in 1997 by William Morrow and Company, Inc. Dr. Satinover is a practicing psychiatrist and former William James Lecturer in Psychology and Religion at Harvard. He holds degrees from M.I.T., the Harvard Graduate School of Education, and the University of Texas. 15 Satinover is so intrigued with the potential of Bible codes that he has earned a masters in physics since completing his book and is now working on a doctorate in the field. D.J. Bartholomew, author of the article, "Probability, Statistics and Theology," in a 1988 issue of the Journal of the Royal Statistical Society. Daniel Michelson, a professor in the Department of Computer Science and Applied Mathematics at the Weizman Institute of Science in Rehovat, Israel, has posted a supportive article at www. 600000men.com/ book/ bo.htm. Third, it should be noted that the research behind WRR's paper was peer reviewed three times by various mathematicians before the editors of Statistical Science would publish it. These unnamed reviewers must have signed off on Dr. Rips 'research or it would not have appeared in that professional journal. In addition, four professors (H. Furstenberg of the Hebrew University of Jerusalem, I. Piatetski-Shapiro of Yale, and David Kazhdan and J. Bernstein of Harvard) have issued a joint statement regarding the results of their review of Dr. Rips 'research stating that the work was carried out by serious researchers, but that it is a controversial topic that may require a higher level of statistical significance than would be required of more routine research. They also stated that the results deserve further study. 16 Finally, we have the chairman of Harvard's mathematics department, Dr. Kazhdan stating that Bible codes are a real phenomenon, but that the conclusions derived from them are left to each individual to decide." (R. Edwin Sherman with Nathan Jacobi, PH.D, and Dave Swaney, Bible Code Bombshell: Compelling Scientific Evidence That God Authored The Bible, 45-49 (Kindle Edition); Green Forest, AR; New Leaf Press)

Later we are told:

"The Christian point of view about the link between the prophecies in these chapters and Jesus Christ is bolstered significantly by the discovery of the great number of codes in this section. There is simply overwhelming evidence of a prophetic concurrence beyond human capability in the huge number of phrases and words straight out of the Gospel's account of Christ's execution that appear in these two chapters of Isaiah. The fact that so many codes in the underlying Hebrew text contain the details of the playing out of the prophecy of Isaiah, Moses and many other Old Testament prophets is totally beyond human comprehension. Could Not Have Been Written After Christ's Death The existence of so many ELSs in this passage also argues vehemently against the possibility that the text of Isaiah 52 and 53 was written following the death of Jesus. If this passage in Isaiah was written after Jesus had died, then why did its author implant such an amazingly complex web of underlying codes authenticating Jesus as the messiah? Such a possibility makes no sense whatsoever. Not only that, but the Dead Sea Scrolls contain complete copies of this passage made 100 years before Jesus was born. In The Dead Sea Scrolls Bible, the authors note that an intact scroll containing the entire Book of Isaiah was found in Cave 1, and that Isaiah and Psalms both have very large manuscripts preserved. 23 Other comments make it clear that Isaiah is the only book for which the complete manuscript was found. Is it not ironic that Jewish people, who to date have been the strongest proponents of Bible/ Torah codes, are faced with the possibility that the most conclusive evidence in their favor was a passage that provided the strongest challenge to their skeptical views about Jesus? What other ironies await us as we continue to explore this incredible labyrinth of ELSs? All that is certain is that the controversies will rage on." (R. Edwin Sherman with Nathan Jacobi, PH.D, and Dave Swaney, Bible Code Bombshell: Compelling Scientific Evidence That God Authored The Bible, 91-92 (Kindle Edition); Green Forest, AR; New Leaf Press)

Why the ELS Codes are Becoming More Popularly Known in Our Day and Age

I must admit: the more I learned about the Bible Codes, the more amazed I was (and have been) by the powerful evidence which they bring to the table. Could it be that perhaps one reason why the Codes are in the Bible is to provide another line of evidence, especially for our generation? After all, it is only with the help of computers that we are able to find many of these Codes now.

"When I first heard about the codes during a trip to Israel in the late 1980s, I was naturally quite skeptical. However, after more than fifteen years of careful evaluation of the phenomenon, I believe that there is powerful evidence that the code is genuine. Additional research during the last six years has provided more evidence that God placed these codes in the Scriptures. They provide fascinating details about historical events that have come to pass thousands of years after the biblical text was written. The Bible Codes provide a new type of evidence that supplements the many other types of evidence that prove the Scriptures are supernatural. This discovery may provide a last measure of incontrovertible evidence to our skeptical generation that the Bible is the inspired Word of God....There is no question that the Bible Codes represent an astonishing new claim that demands a high level of validation before we should accept it. By nature I am a skeptic. When I first heard about this, I thought that the claims of the code researchers seemed unbelievable. That is why I am not offended in the slightest when someone tells me that they cannot accept the Bible Codes as genuine. However, after almost a dozen years of research, I am more convinced than ever that God placed the Bible Codes within the text of the Bible to prove to this skeptical generation through this remarkable new evidence that He inspired the human writers to record His revelation to humanity in the Word of God...With powerful apologetic evidence, Christians can challenge the skeptics in our generation to seriously consider the claims of the Bible that it is the supernatural Word of God. The Lord commands Christians, in the words of 1 Peter, to be prepared to explain and defend the reasonableness of our faith in the Bible and in Jesus Christ. We need to be prepared to persuade men and women to turn from their unbelief to seriously consider the claims of Jesus Christ. "But sanctify the Lord God in your hearts: and be ready always to give an answer to every man that asketh you a reason of the hope that is in you with meekness and fear" (1 Peter 3:15). In light of God's command to defend our faith to our generation of unbelievers, I find it natural that we should from time to time discover new types of evidence in both the text of the Scriptures as well as in the world of science and archeology. I found an interesting quotation from the Christian writer, Joseph Butler, in his The Analogy of Religion that illustrates this point. "Nor is it at all incredible that a book which has been so long in the possession of mankind, should contain many truths as yet undiscovered." (Grant R. Jeffrey, The Signature Of God: Conclusive Proof That Every Teaching, Every Command, Every Promise In The Bible Is True, 224-227 (Kindle Edition); Colorado Springs, Colorado; Waterbrook Press)

Conclusion

In 1994, a paper entitled "Equidistant Letter Sequences In The Book Of Genesis" was published in the well-known journal, *Statistical Science.* The study was overseen by three Israeli mathematicians Doron Witztum, Yoav Rosenberg, and Eliyahu Rips at the Hebrew University and the Jerusalem College of Technology.

The details of the study (as well as their shocking conclusions) are recounted by Missler:

"In 1994, researchers Doron Witzum, Eliyahu Rips, and Yoav Rosenberg caused a great uproar. The men had conceived of an experiment in the mid-1980s, the results of which they eventually submitted to a prestigious peer-reviewed journal called Statistical Science . In their experiment, they formed a list of 34 of the most prominent rabbis in Jewish history along with their dates of birth and death. Remarkably, each rabbi was found in the Bible encrypted with those dates of birth and death. The statistical likelihood of this taking place was about 1 in 775 million, but the statistical review board thought it was contrived. They said, "Let's add another 32 rabbis to your list." The researchers agreed and added 32 additional names, along with their dates of birth and death. These additional 32 were also found. (Dr. Chuck Missler, The Fulcrum of the Entire Universe Isaiah 53: The Pivot Point of All History, 1116-1126 (Kindle Edition); Coeur d'Alene, ID; Koinonia House)

The study in *Statistical Science Journal* concluded with these words:

"We conclude that the proximity of the ELS's (Equidistant Letter Sequences) with related meanings in the Book of Genesis is not due to chance."

We should also consider the amazing work of Professor Harold Gans.

Being a U.S. intelligence expert who has spent years studying complicated foreign intelligence codes for the Armed Forces, as well as a brilliant mathematician who has published in well over 100 prestigious magazines, Gans decided to carefully examine the authenticity of these codes.

When he first heard of equidistant letter skipping in the Hebrew text from his friend Professor Doron Witztum (who was also a skeptic of these matters), he believed that these things were "ridiculous."

Gans created a very sophisticated computer program in 1989 to determine whether these "codes" were actually true, or were the result of sloppy research. For nineteen days and nights, he had his computer carefully examine all of the 78,604 Hebrew letters in the Book of Genesis.

As a result of his careful research, he was forced to conclude that the codes found in the Old Testament through equidistant letter skipping are very real, and cannot be the result of random chance or human design.

He has been so convicted by his careful investigations that he travels around the world, teaching in various synagogues of these matters, and works to show nonbelievers through these evidences that the Bible is, indeed, the inspired Word of God.

It is also worth noting that, when these same studies were conducted using other religious texts besides the Bible, the "codes" were not found.

The evidence is mounting that the Bible Codes are very real, and may not be explained by mere coincidence or unaided human wisdom.

CHAPTER FIVE

SCIENTIFIC FOREKNOWLEDGE OF THE BIBLE WRITERS AS PROOF THAT THE BIBLE IS THE INSPIRED WORD OF GOD

"You will never convince me that the Bible is pro-science! Everyone knows that the writers of the Bible were ignorant shepherds living in caves!"

Johnathan was a very quiet young man.

He was unassuming and reserved.

To every appearance, nothing seemed to upset him.

Everything, that is, except his preconceptions about the Bible.

John had been raised in a Christian home, one where going to church and reading the Bible was strongly emphasized. However, when entering into high school and then later college, Johnathan's faith had been challenged in ways that he had never expected (or been prepared for). As a result, by the time that he was a junior in college, he had become a self-professing agnostic. When we started getting together for Bible studies, he was curious as to my faith in God. After spending several weeks discussing the evidences for God's existence, we had turned our attention to the Bible and science. The common misconception that science and the Bible are at odds and opposed to each other is prevalent in our culture. Many are not aware that not only does the Bible encourage humans to utilize science[128], but the Bible Prophets display remarkable knowledge of scientific facts that were completely unheard of for centuries (even millennia)-some of which are only now being recognized and understood! This stands as another powerful evidence that the Bible is the Word of God.

Let me take you on a tour of some of these evidences.

The Laws Of Thermodynamics

The First and Second Laws of Thermodynamics are two of the most prominent and important laws of existence. Blanchard describes them and shows us why these matter in our study of God:

"Not everyone welcomed the Big Bang concept, some disliking the idea that the universe had a beginning because it strongly implied a supernatural creation. In 1948 Sir Fred Hoyle helped to formulate the 'steady-state 'theory. This maintained that the universe was infinite and eternal and that the entire cosmic process was kept in balance as matter simply sprang into existence out of nothing at a regular rate to replace the matter which had 'died 'through expansion. The biggest problem with this view is that it violates the First Law of Thermodynamics, sometimes known as the law of conservation of mass and energy. This fundamental law, which Isaac Asimov called 'the most powerful and most fundamental generalization about the universe that scientists have ever been able to make',24 states that matter and energy can neither be self-created nor destroyed...The First Law of Thermodynamics clearly supports the idea that an expanding universe must have had a beginning but could not have created itself. The Second Law of Thermodynamics, which states that any isolated physical system becomes less ordered and more random over time, provides another piece for the cosmic jigsaw. Applied very simply and generally, it means that our entire universe is running down. As the rotation of the planets and their moons slows down, and as stars (and whole galaxies) burn themselves out, the matter in our universe is becoming more and more disorganized as its energy is dissipated. The logical consequence of this is that the universe cannot be eternal. If it were, the stars would have ceased to shine long ago and all the energy in our universe would have long since been evenly spread throughout space. At the same time, this suggests that if the universe is becoming less ordered, it must have been more ordered in the past, and have had a highly ordered beginning." (John Blanchard, Does God Believe In

Atheists? 5601-5620 (Kindle Edition); Carlisle, PA; EP Books USA)

These laws were not understood until the last couple hundred years:

> "When steam engines were being developed in the 18th and 19th centuries, much effort was devoted to understanding heat and energy transfer. As a result, two laws of thermodynamics (from the Greek therme = heat) were formulated and have since been found to be generally applicable to all forms of energy and not just to heat energy. The first law of thermodynamics states that energy cannot be created or destroyed—it can be transformed into matter and converted from heat to electricity or to mechanical energy and back again but the total amount of energy always remains constant. The second law of thermodynamics says that, in the absence of any interference, the energy in a system will always tend toward its most probable distribution—a hot cup of coffee left to stand will always get colder, it won't get hotter." (John Hartnett, Alex Williams, Dismantling The Big Bang: God's Universe Rediscovered, 1969-1975 (Kindle Edition); Green Forest, AR; Master Books, Inc.)

However, while these laws have only recently been "formulated," the Bible clearly foretold these laws in detail:

> *Psalm 102:25-27—Of old You laid the foundation of the earth, And the heavens are the work of Your hands. They will perish, but You will endure; Yes, they will all grow old like a garment; Like a cloak You will change them, And they will be changed. But You are the same, And Your years will have no end.*

The Law Of Biogenesis

Throughout Genesis chapter one, we are told about the Law of Biogenesis:

Genesis 1:11-12—Then God said, "Let the earth bring forth grass, the herb that yields seed, and the fruit tree that yields fruit according to its kind, whose seed is in itself, on the earth"; and it was so. And the earth brought forth grass, the herb that yields seed according to its kind, and the tree that yields fruit, whose seed is in itself according to its kind. And God saw that it was good.

Genesis 1:21—So God created great sea creatures and every living thing that moves, with which the waters abounded, according to their kind, and every winged bird according to its kind. And God saw that it was good.

Genesis 1:24-25—Then God said, "Let the earth bring forth the living creature according to its kind: cattle and creeping thing and beast of the earth, each according to its kind"; and it was so. And God made the beast of the earth according to its kind, cattle according to its kind, and everything that creeps on the earth according to its kind. And God saw that it was good.

All of these passages speak to the truthfulness of the well-known and established Law of Biogenesis, which states that life only comes from preexisting life, and that of its own kind. The fact of the Law of Biogenesis continues to stand as an obstacle to the theory of macroevolution, which tries every way possible to undermine this law of science. Yet the Law of Biogenesis stands firm![129]

I still remember one young man and friend I taught the Gospel to who had come to accept Darwinian evolution. When he learned the facts regarding this law and how it undermines Darwin's theory so completely, he wrote a paper for his college regarding the matter. He received a less-than-stellar grade, and he was furious. I still remember our conversation that day:

Jimmy: Dude, I quoted half a dozen books and sources about the Law of Biogenesis! They gave me a D!

Mark: Man, I am sorry to hear that. But honestly bro, it doesn't surprise me. The entire college system in our country caters to Darwinian propaganda. Ben Stein even did a documentary about it a few years ago. I even know one college professor that got "let go" because she refused to tell people Darwin's foolishness is factual. But the important thing is you told the truth!

My friend made the most of the situation, however. He used his research paper in jail ministry, trying to reach people whose faith had been corrupted by a wicked system that has infiltrated our country through public school indoctrination.

Amazingly, the facts of science had only further bolstered and confirmed the Word of God.

Watching Out for the Welfare of Women

In the Old Testament, God had given this directive to the children of Israel:

> *Leviticus 12:1-5—Then the LORD spoke to Moses, saying, "Speak to the children of Israel, saying: 'If a woman has conceived, and borne a male child, then she shall be unclean seven days; as in the days of her customary impurity she shall be unclean. And on the eighth day the flesh of his foreskin shall be circumcised. She shall then continue in the blood of her purification thirty-three days. She shall not touch any hallowed thing, nor come into the sanctuary until the days of her purification are fulfilled. But if she bears a female child, then she shall be unclean two weeks, as in her customary impurity, and she shall continue in the blood of her purification sixty-six days.*
> *(Leviticus 12:1-5)*

Here, the Bible tells us that if a woman in Israel gave birth to a boy, she would be unclean for a period of thirty-three days. However, if she had a female baby, she would be unclean for sixty-six days.

Bonnie had a big problem with the Bible and women! One day during a Bible study, she told me about this deep-seated issue.

Bonnie: I just don't think the Bible really shows that much care and concern for women.

Mark: Hmm. Why do you believe that?

Bonnie: Well, somewhere in the Old Bible (a common euphemism for the Old Testament Scriptures, M.T.), God says women were "unclean" longer for having girl babies than boy babies. Don't you think that is just a bias against women?

Mark: Well, I have not studied about that. Let me find the passage and I will study on it.

After finding the passage here in Leviticus, I was quite amazed indeed to discover what I did. Not only does this passage not show bias against women, it describes God's care and concern for women!

During my research, I found the writings of David L Macho, and his work entitled "Scientific Appreciation Of Leviticus 12:1-5," in *The Journal Of Biblical Literature,* the main idea being research into this passage from none other than John Hopkins University. The result was that blood toxicity among new mothers were nearly double in women who had birthed females than males. Amazingly, the toxicity levels remained higher for women who birthed females than males for an average of some forty days![130] More recent medical research confirm these findings as well.[131]

A text of Scripture which some believe teaches the Lord looking down upon women actually shows His amazing love and concern for them.

Modern Pandemic Lessons from the Bible

Life changed considerably during the Covid pandemic/lockdown.

Yet through the pandemic, we have seen the scientific foreknowledge of the Bible writers demonstrated and affirmed.

For example, throughout Leviticus 13-17, God instructs the Hebrews in dealing with matters of quarantine. These principles are remarkable, especially in light of the contemporary Egyptian medical "knowledge" of Moses' time.

Consider the famous Ebers Papyrus, an ancient Egyptian medical document which advocated treating baldness by applying "a mixture of six fats...(from) the horse, the hippopotamus, the crocodile, the cat, the snake, and the (wild goat)." To cure pink eye, this document advised a person "to apply the urine of a faithful wife."[132]

Moses was raised in this knowledge:

> *Acts 7:22—And Moses was learned in all the wisdom of the Egyptians, and was mighty in words and deeds.*

However, his medical and scientific foreknowledge demonstrates a Source of wisdom far greater than the Egyptians of his time.

Let's notice a few examples.

Quarantine

The Bible specified that people sick with infectious debases were to be quarantined.

> *Leviticus 13:46—He shall be unclean. All the days he has the sore he shall be unclean. He is unclean, and he shall dwell alone; his dwelling shall be outside the camp.*

These ideas of quarantine revealed by God to Israel were often not recognized by the world at large in regard to their scientific wisdom. The fact is: if people had listened to God's directives, millions of lives may have been saved especially from the Black Plague!

> "The continents of Europe and Asia have periodically been engulfed by epidemics of leprosy and plague, especially from 1200 to 1400. More than sixty million people, almost one-third of the population of Europe in the fourteenth century, are estimated to have died by the Black Death (bubonic plague). Those who survived described scenes that sounded like the haunting visions of Dante's descriptions of hell. Renowned doctors of the time were unable to respond effectively to the rapid spread of this disease due to their lack of knowledge. They were reduced to offering medical advice to prevent the plague such as, "Stop eating pepper or garlic." Some suggested the plague was caused by the position of the planets and stars. Mostly, doctors helplessly comforted their dying patients and finally succumbed to the disease themselves. How was this dreaded plague finally stopped? During a trip to Vienna, in the center of the city I examined a strange-looking plague statue dedicated to the Black Death's countless victims and the actions of the church fathers to abolish the curse of that plague. In light of God's advanced health laws, one might expect to learn that it was only after the people began to follow the biblical laws of sanitation and disease control that the epidemic was broken. Several church leaders began to search the Bible to discover whether there was a practical solution. They saw that in Leviticus 13: 46 Moses laid down strict regulations regarding the treatment of those afflicted with leprosy or plague: "All the days wherein the plague shall be in him he shall be defiled; he is unclean: he shall dwell alone; without the camp shall his habitation be." God answered their prayers for deliverance when they finally began to obey His scriptural commands. This divine medical rule demanded that a person who con-

tracted the plague must be isolated from the general population during his infectious period. Fortunately, the church fathers of Vienna finally took the biblical injunctions to heart and commanded that those infected with the plague must be placed outside the city in special medical quarantine compounds. Caregivers fed them until they either died or survived the disease. Those who died in homes or streets were quickly removed and buried outside the city. These biblical sanitation measures quickly brought the dreaded epidemic under control. Other cities and countries rapidly followed the medical practices of Vienna until the deadly spread of the Black Death was halted. Until the twentieth century, nearly every society other than the Israelites kept infected patients in their homes—even after death—unknowingly exposing other people to deadly disease. Even during the Black Death epidemic, patients who were sick or had died were kept in the same rooms as the rest of the family. People often wondered why the disease affected so many people at one time. They attributed the epidemic to "bad air" or evil spirits. However, careful attention to the medical commands of God as revealed in Leviticus would have saved untold millions of lives. Arturo Castiglioni characterized this biblical law with these words: "The laws against leprosy in Leviticus 13 may be regarded as the first model of a sanitary legislation." 9 Moses' instruction to segregate infected patients from their families and other people was one of the most important medical advances in human history. Yet no other ancient nation followed this effective medical regulation. The only reasonable explanation is that Moses received this advanced medical knowledge from God's inspiration." (Grant R. Jeffrey, The Signature of God, Revised Edition: Conclusive Proof That Every Teaching, Every Command, Every Promise in the Bible Is True, 144-146 (Kindle Edition); Colorado Springs, CO; WaterBrook Press)

Not only were the infected to be quarantined, but so also were those who had been exposed to the infected (Leviticus 15:7-8, 11,

18, 24). Does this not powerfully describe the scientific accuracy of the Bible-especially as we have learned during the Covid-19 pandemic?

Carol made the decision to quarantine from nearly all human contact for several months due to her compromised immune system.

Carol: Brother Mark, do you believe that I am sinning by not going to church service during the pandemic?

Mark: Well Carol, the Bible teaches it is a sin to forsake the assembly (Hebrews 10:24-25). However, there are also times the Bible recognizes when people cannot attend church services due to special circumstances. Can you tell me more about what happened at your church?

Carol: Mark, I have been going to church since I was a little girl. I am a baptized and saved believer. The church I was attending does not believe in any kind of social distancing or mask wearing, and they had two people come to church who had gone to a church even in another state. Those two came to church and within two weeks, thirty members of the church were sick at home. Several of them died! The elders of that church said anyone who stopped attending church during that period was going to be disfellowshipped and they told the preacher that he needed to preach from the pulpit that it is all a conspiracy to get rid of the President. If I get this disease, there is a good chance that I will die from it with my immune system!

Mark: Carol, even though we do not live under the Old Testament, the things which are written in the Old Testament are meant to be studied by us and the principles are just as binding even if the specific commands aren't. I do not believe that you are sinning by isolating in this situation. However, I have serious concerns about the elders of your church and their minister.

How many lives may have been saved during the modern pandemic if people had more carefully heeded the Bible's teaching and instruction regarding quarantine? In any case, we see yet another example of how the Bible is scientifically accurate at a time when this science was not even conceived of!

Masks

Another interesting to consider about this passage in Leviticus is its teaching regarding masks!

> *Leviticus 13:46 (MKJV)- And as for the leper in whom the plague is, his clothes shall be torn, and his head shall be bare, and he shall put a covering on his upper lip, and shall cry, Unclean! Unclean!*

While common cloth masks won't stop *every* disease (there are scientific papers on both sides of the debate in regards to Covid-19), it is obvious God thought (and the medical community unanimously agrees) that it is useful for stopping the spread of *some* diseases.

Soap

Soap is a blessing that we often take for granted. Yet the Bible teaching regarding soap is fascinating:

> *Numbers 19:20-22—But the man who is unclean and does not purify himself, that person shall be cut off from among the assembly, because he has defiled the sanctuary of the LORD. The water of purification has not been sprinkled on him; he is unclean. It shall be a perpetual statute for them. He who sprinkles the water of purification shall wash his clothes; and he who touches the water of purification shall be unclean until evening. Whatever the unclean person touches shall be unclean; and the person who touches it shall be unclean until evening.' "*

In this passage, we read about the "water of purification."

"Let's compare modern hand washing with the biblical method in Numbers 19:

• Running water: to rinse off germs. Biblical Method: Water was showered from a hyssop branch.

• Time: to assure a thorough job. Biblical Method: The washings were repeated over a period of seven days. Between washings germs were killed by the sun and by drying.

• Antiseptic soap: to kill germs. Biblical Method: Hyssop contains the antiseptic thymol, the active ingredient in Listerine.

• Vigorous scrubbing: to dislodge germs from crevasses. Biblical Method: The soap contained cedar oil, a skin irritant to encourage scrubbing. The soap also contained wool fibers, making it the ancient equivalent of Lava soap. Once the soap was on you, you had to scrub to get it off.

Centuries before Semmelweis, God had already detailed the most effective method of washing. To prevent the spread of disease, modern science has merely rediscovered the biblical method." (S. I. M.D. McMillen, David E. M.D. M.D. Stern, None of These Diseases: The Bible's Health Secrets for the 21st Century, 425-437 (Kindle Edition); Grand Rapids, Michigan; Revell a division of Baker Publishing Group)

Kyle Butt provides much more in-depth research on the matter:

"With the presence of such symbolism in the Old Testament, it is important that we do not overlook the Old Testament instructions that were pragmatic in value and that testify to a Master Mind behind the writing of the Law. One such directive is found in Numbers 19, where the Israelites were instructed to prepare the "water of purification" that was to be used to wash any person who had touched a dead body. At first glance, the water of purification sounds like a hodge-podge of superstitious potion-making that included the ashes of a red heifer, hyssop, cedar wood, and scarlet. But this formula was the farthest thing from a symbolic potion intended to "ward off evil spirits." On the contrary, the recipe for the water of purification stands today as a wonderful example of the Bible's brilliance, since the recipe is nothing less than a procedure to produce an anti-bacterial soap. When we look at the ingredients individually, we begin to see the value of each. First, consider the ashes of a red heifer and cedar. As most school children know, the pioneers in this country could not go to the nearest supermarket and buy their favorite personal hygiene products. If they needed soap or shampoo, they made it themselves. Under such situations, they concocted various recipes for soap. One of the most oft'-produced types of soap was lye soap. Practically anyone today can easily obtain a recipe for lye soap via a quick search of the Internet (see "Soapmaking," n.d.). The various lye-soap recipes reveal that, to obtain lye, water often is poured through ashes. The water retrieved from pouring it through the ashes contains a concentration of lye. Lye, in high concentrations, is very caustic and irritating to the skin. It is, in fact, one of the main ingredients in many modern chemical mixtures used to unclog drains. In more diluted concentrations, it can be used as an excellent exfoliant and cleansing agent. Many companies today still produce lye soaps. Amazingly, Moses instructed the Israelites to prepare a mixture that would have included lye mixed in a diluted solution. Furthermore, consider that hyssop was also added to the "water of purification." Hyssop contains the antiseptic thymol, the same ingredient that we find today in some brands of mouthwash (McMillen and Stern, 2000, p. 24). Hyssop oil continues to be a popular "healing oil," and actually is quite expensive. In listing the benefits of hyssop, one Web site noted: "Once used for purifying temples and cleansing lepers, the leaves contain an antiseptic, antiviral oil. A mold that produces penicillin grows on the leaves. An infusion is taken as a sedative expectorant for flue, bronchitis, and phlegm" (see "Hyssop"). Other ingredients in the "water of purification" also stand out as having beneficial properties. The oil from the cedar wood in the mixture most likely maintained numerous salutary properties. A Web site dealing with various essential oils noted: "Cedar wood has long been used for storage cabinets because of its ability to repel insects and prevent decay. In oil form, applied to humans, it is an antiseptic, astringent, expectorant (removes mucus from respiratory system), anti-fungal, sedative and insecticide" (" Spa Essential Oils," 2005). Another site, more specifically dealing with the beneficial properties of cedar, explained: Cedar leaves and twigs are in fact rich in vitamin C, and it was their effectiveness in preventing or treating scurvy that led to the tree's being called arbor vitae or tree of life. In addition, recent research has shown that extracts prepared from either Thuja occidentalis or Thuja plicata [types of oriental cedar—KB] do in fact have anti-viral, anti-inflammatory, and antibacterial properties. A group of German researchers reported in 2002 that an extract prepared from cedar leaf, alcohol, and water inhibits the reproduction of influenza virus type A, while a team of researchers in Japan found that an extract of Western red cedar was effective in treating eczema (Frey, n.d). It is interesting to note that this information about the beneficial properties of the ingredients such as cedar, hyssop, and lye in the water of purification is not coming from Bible-based sources. Most of it is simply coming from studies that have been done through cosmetic and therapeutic research. Finally, the Israelites were instructed to toss into the mix "scarlet," which most likely was scarlet wool (see Hebrews 9: 19). Adding wool fibers to the concoction would have made the mixture the "ancient equivalent of Lava ® soap" (McMillen and Stern, 2000, p. 25). Thousands of years before any formal studies were done to see what type of cleaning methods were the most effective; millennia before American pioneers concocted their lye solutions; and ages before our most advanced medical students knew a thing about germ theory, Moses instructed the Israelites to concoct an amazingly effective recipe for soap, that, if used properly in medical facilities like hospitals in Vienna, would literally have saved thousands of lives." (Kyle Butt, Behold! The Word of God, 1310-1348 (Kindle Edition); Montgomery, AL; Apologetics Press)

While there is some history of soap that predates the Bible, what is especially amazing is the specific concoctions used in the "water of purification" that would encourage such concepts as scrubbing and cleanliness.[133]

The Paths Of The Sea

Psalm 8:8—The Bible here references the "paths of the sea." Today, we know that there are indeed paths in the sea. However, that has not always been known! George DeHoff describes how these "paths of the sea" were discovered:

> "Matthew Fontaine Maury, "the pathfinder of the seas", and the founder of the science of Oceanography, was a firm believer in and a close student of the Bible. His teaching caused the Annapolis Academy to be founded and his memory is honored and respected throughout the world. On monument row in Richmond, Virginia, is a statue of the great scientist sitting with the Bible in one hand and his charts of the sea in the other. Behind him is a globe of the earth which he helped to explore. Before Matthew Fontaine Maury lived there were no sailing lanes and no charts of the sea. One day, when he was ill, his son read to him from the eighth Psalm. He read that God put under man "... the fowls of the air, the fish of the sea, and whatsoever passeth through the paths of the sea." "Read that again," he said. Upon hearing it the second time, the venerable scientist said, "If the Word of God says there are paths in the sea, they must be there. I will find them." Within a few years he had charted the principal lanes or paths of the sea and these are followed by oceangoing vessels to this day. How did David know of these paths of the sea?" (George DeHoff, Why We Believe the Bible, 719-729 (Kindle Edition); McLoud, OK; Cobb Publishing)

The Rotundity Of The Earth

The Bible teaches that the Earth is a sphere:

> *Isaiah 40:22—It is He who sits above the circle*
> *of the earth, And its inhabitants are like grass-*
> *hoppers, Who stretches out the heavens like a*
> *curtain, And spreads them out like a tent to*
> *dwell in.*

Notice the phrase used here, "circle of the Earth." It points to the fact that the Earth is spherical in nature:

> "Many Christian authors claim that the Hebrew word for circle here (hug) refers to the earth being a globe. Notice the parallel structure here. The first half of the verse describes the roundness of the earth, followed by a simile about the inhabitants of the earth. The second half of the verse describes the stretching of the heavens (probably a reference to what God did on day two of the creation week), followed by a simile about the heavens. Everyone agrees that the heavens appear to have curvature, whether a dome or a sphere around the earth..."The Hebrew word hug is used only two other times in the Old Testament. One appearance is in Proverbs 8: 27: When he established the heavens, I was there; when he drew a circle on the face of the deep. (The "I" here is a personification of wisdom.) The only other time that this word appears in the Old Testament is Job 22: 14: Thick clouds veil him, so that he does not see, and he walks on the vault of heaven. Note that in the King James Version, this word is rendered "circuit." Also note that if one goes with "vault" as a good translation of hug as the English Standard Version does, a vault is a two-dimensional surface that is curved in a third dimension. This is an apt description of the surface of a sphere, as a vault is generally hemispherical. No wonder flat-earthers generally don't mention Job 22: 14, because that might lead to the conclusion that Isaiah 40: 22 really does describe the earth being spherical. The Hebrew word hug derives from the word chuwg, which appears only once in the Old Testament, in Job 26: 10: He has inscribed a circle on the face of the waters at the boundary between light and darkness. This obviously is a reference to the creation of light on day

one. On a spherical earth, the division between night and day is always a circle. Therefore, this verse appears to be consistent with a spherical earth, too." (Dr. Danny Faulkner, Falling Flat: A Refutation of Flat Earth Claims, 270-271 (Kindle Edition); Green Forest, AR; Master Books)

Our flat-Earth friends contend that if Isaiah wanted to suggest a spherical Earth, he would have chosen a different Hebrew word.

However, Faulkner documents:

"But, more importantly, they say that the Hebrew word hug must mean a circle, not a globe. Their evidence is that the prophet Isaiah used a word meaning "ball" elsewhere, so if Isaiah had meant to convey that the earth was spherical, he would have used this word in Isaiah 40: 22. The verse in question is Isaiah 22: 18: And whirl you around and around, and throw you like a ball into a wide land. There you shall die, and there shall be your glorious chariots, you shame of your master's house. The Hebrew word translated "ball" here is kaddur. It occurs two other times in the Old Testament. One occurrence is in Isaiah 29: 3: And I will encamp against you all around, and will besiege you with towers and I will raise siegeworks against you. Obviously, the meaning here isn't a ball, but a circle. The other time kaddur appears is Ezekiel 24: 5: Take the choicest one of the flock; pile the logs under it; boil it well; seethe also its bones in it. Here, kaddur is translated "pile." Note that in the English Standard Version, a footnote on the word "logs" indicates that the Hebrew word used there literally means "bones." The important thing to recognize is that the Hebrew word kaddur can be translated several ways, such as ball, circle, and a pile, or heap. Therefore, the insistence that kaddur is the appropriate Hebrew word for "ball" is unwarranted. In English, most people don't think of the word "round" to be restricted to two dimensions. Many people speak of the earth being round when they mean that the earth is a globe. But flat-earthers speak of the earth being round, too. That is, roundness applies to either a circle or a sphere (topologically, a sphere is merely a three-dimensional circle)." (Dr. Danny Faulkner, Falling Flat: A Refutation of Flat Earth Claims, 271-272 (Kindle Edition); Green Forest, AR; Master Books)

Despite his defense of the passage, Faulkner believes that Isaiah 40:22 is not conclusive in proving the rotundity of the Earth.

Other scholars disagree.

For example:

"THE SPHERICITY OF EARTH: For a long time people used to think that the earth is flat. It was not considered safe for ships to venture beyond the pillars of Hercules (at the entrance to the straits of Gibraltar) into the Atlantic ocean because at the boundary of the flat earth the ship would fall into the abyss. However, Bible teaches no such error. In Isaiah 40: 22 the "circle of the earth" is mentioned in connection with its shape. The word KHUG used in Hebrew refers to a spherical body. We infer the same from the Lord Jesus when He spoke in Luke 17: 34 to 36 about His second coming. This coming was to be instantaneous yet He said, "I tell you, in that night there shall be two men in bed, the one shall be taken and the other shall be left. Two women shall be grinding together; the one shall be taken the other left. Two men shall be in the field; the one shall be taken and the other left". (Luke 17: 34-36) The Lord Jesus said that He will come in a moment yet three activities corresponding roughly with morning noon and night have been shown to take place at the same moment. Obviously, the reference is to the spherical earth on which alone simultaneity of such events is possible." (Dr. Johnson C. Philip & Dr. Saneesh Cherian, Bible And Modern Science (Christian Apologetics), 562-574 (Kindle Edition))

Others have raised their voice in protest to a flat-earth, based especially on God's revelation in nature (Romans 1:18-20). That the Earth is spherical is not only documented by God's revelation in nature through science and by the Bible, but it was also acknowledged by many both before and after the Middle Ages (although some people during these times held to a belief in a flat-earth):

"Did people in the Middle Ages think that the world was flat? Certainly the writers quoted above would make us think so. As the story goes, people living in the "Dark Ages" were so ignorant rant (or so deceived by Catholic priests) that they believed the earth was flat. For a thousand years they lingered in ignorant obscurity, scurity, and were it not for the heroic bravery of Christopher Columbus and other explorers, they might well have continued in this ignorance for even longer. Thus, it was the innovation and courage of investors and explorers, motivated by economic goals and modern curiosity, that finally allowed us to break free from the shackles forged by the medieval Catholic church.' Where does this story come from? In the nineteenth century, scholars interested in promoting a new scientific and rational view of the world claimed that ancient Greeks and Romans had understood that the world was round, but that this knowledge was suppressed by medieval churchmen. Pro-Catholic scholars responded by making the argument that medieval thinkers did know the world was round.2 Critics, however, dismissed such opinions as mere apologetics. Why did the battle rage over this particular issue? Because a belief in the flat earth was equated with willful ignorance, while an understanding of the spherical earth was seen as a measure of modernity; the side one defended became a means of condemning or praising medieval churchmen. men. For scholars such as William Whewell or John Draper, therefore, Catholicism was bad (since it promoted a flat-earth view), while for Roman Catholics, Catholicism was good (since it promoted modernity). As we'll see, neither of these extremes describes the true state of affairs.3 This equation of rotundity with modernity also explains why nineteenth-century American historians claimed it was Columbus and the early mercantilists who proved the earth was round and thereby ushered in modernity-and America. In fact, it was a biography of Columbus by the American author Washington Irving, the creator of "Rip Van Winkle," that introduced this idea to the world.4 But the reality is more complex than either of these stories. Very few people throughout the Middle Ages believed that the world was flat. Thinkers on both sides of the question were Catholics, and for them, the shape of the earth did not equate with progressive or traditionalist views. It is true that most clerics were more concerned with salvation than the shape of the earth-that that was their job, after all. But God's works in nature were important portant to them as well. Columbus could not have proved that the world was round, because this fact was already known. Nor was he a rebellious modern-he was a good Catholic and undertook his voyage believing he was doing God's work. A transformation was taking place in fifteenth-century views of the earth, but it had more to do with a new way of mapping than with a move from flat earth to round sphere. Scholars in antiquity developed a very clear spherical model of the earth and the heavens. Every major Greek geographical thinker, including Aristotle (384-322 B.C.), Eratosthenes (third century B.C.), and Ptolemy (second century A.D.), based his geographical graphical and astronomical work on the theory that the earth was a sphere. Likewise, all of the major Roman commentators, including Pliny the Elder (23-79 A.D.), Pomponius Mela (first century A.D.), and Macrobius (fourth century A.D.), agreed that the earth must be round. Their conclusions were in part philosophical-a spherical universe required a sphere in the middle-but were also based on mathematical and astronomical reasoning.' Most famous was Aristotle's proof of the sphericity of the earth, an argument used by many thinkers in the Middle Ages and Renaissance. If we examine the work of even early-medieval writers, we find that with few exceptions they held a spherical-earth theory. Among the early church fathers, Augustine (354-430), Jerome (d. 420), and Ambrose (d. 420) all agreed that the earth was a sphere. Only Lactantius (early fourth century) provided a dissenting ing opinion, but he rejected all pagan learning since it distracted people from their real work of achieving salvation.6 From the seventh century to the fourteenth, every important medieval thinker concerned about the natural world stated more or less explicitly that the world was a round globe, many of them incorporating Ptolemy's astronomy and Aristotle's physics into their work. Thomas Aquinas (d. 1274), for example, followed lowed Aristotle's proof in demonstrating that the changing positions sitions of the constellations as one moved about on the earth's surface indicated the spherical shape of the earth. Roger Bacon (d. 1294), in his Opus Maius (ca. 1270), stated that the world was round, that the southern antipodes were inhabited, and that the sun's passage along the line of the ecliptic affected climates of different parts of the world. Albertus Magnus (d. 1280) agreed with Bacon's findings, while Michael Scot (d. 1234) "compared the earth, surrounded by water, to the yolk of an egg and the spheres of the universe to the layers of an onion."7 Perhaps the most influential were jean de Sacrobosco, whose De Sphera (ca. 1230) demonstrated that the earth was a globe, and Pierre d'Ailly (1350-1410), archbishop of Cambrai, whose Imago Mundi (written in 1410) discussed the sphericity of the earth.' Both of these books enjoyed great popularity; Sacrobosco's book was used as a basic textbook throughout the Middle Ages, while d'Ailly's book was read by early explorers like Columbus." (Ronald L. Numbers, Galileo Goes to Jail and Other Myths about Science and Religion, 316-346 (Kindle Edition); Cambridge, Massachusetts: Harvard University Press)

Once again, scientific advance demonstrates the truthfulness of the Bible.

Conclusion

There are many other evidences we could examine which demonstrate the scientific foreknowledge of the Bible writers. Yet these are sufficient to establish the conclusion that the Bible is the Word of God.

EPILOGUE:

WHAT NOW?

We come now to the conclusion of our study. I don't know what your background is, where you were spiritually when you began this book, and where you are now. However, I hope that you have seen from this volume some of the evidence that leads to the conclusion that the Bible is the Word of God.

The entire Message of the Bible revolves around the identity of Jesus Christ, the Son of God, Who came to this world and died for the sins of mankind on the Cross of Calvary (Luke 19:10). Jesus died to pay for your sins, was buried, and arose again the third day (1 Corinthians 15:1-8).

My friend, the God of Heaven loves you, and so do we! Why not obey Him today and be saved from your sins?

> *Acts 2:38—Then Peter said to them, "Repent, and let every one of you be baptized in the name of Jesus Christ for the remission of sins; and you shall receive the gift of the Holy Spirit.*

If I can assist you in any way, you can contact me through my website (www.marktabata.com), or the Facebook page of the church that I work with, the Couchtown church of Christ.

Let me encourage you to visit the church of Christ in your community.

The grace of the Lord Jesus Christ, and the love of God, and the communion of the Holy Spirit, be with you all. Amen.

ENDNOTES

[1] the word "inspiration" comes from the Greek word Theopneustos.

"This term is given to THE MYSTERIOUS POWER EXER-
CISED BY THE DIVINE SPIRIT ON THE AUTHORS OF THE
WRITINGS OF THE OLD AND NEW TESTAMENT, to enable
them to compose that which the church of God has received from
their hands....The historian Josephus, 1 who was the contemporary
of Paul, makes use of a term exactly similar, in his first book
against Appion, in which, speaking of all the prophets, "who," he
remarks, " have composed the twenty-two sacred books of the Old
Testament," he declares, that they wrote according to [or inspira-
tion] which comes from God...These assertions, which are themselves the testimony of the word of God, include already our last
definition of , and lead us finally to characterizes it as—" THAT
INEXPLICABLE POWER WHICH THE DIVINE SPIRIT,
AFORE TIME, EXERCISED UPON THE AUTHORS OF HOLY
SCRIPTURE, TO GUIDE THEM EVEN TO THE WORDS
WHICH THEY HAVE EMPLOYED, AND TO PRESERVE
THEM FROM ALL ERROR, AS WELL AS FROM ANY OMIS-
SION."" (François Samuel R. Louis Gaussen, Theopneustia: The
Plenary Inspiration Of The Holy Scriptures, 260-425 (Kindle Edi-
tion, emphasis added); Miami, FL; Hard Press)

[2] "Paul has not lost his mind but speaks "true and prudent
words" (ἀληθείας καὶ σωφροσύνης ῥήματα , alētheias kai
sōphrosynēs rhēmata), or "the sober truth." The combination of
"true" and "prudent" is common in Greek, as is a contrast between
"prudent" and "mad" (Lucian, Timon 55; Xenophon, Memorabilia
1.1.16; P.Oxy. 1.33; Plato, Phaedrus 244D; Barrett 1998: 1168). In
this context, where Paul has been accused of being crazy, his reply
is that his words are truth. He has not lost control of his thoughts;
they are quite sober and thought through. "The metaphor of things
not being done in a corner refers to no hidden events tucked away
somewhere in the corner out of public sight (BAGD 168; BDAG
209; Malherbe 1985–86; Epictetus, Discourses 2.12.17; Plutarch,
Moralia 777B; Fitzmyer 1998: 764). The idiom means not doing
one's philosophical reflection in a way that is disengaged from the

public. Paul can speak boldly and say that these events were public enough that anyone paying attention could appreciate them. Paul asks the king if he believes the prophets, who declare that such things are possible and a part of God's plan. The issue Paul wants to focus on is God's teaching as set forth in the prophets. "Paul is a model witness and evangelist here. Agrippa is capable of understanding and appreciating what Paul claims (Acts 26:2–3)." (Darrell L. Bock, Acts: Baker Exegetical Commentary On The New Testament,17597-17611 (Kindle Edition); Grand Rapids, Michigan; Baker Academic)

[3]" Do you think that it seems reasonably possible that forty men, from varying backgrounds, and scattered across more than a thousand years in time, could have designed some 66 metal components which accidentally came together to form a precision machine that revolutionized the world? Impossible! Exactly—from the human vantage point! But that is precisely the kind of thing that happened in the case of the Bible. The sacred Scriptures were written by some 40 different persons, over a span of approximately 1,600 years. These authors, from a variety of cultural and educational backgrounds, writing in three different languages (Hebrew, Aramaic, Greek), produced a volume of 66 books that is characterized by such an amazing unity and beautiful continuity as to be inexplicable on the basis of merely human origin." (Wayne Jackson, Eric Lyons, Kyle Butt, Surveying The Evidence,1341-1347 (Kindle Edition); Montgomery, Alabama; Apologetics Press)

[4]"If a forty piece orchestra should suddenly begin to play-in perfect timing, melody, and harmony-it would be evidence of direction by a single mind. If forty archers, in forty different places, widely separated by time, should shoot their arrows and all hit the same target "dead-center" it would be evidence of (proof of) direction by a single mind. If forty men-widely separated in geography, with varied backgrounds, and living over a period of sixteen hundred years-should each write down a few lines, and these lines when brought together constituted a beautiful poem, it would be evidence of direction by a single mind. Because of its marvelous and otherwise inexplicable unity, we believe that the Bible came

from God-that it is miraculously inspired and is divine authority (Deaver, quoted by Charles Pugh, Why I Am A Christian, 42)."

[5]"Since there is such significance in Methuselah's name, let's examine the other names to discover what may lie behind them. (Bear with me on this: it'll be worth it!) The first name, Adam, , adomah, means "man." As the first man, that seems straightforward enough. Adam's son was named Seth, , which means "appointed." "When he was born Eve said, "For God hath appointed me another seed instead of Abel, whom Cain slew."15 Seth's son was called Enosh, , which means "mortal," "frail," or "miserable." It is from the root anash: to be incurable, used of a wound, grief, woe, sickness, or wickedness. It was in the days of Enosh that men began to defile the name of the Living God.16 Enosh's son was named Kenan, from which can mean "sorrow," "dirge," or "elegy." (The precise denotation is somewhat elusive; some study aids unfortunately presume that Kenan is synonymous with "Cainan." Balaam, looking down from the heights of Moab, employed a pun upon the name of the Kenites when he prophesied their destruction.17) We have no real idea as to why these names were chosen for their children. Often they may have referred to circumstances at their birth, etc. Kenan's son was Mahalalel, from , which means "blessed" or "praise"; and El, the name for God. Thus, Mahalalel means "the Blessed God." Often Hebrew names included El, the name of God, as Dani-el, "God is my Judge," Nathani-el, "Gift of God," etc. Mahalalel's son was named Jared, , from the verb yaradh, meaning "shall come down." Some authorities suggest that this might be an allusion to the "Sons of God" who "came down" to corrupt the daughters of men, resulting in the Nephilim ("fallen ones") of Genesis 6.18 Jared's son was named Enoch, , which means "teaching," or "commencement." He was the first of four generations of preachers. In fact, the earliest recorded prophecy was by Enoch,...Enoch was the father of Methuselah, whom we have already mentioned. Enoch walked with God after he begat Methuselah.19 Apparently, Enoch received the prophecy of the Great Flood, and was told that as long as his son was alive, the judgment of the Flood would be withheld. The year that Methuselah died, the Flood came. Methuselah's son was named Lamech, , a root still evident today in our own English word, "lament" or

"lamentation." Lamech suggests "despairing." (This name is also linked to the Lamech in Cain's line who inadvertently killed his son Tubal-Cain in a hunting incident.20) Lamech, of course, is the father of Noah, , which is derived from nacham, "to bring relief" or "comfort," as Lamech himself explains.."Man (is) appointed mortal sorrow; (but) the Blessed God shall come down teaching (that) His death shall bring (the) despairing rest." Here is a summary of God's plan of redemption, hidden here within a genealogy in Genesis!...The implications of this discovery are far more deeply significant than may be evident at first glance. It demonstrates that in the earliest chapters of the Book of Genesis, God had already laid out His plan of redemption for the predicament of mankind. It is the beginning of a love story, ultimately written in blood on a wooden cross which was erected in Judea almost 2,000 years ago. This is also one of many evidences that the Bible is an integrated message system, the product of supernatural engineering. This punctures the you presumptions of many who view the Bible as a record of an evolving cultural tradition, noble though it may be. It claims to be authored by the One who alone knows the end from the beginning.21 It is astonishing to discover how many Biblical "controversies" seem to evaporate if one simply recognizes the unity—the integrity—of these 66 books. Every number, every place name, every detail—every jot and tittle—is part of a tightly engineered design, tailored for our learning, our discovery, and our amazement." (Chuck Missler, *Hidden Treasures In The Biblical Text,* 1443-231 (Kindle Edition); Coeur d'Alene, ID; Koinonoia House)

6"The same person, Jesus Christ, is the central theme of the Bible: it is about Him. It builds to His coming, describes it, and interprets what it means. The golden thread is the redemption of sinful man by the grace of God through faith in the shed blood of the Redeemer. Keep in mind that no human publisher commissioned the writing of such a book. No editor set forth a plan; no editorial committee oversaw its development; no one distributed an outline to the different authors. Despite these facts, there is every sort of literature in the Bible, including prose and poetry; history and law; biography and travel; genealogies, theologies, and philosophies.

And somehow, all of these elements combine to provide an incredible unity from Genesis to Revelation.1 Suppose that forty different artists were to paint a picture without having any idea what the others might be doing—or that others were doing anything at all. Imagine someone collecting these pieces and arranging them all upon a huge wall, and the result was a perfect picture that displayed all the features of Jesus Christ. Or suppose that forty different sculptors, without any knowledge of what the others were doing, each decided to create a piece of sculpture. And when the pieces were brought together, they formed an exquisite statue of Christ. These outcomes are incomprehensible, yet the Bible is a greater accomplishment by far. No other book in all the world has ever been made in this way. Having written a number of books, I know what publishers and editors and editorial committees do. None of this process was involved in writing the Bible. But we see in this book an incredible unity that testifies that the hand that made this book is divine. Writer James C. Hefley says, "The sixty-six books are a perfect whole, a purposeful revelation, a progressive proof that the Bible is more than the work of fallible men."2 (D. James Kennedy & Jerry Newcombe, *What If The Bible Had Never Been Written?* 181-194 (Kindle Edition); Nashville, TN: Thomas Nelson Publishers)

[7]"But what constitutes a contradiction? Most alleged biblical contradictions are not even "apparent" contradictions because there is no necessary conflict between the two propositions....A contradiction is a proposition and its negation (symbolically written, "A and not A") at the same time and in the same relationship. The law of non-contradiction states that a contradiction cannot be true: "It is impossible to have A and not A at the same time and in the same relationship." The last part of this definition is crucially important." (Ken Ham, *Demolishing Supposed Bible Contradictions: Volume One-Exploring Forty Alleged Contradictions,* 13 (Kindle Edition); Green Forest, AR; Master Books).

[8]"Again, the apologist does not have to know the exact solution to an alleged contradiction; he need only show one or more possibilities of harmonization. We act by this principle in the courtroom, in our treatment of various historical books, as well as in

everyday life situations. It is only fair, then, that we show the Bible the same courtesy by exhausting the search for possible harmony between passages before pronouncing one or both accounts false." (Eric Lyons, *The Anvil Rings: Answers To Alleged Bible Discrepancies: Volume 1,* 11; Montgomery, Alabama; Apologetics Press)

[9]"But to make matters even worse, it is alleged that the Bible contains contradictions. That is, the Bible seems to say one thing in one place, and then the opposite in another. Which are we to believe? Obviously, two contradictory statements cannot both be true. While we might come to accept many of the peculiar claims of Scripture, a genuine contradiction cannot be true even in principle. It is not possible to have a sunny night, a married bachelor, dry water, a true falsehood, and so on. Thus, the claim that the Bible contains contradictions is a serious challenge indeed. For if the Bible has even one real contradiction, then it cannot be completely true. Yet the Christian asserts that the Bible is the Word of God and without error. The claim of contradictions is a serious allegation against the Christian worldview, and we must be prepared to defend the Bible against such claims....In this introduction, we've seen that many criticisms of the Bible are not even alleged contradictions, but mere opinions about what is possible. These are not logical problems for the Bible; they are simply psychological problems for the critic. A contradiction would be "A and not A at the same time and in the same relationship." Many alleged biblical contradictions have been asserted. **BUT IN MOST CASES WE FIND THAT A AND NOT A ARE NOT AT THE SAME TIME, OR ARE USED IN A DIFFERENT SENSE OR RELATIONSHIP AND ARE THUS NOT CONTRADICTIONS AT ALL.** The critic sometimes presents a pair of biblical principles as if they were two mutually exclusive options, when, in fact, this is not the case—**A FALSE DILEMMA.** In other instances, we find that the words or phrases have been taken **OUT OF CONTEXT:** poetic passages taken hyper-literally, figures of speech not taken as such, or language of appearance taken as a Newtonian physics. **SOMETIMES CRITICS COMMIT THE FALLACY OF SWEEPING GENERALIZATION:** taking a general principle as if it were universally true, or taking a rule as if it had no excep-

tions. **SOME ALLEGED CONTRADICTIONS ARE NOTH-ING MORE THAN A TRANSLATIONAL OR MANU-SCRIPT ISSUE; THE ORIGINAL TEXT CONTAINS NO CONTRADICTION AT ALL. ADDITIONALLY, A NUM-BER OF CONTRADICTIONS ARE MERELY ERRONE-OUS INFERENCES: THEY EXIST ONLY IN THE MIND OF THE CRITIC, NOT IN THE BIBLICAL TEXT.** One in particular that occurs frequently is when the critic assumes that a number (X) means "only X" when the Bible does not state this. **ALSO, THE BIBLE IS SOMETIMES ALLEGED TO CON-FLICT WITH AN EXTERNAL "FACT." A NUMBER OF THESE CLAIMS STEM FROM A MISREADING OF SCRIPTURE. IN OTHER CASES, THE CRITIC HAS SIMPLY ASSUMED THAT THE BIBLE IS IN ERROR WHEN IT CONTRADICTS A PARTICULAR BELIEF. IN DOING SO, THE CRITIC HAS COMMITTED THE FAL-LACY OF BEGGING THE QUESTION.** Perhaps most signifi-cantly, we have shown that any claim of alleged contradiction ac-tually confirms that the Bible is true. This is because the law of non-contradiction is based on the biblical worldview. When the critic accepts that a contradiction cannot possibly be true, he has implicitly presumed that the Bible must be true." (Dr. Jason Lisle, in Ken Ham, Demolishing Supposed Bible Contradictions Volume One: Exploring Forty Alleged Contradictions, 11-20 (Kindle Edi-tion, emphasis added M.T.); Green Forest, AR; Master Books)

[10]"As we discussed in chapter 4, one of the most important tasks for a detective is to listen carefully when multiple eyewitnesses provide a statement about what they observed at the scene of a crime. It's my job to assemble the complete picture of what hap-pened at the scene. No single witness is likely to have seen every detail, so I must piece together the accounts, allowing the observa-tions of one eyewitness to fill in the gaps that may exist in the ob-servations of another eyewitness. That's why it's so important for eyewitnesses to be separated before they are interviewed. True, re-liable eyewitness accounts are never completely parallel and iden-tical. Instead, they are different pieces of the same puzzle, uninten-tionally supporting and complementing each other to provide all the details related to what really happened....When I first read

through the Gospels forensically, comparing those places where two or more gospel writers were describing the same event, I was immediately struck by the inadvertent support that each writer provided for the other. The accounts puzzled together just the way one would expect from independent eyewitnesses. When one gospel eyewitness described an event and left out a detail that raised a question, this question was unintentionally answered by another gospel writer (who, by the way, often left out a detail that was provided by the first gospel writer)....As someone who was new to the Bible, I began to investigate whether or not anyone else had observed this phenomenon and found that a professor of divinity named J. J. Blunt wrote a book in 1847 entitled Undesigned Coincidences in the Writings of the Old and New Testament, an Argument of Their Veracity; with an Appendix, Containing Undesigned Coincidences between the Gospels and Acts, and Josephus. This was one of the first books about the Bible I ever purchased. In his section related to the Gospels and the book of Acts, Blunt identified the very same inadvertent parallel passages I discovered when examining the Gospels forensically. Blunt described the phenomenon as a series of "undesigned coincidences" and identified over forty locations in the New Testament where this feature of unintentional eyewitness support could be seen on the pages of Scripture. Let me give you a few examples of what we are talking about here....As a cold-case detective, I've experienced something similar to this a number of times. Often, questions an eyewitness raises at the time of the crime are left unanswered until we locate an additional witness years later. This is a common characteristic of true, reliable eyewitness accounts." (Jay Warner Wallace, *Cold-Case Christianity: A Homicide Detective Investigates The Claims Of The Gospels,* 183-187 (Kindle Edition, emphasis added, M.T.); Colorado Springs, CO; DavidCook). He points out the following regarding the "apparent contradictions" between the Gospels:

[11]"The purpose of this brief characterization of each of the three Synoptists has been to furnish some sort of guideline or rationale in accounting for what each Evangelist includes in his record and what he omitted, and for the particular manner of his presentation. But it should be understood that all three of them accurately related the events of Christ's career and the words of His mouth, even

though they included only what was pertinent to their particular approach. When any room is photographed in a person's home, the camera may well capture different views of the contents, depending on the angle from which the picture is shot. All of them are accurate, even though they are by no means identical. The same is true with a classroom of students who are engaged in taking notes on their teacher's lecture. Each student will note at least a few details that are not reported by the others, and yet none of them will be making a false report of what the instructor said. In the same way we are to fit together the testimony of each of the three Synoptists. Each one is on the alert for details that fit in with his own special view of Jesus, and so there are naturally going to be inclusions and omissions that correspond with the particular aim of each Evangelist. (Students of classical Greek literature notice a similar phenomenon in regard to Plato's portrait of Socrates, his revered teacher in Athens, and the quite different emphasis of Xenophon, who was another of Socrates 'pupils. Plato dwells on his teacher's skill in dialogue and his masterful treatment of philosophical themes: Xenophon in the Symposium concentrates on the character and personality of Socrates, as indicated by various anecdotes from personal experience. The two witnesses bring out different aspects of their master, but neither is in error!) As we deal with episodes in our Lord's life that are of such importance that all three (or even John as well) furnish an account, our task is to line them up beside one another and see how each fits in with or supplements the others. In almost every case, a careful consideration will yield a synthetic account that bears a resemblance to a stereophonic player as contrasted with a monaural player, or a trio of monaural recorders. Some writers deprecate Tatian's Diatessaron (which interweaves material from all four Gospels to form a composite, sequential account of Jesus 'works and words), but with dubious justification. Essentially the same method is followed in every inquest or court hearing where a multiplicity of witnesses are to be heard. Each of them may contribute differing details that bear on the case, but the judge and jury that hear the various testimonies are expected to fit together the contribution of each witness into a self-consistent, coherent picture of the entire episode or transaction." (Gleason L. Archer, Jr., New International Encyclopedia of Bible

Difficulties by Gleason L. Archer Jr., 645-646 (Kindle Edition); Grand Rapids, Michigan; Zondervan)

[12]"Most modern English dictionaries define the word "wine" as the fermented juice of grapes. For example, the seventh edition of the Merriam Webster's Collegiate Dictionary defines "wine" as follows: "fermented grape juice containing varying percentages of alcohol." No mention at all is made in this current definition of unfermented grape juice as one of the possible meanings of "wine." Classical dual meaning. This restrictive meaning of "wine" represents, however, a departure from the more classical dual meaning of the word as a designation for both fermented and unfermented grape juice. To verify this fact one needs only to consult some older dictionaries. For example, the 1955 Funk & Wagnalls New "Standard" Dictionary of the English Language defines "wine" as follows: "1. The fermented juice of the grape: in loose language the juice of the grape whether fermented or not." This definition shows that forty years ago the loose usage of "wine" referred to "the juice of the grape whether fermented or not." The dual meaning of "wine" is clearly given in older English dictionaries. For example, the 1828 Webster's Dictionary defines the word "must" as "new wine—wine pressed from the grape, but not fermented." 1 Benjamin Marin's Lingua Britannica Reformata or A New English Dictionary, published in 1748, defines "wine" as follows: "1. the juice of the grape. 2. a liquor extracted from other fruits besides the grape. 3. the vapours of wine, as wine disturbs his reason." 2 It is noteworthy that here the first meaning of "wine" is "the juice of the grape," without any reference to fermentation. The past dual meanings of wine suggest that when the King James Version of the Bible was produced (1604-1611) its translators must have understood "wine" to refer to both fermented and unfermented wine. In view of this fact, the King James Version's uniform translation of the Hebrew yayin and Greek onios as "wine" was an acceptable translation at that time, since in those days the term could mean either fermented or unfermented wine, just as the words it translates (yayin or oinos) can mean either....Examples of the dual usage of oinos abound in secular Greek. A clear example is provided by Aristotle (384-322 B.C.). In his book Meteorologica, he clearly refers to "grape juice" or "must" (gleukos), as one

of the kinds of wine: "For some kinds of wine [oinos], for example must [gleukos], solidify when boiled." 6 In another passage of the same book, Aristotle refers to a sweet grape beverage (glukus) which "though called wine [oinos], it has not the effect of wine, for it does taste like wine and does not intoxicate like ordinary wine." 7 In this text Aristotle explicitly informs us that unfermented grape juice was called "oinos—wine," though it did not have the taste or the intoxicating effect of ordinary wine. Athenaeus, the Grammarian (about A.D. 200), explains in his Banquet that "the Mityleneans have a sweet wine [glukon oinon], what they called prodromos, and others call it protropos." 8 Later on in the same book, he recommends this sweet, unfermented wine (protropos) for the dyspeptic: "Let him take sweet wine, either mixed with water or warmed, especially that kind called protropos, the sweet Lesbian glukus, as being good for the stomach; for sweet wine [oinos] does not make the head heavy." 9 Here the unfermented sweet wine is called "lesbian" because its alcoholic potency had been removed. The methods by which this was done will be discussed later....As in Greek so in Hebrew the term for "wine" (yayin) was used to refer to either fermented or unfermented wine. The Jewish Encyclopedia explains that "Fresh wine before fermenting was called 'yayin mi-gat '(wine of the vat; Sanh 70a)." 14 The Halakot Gedalot, which is the earliest Jewish compen-dium of the Talmud, says: "One may press out a cluster of grapes and pronounce the Kiddush over the juice, since the juice of the grape is considered wine [yayin] in connection with the laws of the Nazirite."...The above survey indicates that the four related words— wine in English, vinum in Latin, oinos in Greek and yayin in Hebrews have been used historically to refer to the juice of the grape, whether fermented or unfermented. This conclusion will become clearer in the next chapter, where we shall examine some of the reasons that the Bible disapproves of fermented wine but approves of unfermented grape juice." (Samuele Bacchiocchi, Wine In The Bible: A Biblical Study On The Use Of Alcoholic Beverages, 124-225 (Kindle Edition); Biblical Perspectives)

[13]"In the original Greek, however, there is no real contradiction between these two statements. Greek makes a distinction between hearing a sound as a noise (in which case the verb "to hear" takes

the genitive case) and hearing a voice as a thought-conveying message (in which case it takes the accusative). Therefore, as we put the two statements together, we find that Paul's companions heard the Voice as a sound (somewhat like the crowd who heard the sound of the Father talking to the Son in John 12: 28, but perceived it only as thunder); but they did not (like Paul) hear the message that it articulated. Paul alone heard it intelligibly (Acts 9: 4 says Paul ēkousen phōnēn —accusative case); though he, of course, perceived it also as a startling sound at first (Acts 22: 7: "I fell to the ground and heard a voice [ēkousa phōnēs] saying to me," NASB). But in neither account is it stated that his companions ever heard that Voice in the accusative case." (Gleason Archer, *The New International Encyclopedia Of Bible Difficulties,* 10056-10068 (Kindle Edition): Grand Rapids, Michigan; Zondervan)

[14]"Both Gospel writers are correct in their assertions. The difficulty is answered when we realize that each Gospel writer used a different time system. John follows the *Roman* time system while Mark follows the *Jewish* time system. According to Roman time, the day ran from midnight to midnight... The Jewish 24 hour period began in the evening at 6 p.m. and the morning of that day began at 6:00 a.m. Therefore, when Mark asserts that at the third hour Christ was crucified, this was about 9 a.m. John stated that Christ's trial was about the sixth hour. This would place the trial before the crucifixion and this would not negate any testimony of the Gospel writers." (Norman Geisler and Thomas Howe, *The Big Book Of Bible Difficulties: Clear And Concise Answers From Genesis To Revelation,* 4368-4371 (Kindle Edition); Grand Rapids, Michigan; Baker Books)

[15]"Notice how Paul's reasons for the head covering for women and its absence for men are loaded with the language of culture. (1) Honor or shame (disgrace) for the man— "any man who prays or prophesies with something on his head disgraces his head, but any woman who prays or prophesies with her head unveiled disgraces her head" (1 Corinthians 11:4- 5). (2) Shame (disgrace) to the woman— "It is one and the same thing as having her head shaved.... If it is disgraceful for a woman to have her hair cut off or to be shaved, she should wear a veil" (1 Corinthians 11:5- 6).

(3) What is accepted as a sign of authority "For this reason a woman ought to have a symbol of authority on her head" (1 Corinthians 11:10). (Angels are perhaps invoked as witnesses to the order of creation.) (4) What is regarded by human beings as natural (that is, what is customarily done)— "Judge for yourselves: is it proper for a woman to pray to God with her head unveiled? Does not nature itself teach you that if a man wears long hair, it is degrading to him, but if a woman has long hair, it is her glory?" (1 Corinthians 11:13- 15). (5) The practice of the churches "We have no such custom, nor do the churches of God" (1 Corinthians 11:16). Honor and shame were major considerations in determining conduct in the societies of the ancient Mediterranean world...Since a culture tends to regard its customs as the "natural" way to do things, as the established order of things, "nature" (physis) had as one of its derived meanings "[accepted] custom." 14 Observe that all of the considerations urged by Paul, with the possible exception of the fifth, refer to conditions or circumstances established by culture— having to do with honor, shame or disgrace, a sign or symbol, the natural or customary, and the customs of others. Where something is not considered a matter of honor or shame, has no symbolic significance, is not regarded as natural, then the specific expression has no force." (Everett Ferguson, *Women In The Church: Biblical And Historical Perspectives*, 386-405 (Kindle Edition): Abilene, Tx; Desert Willow Publishing)

[16]"There is firm evidence that Corinthian women were connected to the cult of Demeter which we know operated in Roman Corinth in Paul's day in the temple on the slopes of the Acrocorinth overlooking the city.59 Curse inscriptions written by women have been discovered there...It can be concluded, therefore, that those wives who undertook religious functions would have covered their heads with the marriage veil, given that all respectable married women would wear their veil outside the home, as Roman law and custom prescribed. This raises the possibility that those who sent messengers to spy out the activities of Christian gatherings could have reported to the men elected to officially supervise women's dress codes in Corinth that some Christian married women were inappropriately attired while engaging in a religious activity...Their deliberate removing of their veils while praying and

prophesying would have sent a signal that they were identifying themselves in this religious gathering with the new women who behaved loosely at banquets which were often held in private homes." (Winter Bruce, *Roman Wives; Roman Widows-The Appearance Of New Women And The Pauline Communities,* 1063-1098 (Kindle Edition); Grand Rapids, Michigan; William B. Eerdmans Publishing Company)

[17]"Over the course of my teaching career one of the biggest misconceptions I've encountered about Bible interpretation is the idea that interpreting what the Bible says symbolically or metaphorically equates to concluding that what you're reading isn't real. This is deeply flawed thinking. But it's nevertheless understandable. Bible teachers and preachers are fond of saying that the Bible needs to be interpreted literally for it to be taken seriously. Taking something "literally" means you're ruling out any type of figurative language. That only makes sense if the biblical authors wanted to be taken that way. Sometimes they didn't (see Day 20). Since they were human, much of what they wrote could have meaning on more than one level. Insisting only on literalism stifles communication. We use words every day in ways that would be comical or offensive if taken literally—and yet we never expect what we say to be denigrated or considered false or phony. When you say on a hot day, "I was roasting out there today"—were you? When you say you're madly in love with your wife, should I presume you're insane for being attracted to her? If your boss is hard-hearted have you just diagnosed arteriosclerosis? When you tell your neighbor his new car is a sweet ride will he ask you not to lick it again? We can laugh at these absurdities, but all of these statements are meant to be taken seriously—they all have meaning that corresponds to reality. Biblical writers didn't live in an alternate universe where people never used figurative language, metaphors, or symbolic references. All of those things are stock elements of the way language works—and our day-to-day reality itself. Pitting "literalism" and "figurative" against each other in some sort of semantic death match demonstrates poor thinking. The reason we can instantly parse when to take a given statement like those above figuratively or literally is because the world we've experienced informs how to

interpret them. In other words, the cumulative effect of our up-bringing, our cultural setting, our experiences, and our worldview wires us in such a way that we intuitively know what is meant. To reject figurative interpretation in the Bible is to deny the biblical writers their humanity. Instead of letting them be the authority for understanding what they wrote, we assume we know better." (Michael S. Heiser, The 60 Second Scholar: 100 Insights That Illumine The Bible, 2543-2556 (Kindle Edition))

[18]"Over the course of my teaching career one of the biggest misconceptions I've encountered about Bible interpretation is the idea that interpreting what the Bible says symbolically or metaphorically equates to concluding that what you're reading isn't real. This is deeply flawed thinking. But it's nevertheless understandable. Bible teachers and preachers are fond of saying that the Bible needs to be interpreted literally for it to be taken seriously. Taking something "literally" means you're ruling out any type of figurative language. That only makes sense if the biblical authors wanted to be taken that way. Sometimes they didn't (see Day 20). Since they were human, much of what they wrote could have meaning on more than one level. Insisting only on literalism stifles communication. We use words every day in ways that would be comical or offensive if taken literally—and yet we never expect what we say to be denigrated or considered false or phony. When you say on a hot day, "I was roasting out there today"—were you? When you say you're madly in love with your wife, should I presume you're insane for being attracted to her? If your boss is hard-hearted have you just diagnosed arteriosclerosis? When you tell your neighbor his new car is a sweet ride will he ask you not to lick it again? We can laugh at these absurdities, but all of these statements are meant to be taken seriously—they all have meaning that corresponds to reality. Biblical writers didn't live in an alternate universe where people never used figurative language, metaphors, or symbolic references. All of those things are stock elements of the way language works—and our day-to-day reality itself. Pitting "literalism" and "figurative" against each other in some sort of semantic death match demonstrates poor thinking. The reason we can instantly parse when to take a given statement like those above figuratively or literally is because the world we've experienced informs how to

interpret them. In other words, the cumulative effect of our up-bringing, our cultural setting, our experiences, and our worldview wires us in such a way that we intuitively know what is meant. To reject figurative interpretation in the Bible is to deny the biblical writers their humanity. Instead of letting them be the authority for understanding what they wrote, we assume we know better." (Michael S. Heiser, The 60 Second Scholar: 100 Insights That Illumine The Bible, 2543-2556 (Kindle Edition))

[19]. "A prophet was the mouthpiece of God. His function is clarified by the various descriptions given him. He was called a man of God (1 Kings 12: 22), revealing that he was chosen of God; a servant of the Lord (1 Kings 14: 18), indicating his occupation; a messenger of the Lord (Isa. 42: 19), designating his mission for God; a seer or beholder (Isa. 30: 10), revealing apocalyptic source of his truth; a man of the Spirit (Hos. 9: 7), showing by whose promptings he spoke; a watchman (Ezek. 3: 17), manifesting his alertness to do the work of God. By far and away, the most common expression was "prophet," or spokesman for God. By his very calling, a prophet was one who felt as did Amos, "The Lord God has spoken; who can but prophesy?" (Amos 3: 8); or, as another prophet who said, "I could not go beyond the command of the LORD my God to do less or more" (Num. 22: 18). As Aaron was a prophet or mouthpiece for Moses (Ex. 7: 1), speaking "all the words that the LORD had spoken to Moses" (Ex. 4: 30), even so God's prophets were to speak only what He commanded them. God said of His prophet, "I will put my words in his mouth, and he shall speak to them all that I command him" (Deut. 18: 18). Further, "You shall not add to the word that I command you, nor take from it" (Deut. 4: 2). In summation, a prophet was one who declared what God had disclosed to him." (Norman L. Geisler & William E. Nix, From God To Us Revised and Expanded: How We Got Our Bible, 35-36 (Kindle Edition); Chicago; Moody Press)

[20]"Second Peter 1: 21 provides a key insight regarding the human-divine interchange in the process of inspiration. This verse informs us that "prophecy [or Scripture] never had its origin in the will of man, but men spoke from God as they were carried along

by the Holy Spirit." The phrase "carried along" in this verse literally means "forcefully borne along." The human wills of the authors were not the originators of God's message. God did not per-
mit the will of sinful human beings to misdirect or erroneously record His message. Rather, "God moved and the prophet mouthed
these truths; God revealed and man recorded His word." 5 Interestingly, the Greek word for "carried along" in 2 Peter 1: 21 is the
same as that found in Acts 27: 15-17. In this passage the experienced sailors could not navigate the ship because the wind was so
strong. The ship was being driven, directed, and carried along by
the wind. This is similar to the Spirit's driving, directing, and car-
rying the human authors of the Bible as He wished. The word is a
strong one, indicating the Spirit's complete superintendence of the
human authors. Yet, just as the sailors were active on the ship
(though the wind, not the sailors, ultimately controlled the ship's
movement), so the human authors were active in writing as the
Spirit directed. This is in keeping with the fact that many Old Testament passages quoted in the New Testament are said to have the
Holy Spirit as their author, even though a human prophet actually
spoke the words (see Mark 12: 36; Acts 1: 16; 28: 25; Hebrews 3:
7; 10: 15,16)." (Ron Rhodes, The 10 Most Important Things You
Can Say to a Mormon, 36 (Kindle Edition); Eugene, Oregon; Harvest House Publishers)

[21]"First, though, let us remind ourselves of several principles
that govern the validity of genuine prophecy. (1) True prophecies
are stated emphatically; they are not couched in the jargon of contingency (unless, of course, contextual evidence suggests that one
is dealing with a conditional prophecy). (2) Generally, a significant
time frame must lapse between the prophetic utterance and the fulfillment, so as to exclude the possibility of 'educated speculation.'
(3) The prophecy must involve specific details, not vague general-
ities. (4) The predictive declarations must be fulfilled precisely and
completely. No mere substantial percentage will suffice. One
should recognize, though, that occasionally a prophecy may contain figurative terminology; this does not, however, militate
against its evidential validity." (Wayne Jackson, 'Babylon: A Test
Case In Prophecy,' in Kyle Butt, *Behold! The Word Of God,* 1598-
1604 (Kindle Edition); Montgomery, Alabama; Apologetics Press)

[22] The 1972 study by John P. Kildahl "The Psychology of Speaking in Tongues" concludes that: "... from a linguistic point of view, religiously inspired glossolalic utterances have the same general characteristics as those that are not religiously inspired." In fact, glossolalia is a "human phenomenon, not limited to Christianity nor even to religious behavior." (Dictionary of Pentecostal and Charismatic Movements by Spittler, P. 340). George Jennings in an article in the Journal of the American Scientific Affiliation expands upon the universality of the experience: "... glossolalia is practiced among the following non-Christian religions of the world; the Peyote cult among the North American Indians, the Haida Indians of the Pacific Northwest, Shamans in the Sudan, the Shango cult of the West Coast of Africa, the Shago cult in Trinidad, the Voodoo cult in Haiti, the Aborigines of South American and Australia, the aboriginal peoples of the subarctic regions of North America and Asia, the Shamans in Greenland, the Dyaks of Borneo, the Zor cult of Ethiopia, the Siberian shamans, the Chaco Indians of South America, the Curanderos of the Andes, the Kinka in the African Sudan, the Thonga shamans of Africa, and the Tibetan monks. An article in the Journal of the American Scientific Affiliation entitled "An Ethnological Study of Glossolalia" by George J. Jennings, March 1968. Other studies and sources reach the same conclusions: "Summary of Behavioral Science Research Data on Glossolalia: 1. Glossolalia is an ancient and widespread phenomenon of most societies, occurring most usually in connection with religion." "Behavioral Science Research on the Nature of Glossolalia", Journal of the American Scientific Affiliation; September, 1968 "There are records of ecstatic speech and the like in Egypt in the eleventh century B.C. In the Hellenistic [Greek] world the prophetess of Delphi and the Sibylline priestess spoke in unknown or unintelligible speech. Moreover, the Dionysianrites contained a trancelike state as well as glossolalia. Many of the magicians and sorcerers of the first century world exhibit similar phenomena." G.R.Osborne, in the Evangelical Dictionary of Theology, 1984, page 1100. "Descriptions of ecstatic speech are common in the study of comparative religions.... The Delphic and Pythian religions of Greece understood ecstatic behavior and speech to be evidence of divine inspiration by Apollos." C.M.

Robeck, Jr., in The International Standard Bible Encyclopedia, Vol. 4, 1988, page 872. "... Glossolalia is a very ancient practice it is still practiced nowadays in many religions, especially those where one seeks contact with the spirit world (witchcraft/ shamanism, voodoo) or a union mystical with the "All". Mohamed, the founder of Islam, is probably the most famous of those who have practiced glossolalia." "Glossolalia (Tongues) and 1 Corinthians 14" Bruno D. Granger http:// www.apologetique.org/ en/ rticles/ neomontanism/ BDG_glossolalia_en.htm "Enthusiastic, ecstatic, mystic, possession, trance and other kindred phenomena have long been of interest to anthropologists. Cross-cultural reviews of ethnographic data on glossolalia in particular have been published by L.C. May, Jennings, M. Eliade, among others. The practice was known in ancient India and China, and ethnographies describe glossolalia in almost every area of the world... speaking-in-tongues is widespread and very ancient." E. Mansell Pattison Behavioral Science Research On The Nature Of Glossolalia Journal of the American Scientific Affiliation, September 1968 Research conducted by Al Carlson at the University of California and Werner Cohn at the University of British Columbia indicate that anyone can produce glossolalic speech which sounded genuine even to believers. Jimmy Jividen, "Glossolalia: from God or man?" p 163. "This survey has shown that speaking-in-tongues is widespread and very ancient. Indeed, it is probably that as long as man has had divination, curing, sorcery, and propitiation of spirits, he has had glossolalia ... Whatever the explanation, it is clear that pagans as well as Christians have their glossolalia experiences." Jimmy Jividen, "Glossolalia: from God or man?" p 74,75 "It should be noted that, while there are Hellenistic parallels for tongues, there is also an OT basis. Thus the seers of 1 Sam. 10: 5ff. seem to be robbed of their individuality, and their fervor finds expression in broken cries and unintelligible speech (cf. 2 Kgs. 9: 11). Drunkards mock Isaiah's babbling speech (Is. 28: 10-11). The later literatare, e.g., Eth. En. 71: 11, gives similar examples of ecstatic speech (not necessarily speaking in tongues)." The Theological Dictionary of the New Testament, Abridged in One Volume. Kittel, Gerhard, and Friedrich, Gerhard, Editors (Grand Rapids, MI: Eerdmans, 1985) Johannes Behm. Unabridged edition of the TDNT, Volume I, page

722. "Glossolalia is an ancient and widespread phenomenon of most societies, occurring most usually in connection with religion." Behavioral Science Research on the Nature of Glossolalia Journal of the American Scientific Affiliation, September, 1968 The Term "tongues" predates Christianity and the New Testament and in fact was common in the Greek, Roman, and other cultures. "... the significance of the term 'glossolalia', or 'speaking in tongues', comes to the fore. 'The gift of tongues and of their interpretation was not peculiar to the Christian Church, but was a repetition in it of a phrase common in ancient religions. The very phrase glossais lalein, 'to speak with tongues,' was not invented by the New Testament writers, but borrowed from ordinary speech." Encyclopedia Britannica (1911), s.v, "Gift of Tongues," by Fredrick C. Conybeare, 27: 10. "Once they began to commune with that deity, they would begin to speak the language of the gods. This was a very common practice in their culture. In fact, the term used in 1 Corinthians to refer to speaking in tongues (glossais lalein) was not invented by Bible writers. It was a term used commonly in the Greco-Roman culture to speak of the pagan language of the gods which occurred while the speaker was in an ecstatic trance. By the way, this language of the gods was always gibberish." "The Truth about Tongues--Part 1" John MacArthur Tape GC 1871". (C. Alan Martin, Scientific Observations of Speaking in Tongues, 437-516 (Kindle Edition))

[23]"While living with the Native Americans in New Mexico, I witnessed a similar ritual several times. The Indians would eat the hallucinogenic peyote, then sit in a circle and chant and pound drums for hours. Before long, several were spasmodically muttering as they experienced their tormenting visions. Today the charismatic churches are by far the most popular among the Native Americans because it is such an easy and natural transition from their old religions. Among many heathen African tribes, in order to invoke the blessing of their gods, the people would sacrifice a chicken or goat and then dance around a fire for long hours, chanting songs to the hypnotic rhythm of a pounding drum. Eventually some of the people would become possessed by their gods and begin speaking the eerie languages of the spirit world. Then the

local witch doctor or priest would translate the messages. This ritual is still practiced today among the Voodoo Catholics in the West Indies. This pagan practice first found its way into the North American Christian churches in the early 1800s. Many of the African slaves who were brought to America and forced to accept Christianity were unable to read the Bible for themselves. Even though they came from a variety of tribes in Africa, one practice most tribes held in common was the "Spirit Dances" with the "spirit-possessed" person muttering. The slaves mistakenly associated this with the Christian "gift of tongues" and began to incorporate a modified version into their meetings. These frantic services, which were accompanied by heavy rhythmic music, began to spread at first only in the South and the participants were mocked by the mainline denominations as "Holy Rollers." Some even went so far as to grab venomous serpents during their possessed trances as a means of proving that they had the "spirit."...The national expansion of the Pentecostal movement among Caucasians began in Los Angeles at the Apostolic Faith Gospel Mission on Azusa Street in 1906. The leader was a black former holiness preacher named William Seymour. From there, leaders continued to refine the doctrines and make them more attractive and palatable to other mainline Christians." (Doug Batchelor, *Understanding Tongues,* 248-279 (Kindle Edition); Roseville, CA; Amazing Facts, Inc.).

[24]"Using historical and archaeological data, researchers established several facts: (1) Inquirers visited the oracle at a complex underground location. (2) Before presenting an inquiry, visitors faced a month of mind-altering experiences. These included solitary confinement in a room plastered with dreadful pictorial representations of the underworld. (3) Visitors lived for a month in extremely cramped quarters, shut off from natural light. (4) The only light came from lamps probably burning hashish. The psychological setting, coupled with the inhalation of vast amounts of hashish, possible bathing in drugged water, and ingestion of drugs by various mechanisms, guaranteed vivid, strong, and repeated hallucinations." (Kenny Barfield, *The Prophet Motive: Examining The Reliability Of The Biblical Prophets,* 195; Nashville, TN: Gospel Advocate Company)

[25]"Archaeologists and geologists alike have studied the topography at Delphi in search of evidence of the chasm that would allow the passing of gasses through the earth which could have the intoxicating effect described by these two authors. Delphi seems like a good candidate for such a fissure given its rocky morphology and steep cliffs, and the most systematic study of the area of Delphi was conducted by a team comprised of a geologist, an archaeologist, an oceanographer and a toxicologist. The results of this study by de Boer, Hale, Chanton, and Spiller were published in various academic places and even made The New York Times. The emphasis of their arguments and interpretation of their results tended to change according to the main audience of each publication, but the gist of their arguments appeared to confirm the presence of intoxicating vapors at Delphi. (For a good overview of the de Boer team arguments in the different publications see Lehoux, 2007, 41-48.) More specifically, the team claimed to have found two fault lines crossing beneath the temple at Delphi, which they related to the chasm, and to have discovered trace amounts of ethylene in the nearby spring, which they claimed could have been released in much greater amounts and in the form of gas in antiquity from the presumed fissure in the ground. It might have been these vapors that put the Pythia into a trance-like state experienced by the shepherd and his goats mentioned in the ancient sources. Once affected by the gases that flooded the room in which the Pythia sat, the woman spoke in disjointed verses and utterances that might have been interpreted into more coherent prophesies for the people consulting the oracle." (Charles River Editors, The Oracle of Delphi: The Ancient World's Most Famous Seer, 461-472 (Kindle Edition))

[26]"The cult of worshipping Pluto was probably imitated from the cults of Serapis in Egypt . Strabon (Book XIV) mentions three sites in Asia Minor where Pluto was worshipped. In the region of Nysa and Acharaka he describes a temple for Pluto and Kore, as well as a grotto (the Charonion). Somewhere in the vicinity is Limon (λειμ v, the meadow), where similar rites were practiced . As a third Plutonium, Strabo mentions the famous Hierapolis with its hot water ponds, its calcareous hot water falls (nowadays Pamukkale), and its Charonion (Strabon XIV). Pilgrims prayed for

health and cure and/or asked for prophecies. Priests dealt with the gods of the underworld. The priests, rather than the patients, incubated, i.e. immersed themselves in the natural environmental phenomena of the site. The patients subsequently followed the recipes and cures that were prescribed according to the dreams of the priests during incubation. The prerequisites of prophecies and dreams were among other parameters (drugs, hallucinogenic plants, and mushrooms) attributed to the presence of geogenic gases. Lack of oxygen and an increase in carbon dioxide can cause hallucinogenic effects in humans (see also Ref.)." (Philip Wexler, *History OF Toxicology And Environmental Health: Toxicology In Antiquity, Volume I,* 94-95 (Kindle Edition); Waltham, MA; Academic Press)

[27]"Quatrain 2–24 reads: "Beasts mad with hunger will swim across rivers, Most of the army will be against the Lower Danube [Hister sera]. The great one shall be dragged in an iron cage when the child brother [de Germain] will observe nothing." This is allegedly a prophecy concerning Adolf Hitler. According to followers of Nostradamus, the lower portion of the Danube is known as either "Ister" or "Hister" (Randi, 213), which seems to be close enough to "Hitler" for their purposes. However, the substitution of "1" for "s" in Hister, and the inversion of "t" and "s," is totally arbitrary. In another quatrain (4–68), Nostradamus mentions the Lower Danube in conjunction with the Rhine ("De Ryn"). But if "Hister" refers to Hitler, then to what does "De Ryn " refer? Followers of Nostradamus are inconsistent, treating one river as an anagram and taking the other literally. The Latin phrase de Germain should be interpreted "brother" or "near relative," not "Germany" (Randi, 214). Even if these highly questionable interpretations are allowed, the prophecy is still quite ambiguous. What are we to make of the "Beasts" and the "iron cage"? To say that Adolf Hitler ("the great one") will be "dragged in an iron cage" while Germany "will observe nothing" is so ambiguous and confusing it renders the entire prophecy meaningless." (Norman L. Geisler, Baker Encyclopedia of Christian Apologetics (Baker Reference Library), 544 (Kindle Edition); Grand Rapids, Michigan; Baker Books)

[28]"Nostradamus was a sixteenth-century French astrologer and physician. If anything, he was an occultic prophet, not a biblical prophet. He relied quite heavily on horoscopes and other occult methods of divination. His brand of prophecy thus stands condemned by Scripture (Deuteronomy 18:9-14). Many of Nostradamus's predictions are esoteric, vague, and open-ended. ended. This is why his predictions have been interpreted in so many different ways by Nostradamus enthusiasts. This is unlike the biblical prophecies, which are much more straightforward and precise. (Micah 5:2, for example, predicted the Messiah would be born in Bethlehem. Isaiah 7:14 predicted He would be born of a virgin.) How do we account for the appearance of Nostradamus having predicted certain events accurately? There are a number of possible explanations. It may be that Satan inspired these predictions, and even though Satan is not omniscient (all-knowing) like God is, he is a good guesser. Or, it may be that Satan inspired Nostradamus to utter a prophecy and then Satan worked in the world in such a way to bring about some semblance of a fulfillment, thereby lending credence to Nostradamus as a "prophet." Perhaps Satan's goal was to use Nostradamus as a means of drawing other people into occultism. Clearly, though, he was not a biblical prophet." (Ron Rhodes, The Popular Dictionary of Bible Prophecy: More than 350 Terms and Concepts Defined, 2155-2161 (Kindle Edition); Eugene, Oregon; Harvest House Publishers)

[29]" His prophecies, according to the account in the first two quatrains, were obtained by scrying, using a bowl of water on a tripod as a reflecting surface; SEE SCRYING. They are written in an exceptionally obscure style, full of words borrowed from other languages, and have been interpreted and reinterpreted in different ways for centuries. . Some appear to be remarkably accurate predictions of events centuries after Nostradamus' time, others are so cryptic that it's anyone's guess what they mean, and still others have failed to turn out as predicted; the "Great King of Terror" expected in 1999, for example, does not seem to have put in an appearance." (John Michael Greer, The New Encyclopedia of the Occult, 7477-7481 (Kindle Edition); St. Paul, Minnesota; Llewellyn Publications)

[30]" The literature that appears to have influenced him the most, and from which he quotes extensively, is an occult book "De Mysteriius Egyptorum" by a fourth century Neo-Platonist named Tamblichus. Nostradamus wrote that he would spend hours in his study reading his "secret forbidden books" and meditating. Following the methods of his occult masters, he placed a brass tripod in the room, on which stood a bowl of water. He would gaze at this water intensely until it became cloudy, touching it with a ceremonial occult wand engraved with hieroglyphics. This was the same method used by the ancient Apollonian prophetess at the Oracle of Branchus in Classical Times. Thereafter, he moistened his robe and feet, still staring into the water.. which would now begin to clear, revealing pictures of the future. What happened next was a dramatic experience for him. He testified that "a power" was evoked and came to him. He was so terrified by this "being" or presence that he would begin to tremble with fear. He both saw and heard the power speak and described it as a "divine splendour .. the god sits nearby." Suddenly his body would be possessed by this great power to such an extent that he felt disembodied, in a trance-like state as though "everything is beneath his feet." He experienced a "sensation of bodilessness" but, once "the gift" possessed him, he felt at peace. He speaks of emptying his mind, heart and soul of all care, concern and worry in order to ensure calm and tranquillity of spirit, and records the importance of the tripod in achieving this state of bliss. His mind and intellect were now available to "heavenly beings" for their own purposes. As the "sacred prayers, or his invocations to the spirits, are completed he is possessed. His body, together with "the forehead, senses and head" are under the control of that power. "A small flame", he writes, would come upon him and he would hear a powerful voice within him.in him. He does not predict anything, but merely records what he sees in the mists and what the voice tells him. He says that he saw "as in a burning mirror" the events and calamities to come upon the inhabitants of the earth. The voice tells him what his is seeing and he writes it down. He declares quite openly that he used the "aid of astronomy .. other methods.. and even the Holy Scriptures" to bring himself into the place where these revelations were available to him, recording that he could not draw on this power at will."

(Val Waldeck, The Truth About NOSTRADAMUS: Prophet or Clairvoyant?, 219-237 (Kindle Edition); Durban. Spite Africa)

[31]"Typology is one of the most difficult parts of interpreting prophecy. The word type (Greek, tupos) is used quite loosely in the New Testament. Sometimes it refers to a figure or a divinely intended resemblance. Typology illustrates the principle that prophetic utterances somtimes have a latent and deeper meaning than at first appears. Types prefigure coming realities, whereas prophecies delineate the future. The Passover lamb of the Jews is a type of Christ (1 Corinthians 5: 7). This interpretation does not deny the historicity of Passover lambs vicariously slain in every Jewish home, but it finds a higher application of the Passover lambs in Christ, the Lamb of God. Here are some rules about the use of types as explained by Paul Lee Tan: • Typological interpretation is not a different method of interpretation. The interpretation of a type arises from the text and has a higher application of the same sense of that text. • Typological interpretation is therefore the unfolding of the literal sense of the type, not the allegorization of that which is typified. • When an Old Testament element is said to be a type of an element in the New, this does not mean that one equals the other. • Some fanciful typologists see types lurking everywhere and anywhere in Scripture. Careful interpreters will avoid this. • Some go to the other extreme and say that a type is not a type unless the New Testament specifically says so. • Types must be based on either the explicit or the implicit teachings of Scripture. Imagination has no place in typology. (See Tan, pp. 169-71.)" (Ed Hindson, Mark Hitchcock, Tim LaHaye, The Harvest Handbook™ of Bible Prophecy: A Comprehensive Survey from the World's Foremost Experts, 168-169 (Kindle Edition); Eugene, Oregon; Harvest House Publishers)

[32]"When Were Biblical Prophecies Made? According to this objection, all biblical prophecies with enough specificity to be unexplainable were made after the events. Daniel's amazing statements were made quite late, and Isaiahs predictions about Cyrus were edited in after he arrived on the scene. They were recording history, not uttering prophecies. For discussions of the dating of these two books, see DANIEL, DATING OF, and ISAIAH, DEUTERO.

Neither these nor other charges of post-dated prophecies have any foundation in fact. And many fulfillments have occurred long after the writings are known to have existed." (Norman L. Geisler, Baker Encyclopedia of Christian Apologetics (Baker Reference Library), 615 (Kindle Edition); Grand Rapids, Michigan; Baker Books)

[33]" Only God can know the future. If, then, we are able to establish the fact that the prophets announced—many years in advance—truths regarding the desolation of Babylon, it would amount to a demonstration that ultimately the biblical record was given by God Himself. These matters never could have been known by mere chance. There is an interesting passage in the book of Jeremiah that illustrates this point. On a certain occasion in the prophet's ministry to Judah, Jeremiah was told by the Lord that his cousin, Hanamel, would arrive soon, offering to sell him a parcel of land in the town of Anathoth. Presently, Hanamel came to the prophet and made that very offer. Jeremiah subsequently uttered this significant statement: "Then I knew that this was the word of Jehovah" (Jeremiah 32: 8, emp. added). When a prophecy is made—and the prediction comes to pass—one can know that God has spoken, provided other prophetic guidelines are in place." (Wayne Jackson, 'Babylon: A Test Case In Prophecy,' in Kyle Butt, Behold! The Word Of God, 1591-15999 (Kindle Edition); Montgomery, Alabama; Apologetics Press)

[34] "But in this preliminary discussion we shall be centering our attention on the linguistic evidence in Daniel that tends to eliminate all possibility of dating the composition of Daniel any later than the Persian period. With the wealth of new data from the manuscripts of the Dead Sea caves (the Qumran literature), it is possible to settle this question once and for all. Now that we have at least one fairly extensive midrash originally composed in third-century B.C. Aramaic and several sectarian documents in second-century Hebrew, it has become possible to perform a careful linguistic comparison of the Aramaic and Hebrew chapters of Daniel and these unquestionably third-or second-century B.C. documents, which were close to the era of the Maccabean struggle. If Daniel had in fact been composed in the 160s, these Qumran manuscripts

should have exhibited just about the same general characteristics as Daniel in the matter of vocabulary, morphology, and syntax. Yet the actual test results show that Daniel 2–7 is linguistically older than the Genesis Apocryphon by several centuries. Hence these chapters could not have been composed as late as the second century or the third century, but rather—based on purely philological grounds—they have to be dated in the fifth or late sixth century; and they must have been composed in the eastern sector of the Aramaic-speaking world (such as Babylon), rather than in Palestine (as the late date theory requires)." (Gleason L. Archer Jr., New International Encyclopedia of Bible Difficulties, 584-585 (Kindle Edition); Grand Rapids, Michigan; Zondervan)

"Gleason Archer of the syntax and morphology, the use of postbiblical words, postbiblical pronunciation and spelling, and words used with a postbiblical meaning, he concluded: In light of all the data adduced under the four categories just reviewed, it seems abundantly clear that a second-century date for the Hebrew chapters of Daniel is no longer tenable on linguistic grounds. In view of the markedly later development exhibited by these second-century documents in the areas of syntax, word order, morphology, vocabulary, spelling, and word-usage, there is absolutely no possibility of regarding Daniel as contemporary. On the contrary the indications are that centuries must have intervened between them ... Otherwise we must surrender linguistic evidence altogether and assert that it is completely devoid of value in the face of subjective theories derived from antisupernaturalistic bias . . . If all of the book was written even as early as the third century (and there really is nothing in the linguistic data to militate against a late sixth-century composition by the ostensible author himself), the supernatural element of fulfilled prediction would still remain. 51 This conclusion also seems to be supported by a comparative analysis of the Aramaic of Daniel with the Aramaic Elephantine Papyri from Upper Egypt, which are dated to the fifth century BC. British Egyptologist Kenneth Kitchen demonstrated that 90 percent of Daniel's Aramaic vocabulary occurred in documents dated to the fifth century BC or earlier, that Persian loanwords were Old Persian, and that Greek loanwords also could precede the fifth century BC. In addition, some syntactical forms in Daniel were shown to have not survived beyond the fifth century BC, precluding any later date. 52 He thus concluded: "The Aramaic of Daniel (and of Ezra) is simply a part of Imperial (Official) Aramaic—in itself, practically undateable with any conviction within c. 600 to 330 BC" 53 Kitchen's view was supported by University of Liverpool Semiticist Alan Millard, 54 as well as by the leading Aramaist E. Y. Kutscher, who showed from Daniel's Aramaic word order that the provenance was Eastern (Babylon), not Western (Palestine), as the Maccabean date required." (Randal Price, Zondervan Handbook of Biblical Archaeology: A Book by Book Guide to Archaeological Discoveries Related to the Bible, 179 (Kindle Edition); Grand Rapids, Michigan; Zondervan)

[35] 35 "They know the truth of the matter, yet wilfully conceal it from the public. This goes for every item of evidence that we have looked at in this present study. But while that is not surprising considering the school to which the critics belong, it is surprising to see such evidence kept out of the public eye by seemingly conservative scholars. They generally discuss the evidences among themselves, and very ably too, but the discussion is held in scholarly papers which few members of the public will ever get to know about, let alone see; and those who do get to see them will often be confused by the nit-picking pedantry that has become the obscuring fare of scholarship these days. This evidence should have been trumpeted from the housetops from day one, yet it has been kept under wraps even by those who should have loudly advertised it. We have seen for ourselves in this present study the formidable amount of evidence, both written and archaeological, that demonstrates the authenticity, historicity, and integrity of the Book of Daniel. We could hardly ask for better. Yet, it is certain, none of this will make any difference at all to what our schools, colleges, seminars and universities teach concerning the Book of Daniel - nor any other part of the Bible come to that. All we can hope for at this stage is that the evidence which has now come to the surface will be able at long last to circulate amongst those, especially our younger students, who could most easily be misled by what the critics say. It is an understated fact that wherever the Bible can be tested historically, it always shows itself to be astonishingly accurate in its statements. Being buried in obscure scholarly papers that

are scattered around the world, finding the evidence for a given fact is never easy. Sometimes, as I know too well, it can take a lifetime to track down just one solitary item. Yet such research is always rewarded with exonerating evidence of such high quality that, while it can certainly be ignored by the critics, it can never be answered. The Bible is an astonishing Book. It claims to be the Word of God and to speak in perfect Truth. Moreover, and with a breathtaking audacity, it invites us –no, it challenges us -to put it to the test, and test it we must. I have been conducting such tests for more than forty years now, many of those tests being cruel and harsh –unreasonably so for any historical document -yet not once have I ever come across a statement from the Bible that has proved to be untrue, inaccurate, naive, falsely confident, or even an out-right lie. 3 What the Greeks would have called that, I just don't know, but I call it a phenomenon." (Bill Cooper, The Authenticity Of The Book Of Daniel, 1366-1382 (Kindle Edition))

[36] For example: "Cerinthus, too, through written revelations by a great apostle (as he would have us to believe!) brings before us fantastic things. And he pretends these things were shown him by angels. He alleges that after the resurrection, the kingdom of Christ is to be on earth and that the flesh dwelling in Jerusalem is again to be subject to desire and pleasures. And being an enemy to the Scriptures of God and wishing to deceive men, he says that there is to be a space of a thousand years for marriage festivals. (Eusebius, quoting Caius (c. 215, W), 5.601.)

Again:

"The doctrine taught by Cerinthus is this: that there will be an earthly reign of Christ. Since Cerinthus was himself a man devoted to the pleasures of the body, and completely carnal in his dispositions, he imagined that the kingdom would consist in those kinds of gratifications on which his own heart was set. (Dionysius of Alexandria (c. 262, E), 6.82.)

Again:

"They are not to be heard who assure themselves that there is to be an earthly reign of a thousand years. They think like the heretic Cerinthus. For the kingdom of Christ is already eternal in the saints—even though the glory of the saints shall be manifested after the resurrection.(Victorinus (c. 280, W), 7.360; see also 5.147.)

[37]"The lion and eagle are both symbols of Babylon (Jeremiah 49:19; 50:17, 44; 48:40; 49:22; Ezekiel 17:3, 12). The wings represent speed; the rapidity of the Babylonian conquest of the old Assyrian Empire." (Emanuel B. Daugherty, *A Commentary On The Book Of Daniel,* 134; Bethlehem, W.V.)

[38]"Second, statues of winged lions, which are believed to have been representative of the empire, have been found in the ruins of Babylon, and lions adorned the famous Ishtar Gate. Although the text does not specifically interpret the rest of the verse, the meaning of the symbolism would naturally be expected to be found in the descriptions of Nebuchadnezzar (who embodied the Babylonian Empire) presented elsewhere in the book." (Stephen R. Miller, *The New American Commentary Volume 18: Daniel-An Exegetical And Theological Exposition Of Holy Scripture,* 197 (Kindle Edition); Nashville, TN: B&H Publishing Group)

[39]"The bear with one side higher than the other represented the combined empire of the Medes and Persians. The beast corresponds to the chest and arms of silver. Babylon, in fear of Cyrus, formed a coalition with the kingdoms of Egypt and Lydia. These are represented by the three ribs in the bear's mouth, which proved to be no match for the armies of Cyrus. Lydia fell to the Persians in 544 BC; Babylon, in 537 BC; and Egypt, in 523 BC." (Ken Johnson, *Ancient Book Of Daniel,* 85 (Kindle Edition)

The third kingdom is identified as a leopard with four wings and four heads. The leopard in the Bible is used for the imagery of *speed and rapidity (*cf. Habakkuk 1:8). The third great kingdom which arose after the Medes and the Persians was the kingdom of Greece, under the guidance of Alexander the Great. His rise to power and conquest of the known world was very rapid, and the image of a leopard perfectly describes him. Alexander's kingdom was divided up four ways at the time of his death. The Grecian Empire came under the leadership of four great "heads" of state: Cassander, Ptolemy, Lysimachus, and Antiognus.

[40]"The historian Machiavel, without the slightest reference to this prophecy, gives the following list of the nations which occupied the territory of the Western Empire at the time of the fall of Romulus Augustulus, the last emperor of Rome. The Lombards, the Franks, the Burgundians, the Ostrogoths, the Visigoths, the Vandals, the Heruli, the Sueves, the Huns, and the Saxons; ten in all." (Henry Grattan Guinness, The Divine Program of the World's History, 4115 (Kindle Edition); Harley House Row)

[41] "...attempting to change the "set times" or implement a new table of religious festivals (v. 25c; cf. Redditt, 131, who identifies the "sacred seasons" [NRSV] as the Sabbath and annual festivals); and attempting to change the laws or impose a new morality (v. 25d; this assumes that the word "laws" [NIV, though the Aram. d t is singular] refers to the Mosaic code; cf. Goldingay, 146, n. 25. b-b, who understands "times and law" as a type of hendiadys meaning "times set by decree")." (Temper Longman III & David E. Garland, Daniel–Malachi (The Expositor's Bible Commentary Book 8), 143 (Kindle Edition); Grand Rapids, Michigan; Zondervan)

Albert Barnes agrees with this interpretation:

"The word "times" - זמנין zîmnîyn - would seem to refer properly to some stated or designated times - as times appointed for festivals, etc. Gesenius, "time, specially an appointed time, season:" Ecc 3:1; Neh 2:6; Est 9:27, Est 9:31. Lengerke renders the word Fest-Zeiten - "festival times," and explains it as meaning the holy times, festival days, Lev 23:2, Lev 23:4, Lev 23:37, Lev 23:44. The allusion is, undoubtedly, to such periods set apart as festivals or fasts - seasons consecrated to the services of religion and the kind of jurisdiction which the power here referred to would hope and desire to set up would be to have control of these periods, and so to change and alter them as to accomplish his own purposes - either by abolishing those in existence, or by substituting others in their place. At all times these seasons have had a direct connection with the state and progress of religion; and he who has power over them, either to abolish existing festivals, or to substitute others in their places, or to appoint new festivals, has an important control over the whole subject of religion, and over a nation. The word rendered "laws" here - דת dâth - while it might refer to any law, would more properly designate laws pertaining to religion. See Dan 6:5, Dan 6:7, Dan 6:12 (Dan 6:6, Dan 6:9, Dan 6:13); Ezr 7:12, Ezr 7:21. So Lengerke explains it as referring to the laws of religion, or to religion. The kind of jurisdiction, therefore, referred to in this place would be what would pertain to the laws and institutions of religion; it would be a purpose to obtain the control of these; it would be a claim of right to abolish such as existed, and to institute new ones; it would be a determination to exert this power in such a way as to promote its own ends."

[42] "The Venerable Bede, who lived in the north of England at the close of the seventh century, was an historical interpreter of the Apocalypse. Here is a copy of his commentary. He takes the first seal to represent the triumphs of the primitive Church. He expounds the lamb-like beast of Revelation 13 as a pseudo-Christian false prophet. Ambrose Anspert wrote a copious commentary on the Apocalypse in the middle of the eighth century. He expounds the second beast of Revelation 13 as meaning the preachers and ministers of antichrist, and teaches that antichrist will be "pro Christo," or in Christ's place. It is a remarkable fact that he expounds the grievous "sore," or ulcer, poured out under the first vial, as meaning infidelity. This is the general view at the present day among historical interpreters. They consider the infidelity of the French Revolution to be the fulfillment of this vial. Haymo's commentary, written in the ninth century, is for the most part abridged from Anspert. Andreas, who was Bishop of Caesarea, states definitely that the Apocalypse was a prophecy of the things to happen from Christ's first coming to the consummation. He interprets the "hundred and forty-four thousand" as meaning true Christians, and antichrist to be a Roman king and "pseudo-Christ," or false Christ." (Henry Grattan Guinness, Romanism and the Reformation: From the Standpoint of Prophecy, 1711-1718 (Kindle Edition); Harley House)

[43] "Shortly after A.D. 476, "three" of the "ten horns" resisted the growing political influence of the papacy, and one by one, they were systematically "plucked up by the roots" and destroyed. The Heruli were wiped out in A.D. 493, the Vandals in A.D. 534, and

the Ostrogoths were eliminated in A.D. 538. No modern European nation can trace its roots back to these "three" powers. They're gone. And so far, these historical clues (taken together) can apply to no other organization except the Roman Church." (Steve Wohlberg, Decoding The Mark Of The Beast, 158 (Kindle Edition); Goldwater, MI; Remnant Publications)

[44] "The sixth-century BC Cyrus Cylinder, which many have recognized as the first charter of human rights, is a clay record written in Babylonian cuneiform of Cyrus's victory over Babylon. Worthy of note, the cylinder gives permission to worship freely and to rebuild destroyed cities and worship centers. Though the Jews were not mentioned by name in the cylinder, they were free to return to their homeland that lay in ruins. Later some did under Ezra, Nehemiah, and Zerubbabel, but many stayed and lived within Persian society (see the book of Esther). In addition to the Cyrus Cylinder, Ezra 1:2-4 and 6:3-5 state that Cyrus believed he had been charged and authorized by God to rebuild the ruined temple in Jerusalem, and that the Jews should return to pursue the endeavor. Cyrus lived nearly a decade longer, only to be killed in a battle he personally led in 530 BC. His stone tomb pictured here, which was looted prior to its discovery, resides about one mile outside the palaces at Pasargadae.* It stands over 30 feet tall; its interior measures only 80 square feet. Cyrus as a historical figure has been confirmed through a variety of material remains, including palace wall reliefs, his tomb, and building bricks that bear his name." (Joseph M. Holden & Norman Geisler, The Popular Handbook of Archaeology and the Bible: Discoveries That Confirm the Reliability of Scripture, 3286-3293 (Kindle Edition); Eugene, Oregon; Harvest House Publishers)

[45] "The prophet Ezekiel (590 B.C.) was aware of Jeremiah's prophecy that the Jews would be able to return to their land from Babylon after seventy years (in 536 B.C.). However, God gave Ezekiel a new revelation that looked much further into the future, revealing how long it would be until the Jews would finally reestablish their nation in the last days. The prediction is found in Ezekiel 4: 3–6...In this passage, Ezekiel declares that each day represents one biblical year. This means Israel would be punished for

a combined period of 430 years (arrived at by adding 390 years plus another 40 years). The beginning point occurred in the spring of 536 B.C., at the end of the first 70 years of predicted captivity in Babylon (see Jeremiah 25: 11). However, in the month of Nisan in 536 B.C., only a small remnant of the Jews from the southern kingdom (Judah) chose to leave Babylon and return to Jerusalem. The Jewish exiles who remembered their former homes in Israel were now more than 70 years old. Their children who had been born in Babylon had little attachment to the former home of their parents. The vast majority were happy to remain in the Persian Empire as colonists rather than travel six hundred miles to rebuild the devastated colony of Israel. God decreed to Ezekiel a period of punishment of 430 years for Israel's and Judah's sin (390 years + 40 years = 430 years). However, when we deduct the 70 years of punishment that the Jews already had endured during the 70-year Babylonian captivity, there still remained 360 years of further punishment beyond the year 536 B.C....Since the majority of the Jews refused to repent after the Babylonian captivity ended, the period of 360 years of further punishment declared by Ezekiel 4: 3–6 was to be multiplied by seven. This meant that the Jews would remain without an independent nation for another 2,520 biblical years, starting from 536 B.C. The period of punishment was to last 2,520 biblical years (of 360 days each), rather than 2,520 calendar years (of 365.25 days)....**Ezekiel's prophecy declared that the end of Israel's punishment and her final restoration to the Promised Land would be accomplished in 2,520 biblical years of 360 days each, or 907,200 days. To convert this into our calendar year of 365.25 days we simply divide 907,200 days by 365.25 days, or 2,483.8 of our modern calendar years. So Israel's worldwide captivity would end precisely 2,483.8 calendar years after the end of the Babylonian captivity (the spring of 536 B.C.). In these calculations we must keep in mind that the year 1 B.C. was immediately followed by the year A.D. 1. There was no year zero....The Babylonian captivity ended in the spring of 536 B.C., or 536.4 B.C. Subtract 536.4 from the duration of Israel's captivity (see Ezekiel 4: 3–6, as discussed above), which is 2,483.8 calendar years. The result is A.D. 1947.4. Now adjust for the fact there was no year zero between 1 B.C. and**

A.D. 1, so the end of Israel's captivity would occur, on our modern calendar, in the year 1948.4. On the afternoon of May 14, 1948, the Jews proclaimed the independence of the reborn State of Israel. As an old rabbi blew on the shofar, a ram's horn, the Jewish people celebrated the end of their worldwide dispersion and captivity. At midnight, as May 15, 1948, began, Israel officially became an independent nation. ...God remains in full control of the events of humanity and the world. The universe is unfolding precisely as our Lord ordained millenniums ago." (Grant R. Jeffrey, The Signature Of God: Conclusive Proof That Every Teaching, Every Command, Every Promise In The Bible Is True, 161-164 (Kindle Edition, emphasis added M.T.); WaterBrook Press @Books)

" 360 x 7 = 2,520 prophetic years; 2,520 x 360 = 907,220 days 907,220 days on the modern calendar is 2,483 yrs & 285 days 2,483 yrs x 365.25 = 906915; 907200 – 906915 = 285 days August 3, 537 BC + 2,483 yrs = August 3, AD 1946 Add 1 year (no 0 Year) = AD 1947; Add 285 days = May 14, AD 1948" (Ken Johnson, Th.D., Ancient Prophecies Revealed, 206 (Kindle Edition))

[46]"THE following list contains the passages in the Old Testament applied to the Messiah or to Messianic times in the most ancient Jewish writings. They amount in all to 456, thus distributed: 75 from the Pentateuch, 243 from the Prophets, and 138 from the Hagiographa, and supported by more than 558 separate quotations from Rabbinic writings. Despite all labour and care, it can scarcely be hoped that the list is quite complete, although, it is hoped, no important passage has been omitted. The Rabbinic references might have been considerably increased, but it seemed useless to quote the same application of a passage in many different books. Similarly, for the sake of space, only the most important Rabbinic quotations have been translated in extenso. The Rabbinic works from which quotations have been made are: the Targumim, the two Talmuds, and the most ancient Midrashim, but neither the Zohar (as the date of its composition is in dispute), nor any other Kabbalistic work, nor yet the younger Midrashim, nor, of course, the writings of later Rabbis. I have, however, frequently quoted from the well-known work Yalkut, because, although of comparatively

late date, it is really, as its name implies, a collection and selection from more than fifty older and accredited writings, and adduces passages now not otherwise accessible to us. And I have the more readily availed myself of it, as I have been reluctantly forced to the conclusion that even the Midrashim preserved to us have occasionally been tampered with for controversial purposes. I have quoted from the best edition of Yalkut (Frankfort a. M., 1687), but in the case of the other Midrashim I have been obliged to content myself with such more recent reprints as I possessed, instead of the older and more expensive editions. In quoting from the Midrashim, not only the Parashah, but mostly also the folio, the page, and frequently even the lines are referred to. Lastly, it only remains to acknowledge in general that, so far as possible, I have availed myself of the labours of my predecessors—specially of those of Schöttgen. Yet, even so, I may, in a sense, claim these references also as the result of my own labours, since I have not availed myself of quotations without comparing them with the works from which they were adduced—a process in which not a few passages quoted had to be rejected. And if any student should arrive at a different conclusion from mine in regard to any of the passages hereafter quoted, I can at least assure him that mine is the result of the most careful and candid study I could give to the consideration of each passage. With these prefatory remarks I proceed to give the list of Old Testament passages Messianically applied in ancient Rabbinic writings." (Alfred Edersheim (edited by Robert C. Newman), Messianic Passages In The Old Testament As Cited In Rabbinic Literature (IBRi Occasional Papers Book 35), Interdisciplinary Biblical Research Institute)

[47]" I am aware also that in recent times many intelligent Jews, backed by rationalistic, so-called Christians, who, in this respect, are even less conscientious and consistent than their Israelitish champions, deny that there is the hope of a Messiah in the Old Testament Scriptures, and assert that the prophecies on which Christians ground such a belief contain only "vague anticipations and general hopes, but no definite predictions of a personal Messiah," and that consequently the alleged agreement of the gospel history with prophecy is imaginary. But on this I may be permitted to ask, first of all, How is it that it is only within very recent years,

since special efforts were beginning to be made on the part of Christians to show that in Jesus of Nazareth the predictions have received their fulfilment, that attempts are made on the part of some representatives of the synagogue to eliminate the Messianic meaning from those predictions? Does it not appear very much as if this new mode of interpretation was adverted to as a convenience and for argument's sake rather than from a desire to arrive at the truth or from a sincere belief that it is more in accordance with facts? The famous Joseph Albo, of the fifteenth century, author of the "Hikrim," quotes Hillel as an authority when he reproves Maimonides for laying down the belief in a Messiah as a fundamental doctrine of Judaism, and goes on to say, "And there is neither in the law or in the prophets any prediction that must necessarily indicate the appearance of a Messiah" (" Sepher Ikarim Oratio IV" c. 42). A rather bold assertion this! and as for Hillel, had Maimonides lived he might have replied that his (Hillel's) view was an isolated one in the Talmud. Since Albo there have been such isolated cases as Slavador and others of the rationalistic school who have held the same views, but their numbers have increased at the present day to legion, and in many cases they have been driven to it out of a feeling of despair and of hope deferred." (David Baron, Rays of Messiah's Glory, 58-72 (Kindle Edition))

[48] In addition to the broad strokes portraying the Messiah as a reigning king and suffering servant, there are a host of more specific, detailed prophecies that relate to His coming. In regard to the number of Messianic prophecies, Santala wrote: "It is estimated that the Old Testament contains altogether some 456 prophecies concerning Christ. Of these 75 are to be found in the Pentateuch, 243 in the Prophets and 138 in the 'Writings 'and Psalms" (1992, p. 149; cf. Free and Vos, 1992, p. 241)." (Kyle Butt, *Behold! The Word Of God,* 2316 (Kindle Edition); Montgomery, Alabama; Apologetics Press)

[49]"To summarize the point of this section, Rashi and other medieval Jewish interpreters, in seeking a polemical tool to combat Christian interpretation of the Old Testament, adjusted the meaning of peshat, changing it from the literal (or literary) sense to the historical sense. They then used the peshat, even if it contradicted

the messianic interpretation of earlier rabbinic sages, to combat the messianic interpretation of the Old Testament and the identification of Jesus as the Messiah." (Michael Rydelnik, The Messianic Hope: Is the Hebrew Bible Really Messianic? (NAC Studies in Bible & Theology Book 9), 127-128 (Kindle Edition); Nashville, TN: B&H Publishing Group)

[50]"Now, this is just a sampling from the first few pages of the Talmud, pages which are certainly reflective of the Talmudic use of the Hebrew Scriptures, but already we found: (1) verses cited to support positions which barely relate to the discussions at hand; (2) verses cited in somewhat what contrived ways to support various positions; (3) a verse cited, discussed, and ultimately interpreted contrary to its clear, contextual meaning; (4) a verse that is actually misquoted, with key names being reversed; (5) plays on words, with no attempt to elucidate the primary (or, original) meaning of the text.14 Do I write this to demean the Talmud? Absolutely not. Rather, my purpose is to illustrate that: (1) Jewish interpretation and use of Scripture in the first five-plus centuries of this era was much more free-flowing than our contemporary, historical-grammatical approach. (2) Verses from the Tanakh could be cited on many different levels and for many different purposes. (3) Editorial or copyist errors could easily creep into the texts. (4) The use of the Hebrew Bible in the New Covenant Scriptures is completely in line with the Jewish interpretive methods of the day, with this one caveat: In many ways the use of the Tanakh in the New Testament is more restrained, contextual, and sober than its use in the Rabbinic writings. An analysis of the use of the Tanakh in the Dead Sea Scrolls, representing Jewish biblical interpretation contemporaneous with and immediately mediately prior to the New Testament period, offers further support for this position....This, then, was the perspective of Matthew and his fellow authors who penned the Messianic Scriptures. Messiah did come at the time appointed by the peshat (that is, the plain, historical sense) of Scripture and he did fulfill what had to be fulfilled during that phase of his mission-again, according to the plain, historical sense of the Tanakh-and he continues to accomplish that mission-once again, according to the plain, historical sense of the Tanakh (see vol. 1, 2.1; vol. 3, 4.32-4.33, for more on this). And so, the

New Testament authors started with that reality: Messiah has come in accordance with the true and literal meaning of the Hebrew Scriptures, announced by angels and confirmed by miracles, and based on that reality, they then turned to their Bible and saw prophecies and allusions and types of the Messiah siah throughout the Scriptures, just as the rabbis saw references to the Torah everywhere in the Scriptures, even where those references were entirely midrashic or allegorical." (Michael L. Brown, Answering Jewish Objections To Jesus: Volume Four-New Testament Objections, 7; 37 (Kindle Edition); Grand Rapids, Michigan; Baker Books)

[51]"There are an estimated 3,000 languages (not counting dialects) and more than 66,000 letters which make up the alphabets for these languages. Only one language and one alphabet is Divinely created, the letters having been formed and shaped by G-d alone. That language is Lashon HaKodesh, biblical Hebrew. It is no wonder, then, that the Hebrew letters are multifaceted. The letters of the Hebrew alphabet, the alef-beis, are so rich with meaning that even Judaism's greatest scholars had to engage in lengthy study to understand why G-d made them as He did. Traditionally, Hebrew letters possess: 1) Design—the specific way each letter is formed. This form represents the Divine energy within each letter. 2) Gematria—each of the letters of the alef-beis represents a certain number, e.g., alef = 1, beis = 2, etc. 3) Meaning—each letter has many meanings, e.g., the letter alef stands for chief, to learn, wondrous, and much more. Beis means house, etc. 4) Nekudos(vowels)—most letters have a vowel that tells us how it is to be pronounced. 5) Crowns—some letters in the Torah have crowns—little lines drawn on the top of Hebrew letters—which add strength to the letters, e.g. . Rabbi Akivawas famous for his expositions upon them. The crowns have their own special meanings beyond the scope of this work. 6) Cantillation—each word in the Torah has a musical note." (Rabbi Aaron L. Raskin, Letters Of Light: The Power And Essence Of The Alef-Beis In The Light Of Kabbalah And Chassidus, 68-87 (Kindle Edition): Brooklyn, N.Y.; Sichos In English)

[52]"The Hebrew language has some distinctive characteristics that no other language on the planet Earth has. All the early languages were written without spaces between the words, and the Hebrew language is self-parsing. In Hebrew, there are five letters that have a slightly different shape when they're used as the last letter of a word. Because of that, it's possible to read Hebrew without spaces between the letters. There are only consonants in Hebrew, and no vowels. It's what's called a consonantal script. The meaning of a word derives from a root of three letters, and each three letter root word can be expanded to create all manner of other words. Prefixes and suffixes can be added to those three letters, forming different parts of speech or even entirely new words; the meaning is related to those three base letters. The particular meaning of the word depends on how it's pronounced when vowel sounds are added. For instance, the three letters sfr create the word for "book" and it's pronounced "sapher." A writer, on the other hand, somebody who makes books, would be called a "sopher"-same letters. The plural form requires a "ym" ending-sfrym"–sefarim." The pronunciations are therefore very important. It's not difficult for a native speaker to vocally add the appropriate vowels. We often use the consonants "bldg" for "building" and we understand the word even with the vowels (and one consonant) removed. Native speakers would naturally read the words correctly. The root consonants are designed to give Hebrew a semantic backbone and stability not characteristic of Western languages. It also leads to word play. Verb usage is dependent on the context, and the language lends itself to puns. There's often far more meaning implied in the Hebrew sentence than there would be in a Greek sentence....One of the peculiarities of the Hebrew language is that the alphabet is not just phonetic, but also symbolic. The alphabet of most languages are phonetic. Words can be sounded out if the letter sounds are known. Hebrew is phonetic, but it is a special language, because it is also symbolic. Individual letters can have their own meanings. Early in Hebrew writing, the letters were also pictographs. Aleph, for instance, was shaped like the head of an ox and represented strength and leadership. The letter kaf was originally shaped like a hand, and "kaf" means "palm of the hand" or "to coerce." The Hebrew language is astonishingly vivid, concise

and simple. It is also so dense that it makes it difficult to translate fully. While the Greek language is precise, each word holding a specific intended meaning, Hebrew leaves many ideas to be "understood." It requires the reader to fill in the blanks. It often takes two or three times as much space to translate the Hebrew into English because the words carry so much significance on their own." (Chuck Missler, How We Got Our Bible, 445-491 (Kindle Edition); Coeur d'Alene, ID; Koinonia House)

[53]"LOOK AT THE PICTURE MESSAGE HIDDEN IN THE FIRST SIX HEBREW LETTERS OF 'IN THE BEGINNING': The Son Of God pressed by his own hand to a cross.....Are we really surprised that God would inscribe his most awesome work with the name of Yeshua Ha-Mashiach? Isn't this where He would encode His most important message on the billboard of the first words in His Revelation? Guess what. He did! Words fail! Simply contemplate the wonder of this revelation and worship your Savior! Let this revelation soak into your soul that the Lord God, our Savior Yeshua Ha-Mashiach, revealed His redemptive purpose in the very first words of Holy Writ. Can there be any doubt that the Messiah, Yeshua Ha-Mashiach, is hidden in plain sight inside the letters of the Hebrew aleph-beyt?" (C.J. Lovik, The Living Word In 3D-Volume One, 27-28 (E-Book); Rock Island Books)

[54]" Genesis 3: 15, the first messianic prophecy we studied, says the Seed of the woman would crush the head of the serpent. This is an interesting phrase, since seed (" offspring" or "descendant") is usually associated with men. For example, the "descendant of Abraham" (Isa. 41: 8), "Jacob's descendants" (Ps. 22: 24), and the "offspring of David" (Jer. 33: 22). Isaiah 7: 14 sheds further light on this by revealing that the promised Seed would be born of a virgin. Since the Messiah would not have a biological human father, it makes perfect sense that the Messiah is associated with the woman in Genesis 3: 15. The virgin birth is spiritually significant, for the Messiah's unique birth points to His identity as Immanuel, "God with us." The Messiah, the One "born of a woman" (Gal. 4: 4), would be different than any other king in the history of Israel." (Rabbi Jason Sobel, Mysteries of the Messiah: Unveiling Divine

Connections from Genesis to Today, 10 (Kindle Edition); Nashville, TN; W Publishing Group, an imprint of Thomas Nelson)

[55]" Theologians have known these key verses since the time when the Scriptures could only be read in Hebrew, Greek, and Latin as the "protoevangelium," or the first gospel. Perhaps you ask, how did the devil bruise His heel? It may have been the natural result of crucifixion. As a crucifixion victim fights for air, he is forced to push up on his feet so that he can take each breath. That means pushing his full weight upward with one heel, as His feet were nailed together. Because a crucifixion victim had one heel pushed into the cross, that one heel—not both heels, interestingly—would bear a tremendous amount of weight and was, thus, badly bruised." (Joseph Farah, The Gospel in Every Book Of The Old Testament, 24 (Kindle Edition); Washington, D.C.; WND Books)

[56]" Gen. xlix. 10 [The scepter shall not depart from Judah, Nor the ruler's staff from between his feet, Until Shiloh comes, And to him [shall be] the obedience of the peoples]. This well-known prediction (on which see the full and interesting discussion in Raym. Martini, Pugio Fidei) is in Yalkut, u. s., applied to the Messiah, with a quotation of Ps. ii. 9 [You shall break them with a rod of iron, You shall shatter them like earthenware]. This expression 'Shiloh' is also applied to the Messiah, with the curious addition, that in the latter days all nations would bring gifts to Him. Alike the Targum Onkelos, Pseudo-Jonathan, and the Jerusalem Targum, as well as Sanh. 98 b, the Midrash on the passage, and that on Prov. xix. 21, and on Lam. i. 16, where it is rendered shelo, 'whose it is,' refer the expression 'Shiloh,' and, indeed, the whole passage, to the Messiah; the Midrash Ber. R. (99, ed. Warsh. p. 178 b) with special reference to Is. xi. 10" (Alfred Edersheim (edited by Robert C. Newman), Messianic Passages In The Old Testament As Cited In Rabbinic Literature (IBRi Occasional Papers Book 212-218 (Kindle Edition)), Interdisciplinary Biblical Research Institute)

[57]"The key word is "Shiloh." This was the name of a town that was later built near Bethel. For a while during the period of the judges, the tabernacle was set up there; but it never was a very

important town and was later destroyed by the Philistines. It is obvious that the prophecy cannot refer to this town, though it is perhaps possible that the town itself was originally named in commemoration of the prophecy and the One to whom it referred. The context makes it certain that Shiloh is intended to be the name or title of a person. It is "unto him that peoples shall gather." The form of the word is related to the word for "peace" (shalom), and probably it means "The One Who Brings Peace." In any case, it was accepted, by both certain ancient Jewish commentators and the early church, as prophetic of the promised Messiah, although its use as a specific title of Messiah dates from the Reformation." (Henry Morris, Genesis Record, The: A Scientific and Devotional Commentary on the Book of Beginnings, 639 (Kindle Edition); Grand Rapids Michigan; Master Books)

[58]"It is a Messianic passage that implies the scepter shall not depart from Judah. The "scepter" refers to the tribal identity and the right to apply Mosaic Laws. Even when the Jews were in captivity in Babylon for seventy years (606-537 B.C.), they were allowed to retain their tribal identity. They had their own logistics and judges (Ezekiel 1: 5, 8). The proper translation would then be: "the scepter will not depart from Judah until He comes to whom it belongs." The early Rabbis and Talmudic authorities all through the rabbinical literature understood the meaning. After Herod the Great died in 6-7 A.D., Archelaus, the second son of Herod the Great, was appointed "Entharch" by Caesar Augustus. However, Archelaus was badly rejected, dethroned and banished, according to Josephus. 33 Herod's first son, Herod Antipater, had been murdered by Herod the Great, along with other family members. 34 Caponius was appointed Procurator at that time. The legal power of the Sanhedrin was immediately restricted, and the adjudication of capital cases (jus gladii) was lost. This was normal Roman policy. 35" (Chuck Missler, The Christmas Story: What Really Happened, 857-868 (Kindle Edition); Coeur d'Alene, ID; Koinonia Institute)

[59]"Rabbi Rachmon says, "When the members of the Sanhedrin found themselves deprived of their right over life and death, a general consternation took possession of them; they covered their

heads with ashes, and their bodies with sackcloth, exclaiming: 'Woe unto us, for the scepter has departed from Judah, and the Messiah has not come!'" 21/28-30" (Josh McDowell, *Evidence That Demands A Verdict: Historical Evidences For The Christian Faith -Volume One,* 168-169 (Kindle Edition); Nashville, TN: Thomas Nelson Publishers)

[60]"On Ps. xxii. 7 [All who see me sneer at me; They separate with the lip, they wag the head, [saying]] (v 8 in the Hebrew) a remarkable comment appears in Yalkut on Is. lx., applying this passage to the Messiah (the second, or son of Ephraim), and using almost the same words in which the Evangelists describe the mocking behaviour of the Jews at the Cross. Ps. xxii. 15 [My strength is dried up like a potsherd, And my tongue cleaves to my jaws; And You lay me in the dust of death] (v 16 in the Hebrew). There is a similarly remarkable application to the Messiah of this verse in Yalkut." (Alfred Edersheim (Edited by Robert C. Newman), Messianic Passages in the Old Testament as Cited in Rabbinic Literature (IBRI Occasional Papers Book 35), 538-544 (Kindle Edition); Interdisciplinary Biblical Research Institute www.ibri.org)

[61]" Actually, Psalm 22 is the prayer of a righteous sufferer, brought down to the jaws of death and then rescued and raised up by God in answer to prayer, a glorious testimony to be recounted through the ages. As such, it applies powerfully to Jesus the Messiah, the ideal righteous sufferer, surrounded by hostile crowds, beaten, mocked, crucified, and seemingly abandoned by man and God, but delivered from death itself and raised from the dead by the power of God, a story now celebrated around the globe. That's why he quoted words from this psalm with reference to himself when he hung on the cross. How strikingly they apply to him! What is also interesting is that some of the great Rabbinic commentators-including Rashi-interpreted the psalm as a prophecy of Israel's future suffering and exile, not as the story of David's past suffering. Not only so, but a famous Rabbinic midrash composed about twelve hundred years ago said that David spoke of the Messiah's sufferings in Psalm 22. We can therefore say with confi-

dence that the application of this psalm to the death and resurrection of the Messiah is in keeping with the clear meaning of the text." (Michael L. Brown, Answering Jewish Objections to Jesus : Volume 3: Messianic Prophecy Objections, 117 (Kindle Edition): Grand Rapids, MI: Baker Books)

[62]"Although overlooked by most contemporary commentators across the board, the position of Ps 22 in the Psalter is essential to interpretation, and it supports the view of the NT gospel writers. The immediately previous psalms, as well as the entire preceding sequence from the book's introduction (Pss 1–2) onward, support a messianic reading....Psalm 22 is messianic, not simply because Mark and Matthew understood it as such, but because that was the clear intent of the Psalter's author and composer. In fact, when the literary context of the Psalter is examined carefully, the views of Matthew and Mark make perfect sense. The angst is a result of adopting a hermeneutical stance at odds with that of the Psalter's composer." (Robert L. Cole, "Psalm 22: The Suffering Of The Messianic King," in Michael Rydelnik & Edwin Blum, The Moody Handbook of Messianic Prophecy: Studies and Expositions of the Messiah in the Old Testament, 529-530 (Kindle Edition); Chicago; Moody Publishers)

[63]" Rather, the sequence and order of the Psalms reveal a planned strategy and meaning for individual psalms as well as the entire book. 10 Evidence for this exists at the linguistic and thematic levels from psalm to psalm, groups of psalms, the five books of the Psalter, the superscriptions, and the shape of the whole. 11 Superscriptions are present in almost every case throughout Book I, and so with Ps 22.12 From Pss 19 through 21 the identical term is repeated, which could be translated "for/ of the leader, a psalm of David." The first term lamnaṣṣêaḥ (Piel ptc), is common in the Psalter titles, but its meaning is difficult to pinpoint, as in many cases of vocabulary in the titles. It is used as an infinitive (Piel) in Chronicles for the direction of temple service appointed by David (1Chr 23: 4). Temple service included gatekeepers, officers and singers. 13 The plural of the same participle is also found in the context of temple service in 2Chr 2: 2, 18 and 23: 13.14 The term in Psalms is associated specifically with the service of music, as

the accompanying term "song/ psalm" illustrates. 15 Music performed by the Levitical figures appointed by David is specifically
defined as the practice of prophesying under the direction of the
king (1Chr 25: 1, 2, 5). David's words themselves are portrayed as
prophetic in the Psalter, 16 and defined as so explicitly in David's
last words (2Sm 23: 1-3). 17 The term occurs only in the verses
cited from 2 Chronicles and the Psalm headings. Common to both
contexts are the topics of David, Levitical figures, prophecy, and
music. The Levitical musical service under David's direction,
whether composed by him or the priestly figures themselves, was
considered prophecy. The implication is that Ps 22 is to be considered likewise as a prophetic utterance of David used by the priestly
singers. David the king is therefore portrayed deliberately as a
priestly figure. His prophetic portrayal as priest and king has been
exhibited at the very beginning in the first two psalms. 18 The title
of Ps 22 likewise gives him priestly trappings by his association
with singing "a psalm/ song of David" and a "choir director." It is
also significant that the final strophe of Ps 22 (vv. 22-31) portrays
the formerly persecuted and deceased speaker of the first two stro-
phes as now praising God within a great congregation of the faithful. The final verses (27-31) locate this congregational praise in the
mouth of resurrected ones and future generations from all nations
(vv. 27-31). The two elements at the beginning and end of Ps 22 '
s superscription19 function likewise as a link to the psalms before
and after. This practice can be seen in other psalm sequences. 20
For example, the lengthy superscription of Ps 88 matches the previous Ps 87 in its first third, and the following Ps 89 in its final
words. The intervening third matches the content of the psalm itself. The situation in Pss 19–23 is similar although not identical.
Nonetheless, the binding function of the superscription content is
explicit and functions as another signal to read them continuously.
Psalm 22 opens with the phrase "for the choir director," and ends
with "a Davidic psalm." These two phrases at either end of the
lengthy superscription of Ps 22 match exactly the content of the
titles of Pss 19–21. Psalm 23 's brief title matches exactly the final
two words of the previous four. The central phrase of Ps 22 's superscription, "according to 'The Deer of the Dawn,'" is difficult to
comprehend in light of the content of the psalm itself. 21 It is clear

however that the beginning and end of this Hebrew title create linguistic linkage to the previous and following psalms." (Robert L. Cole, "Psalm 22: The Suffering Of The Messianic King," in Michael Rydelnik & Edwin Blum, The Moody Handbook of Messianic Prophecy: Studies and Expositions of the Messiah in the Old Testament, 530-531 (Kindle Edition); Chicago; Moody Publishers)

[64]"Verse 27 also has resonance and reference to the Abrahamic covenant of Gn 12: 2, 3 and its reiteration to Jacob in Gn 28: 13, 14. The identical phrase, "all the families of ..." in Ps 22: 27b is also found in the Genesis passages of promise to the patriarchs. Reference to the nations of Ps 22: 28 also repeats a common term found in the repeated patriarchal covenant (Gn 18: 18; 22: 18; 26: 4). Likewise, the seed of Ps 22: 23(2x) and 30 is a dominant term in the patriarchal promises (Gn 13: 15, 16; 17: 7, 8, 10, 19; 22: 17[2x], 18; 26: 4[2x]; 28: 13, 14; 48: 4). The twice-repeated "worship" of Ps 22: 27-29, 30 and reference to "service" to the king of 22: 30, likewise dominate the patriarchal covenantal declarations (Gn 25: 23; 27: 29, 40; 37: 9, 10; 49: 8). The twice-repeated use of "assembly/ congregation" in Ps 22: 22, 25 also represents a common term in Genesis patriarchal narratives (Gn 28: 3; 35: 11; 48: 4). These numerous linguistic parallels indicate that this third strophe of Ps 22 sees the deliverance and rescue of the messianic king out of death as fulfillment of the eternal covenant with Abraham, Isaac, Jacob, and Judah. It is through his torment and death and subsequent resurrection that the many nations receive the blessings of Abraham." (Robert L. Cole, "Psalm 22: The Suffering Of The Messianic King," in Michael Rydelnik & Edwin Blum, The Moody Handbook of Messianic Prophecy: Studies and Expositions of the Messiah in the Old Testament, 539 (Kindle Edition); Chicago; Moody Publishers)

[65]" Psalm 22 is a psalm describing the suffering, torment, and finally death of the messianic king who has been the book's focus since Pss 1–2. The description of his cruel torment and torture is graphic and certainly was never true of David. Neither did David's suffering of whatever type ever bring about the worldwide worship and praise depicted in the final strophe of the psalm. David's words

here are prophetic of a future royal descendant according to the covenant made with him. His suffering and death in Ps 22 are followed by glorious resurrection into the paradise of God in Ps 23. This is a theme and topic repeated in psalms before Ps 22 and following as well. His joy and universal worship described in vv. 22-31 following the suffering and death of vv. 1-21 demonstrate that his suffering would have worldwide and universal effect and influence. The interpretation of Psalms and the rest of the Scriptures by Christ in Lk 24: 25-27 and 44-47 is borne out by the Hebrew text of Ps 22 in its context. He did indeed have to suffer these things and "enter into His glory" as the Scriptures, including the Psalms, prophesied." (Robert L. Cole, "Psalm 22: The Suffering Of The Messianic King," in Michael Rydelnik & Edwin Blum, The Moody Handbook of Messianic Prophecy: Studies and Expositions of the Messiah in the Old Testament, 539-540 (Kindle Edition); Chicago; Moody Publishers)

[66]"(2) Remez (" hint")—wherein a word, phrase or other element in the text hints at a truth not conveyed by the p'shat. The implied presupposition is that God can hint at things of which the Bible writers themselves were unaware." (David H. Stern, Jewish New Testament Commentary, 752 (Kindle Edition); Clarksville, Maryland; JEWISH NEW TESTAMENT PUBLICATIONS, INC.)

"Let me illustrate: If you look at a drop of water with the naked eye, you see just one drop of water. But if you put that drop of water under a microscope, you see a whole world of life within it, things that you could never see without the magnification. So it is with the Word of God. You may see just one word, but put that word under a spiritual microscope, and you will see a whole world of life within it that you hadn't even begun to imagine. The Jewish Talmud* teaches that there are "seventy faces" to Torah.* That is, every verse could have seventy different shades of meaning. The Word of God is pictured as a gemstone that is taken out to the sunlight. When the light reflects off the gemstone, it displays many different colors. To be sure, there is a literal meaning to every verse, and the Talmud does warn that we are never to wander away from the pashat, or the literal meaning. Yet the literal interpretation is like the surface of the ocean. It is beautiful and vast, but if you dive beneath that surface—similar to observing that drop of water under a microscope—you will find a brand-new world filled with amazing wonders. This, again, is how it is with the Word of God." (Chaim Bentorah, Hebrew Word Study: Revealing the Heart of God, 234-240 (Kindle Edition); New Kensington, PA; Whitaker House).

[67]"We were there together," says Papa (98). Mack is shocked: "At the cross? Now wait, I thought you left him—you know '— My God, my God, why hast thou forsaken me?' "… "You misunderstand the mystery there. Regardless of what he felt at that moment, I never left him." "How can you say that? You abandoned him just like you abandoned me!" "Mackenzie, I never left him, and I have never left you." "That makes no sense to me," he snapped. (98) On the cross Jesus bore the Great Sadness of the world; he gave himself into the trauma of our darkness. Immersed in our contempt, he lost touch with his Father's love and with the comfort of the Holy Spirit. "My God, My God, why have You forsaken Me?" 44 But even this cry of despair was also a cry of solid hope; indeed, a sermon of victory. 45 For the psalm from which Jesus quotes goes on to say: "For He has not despised nor abhorred the affliction of the afflicted; nor has He hidden His face from him; but when he cried to Him for help, He heard." 46 In quoting this psalm, which ends in astonishing triumph, Jesus is interpreting his death, as if to say, "It may look to you, as Isaiah foresaw, 47 that my Father is forsaking me. But nothing could be further from the truth, as you will soon see." Breathing his last breath in the darkness, Jesus gave himself completely into his Father's hands in helpless trust. "Father, into Your hands I commit My spirit." 48 In the words of Papa, "Don't forget, the story didn't end in his sense of forsakenness. He found his way through it to put himself completely into my hands. Oh, what a moment that was!" (96). This is how the Father, Son, and Spirit made their way into Adam's shack—and into Mackenzie's, and ours. And this is why Papa has nail scars on her wrists, and if Sarayu manifested physically, they would be seen on her wrists as well. For in the oneness of the blessed Trinity, the Father and the Holy Spirit suffered Jesus 'hell with him. They shared fully in his trauma, feeling his abuse, tasting

the salt of his tears, and (I should hasten to add) sharing his humble restraint in the teeth of such sickening injustice. They chose the way of submission, of other-centered love, of grief and shared sorrow, and in doing so drew our very hell into the bosom of the Father and into the dwelling of the Holy Spirit. Jesus entered into the den of our iniquity, thereby establishing a real relationship between the blessed Trinity and us in our twisted prejudice. Jesus reached us in our fallen minds, personally closing the abyss between his Father's dream for our adoption and our insane blindness. The death of Jesus was an act of inclusion: he was including the real us, the fallen, helpless, broken, rebellious us in his fellowship with his Father. In dying, Jesus became the mercy seat, the place where the blessed Trinity personally suffered and endured sinners and their sin in astonishing mercy. It deserves repeating again: the gospel is not the news that we can accept an absent Jesus into our lives. The gospel is the news that the Father's Son has received us into his." (C. Baxter Kruger, The Shack Revisited: There Is More Going On Here than You Ever Dared to Dream, 192-195 (Kindle Edition); New York, NY; Faith Words)

[68]"We were clearly moving toward the climax of our discussion. The clues Kreeft had mentioned at the outset of our interview were converging, and I could sense an increasing passion and conviction in his voice. I wanted to see more of his heart—and I wouldn't be disappointed. "The answer, then, to suffering," I said in trying to sum up where we've come, "is not an answer at all." "Correct," he emphasized, leaning forward as he pleaded his case. "It's the Answerer. It's Jesus himself. It's not a bunch of words, it's the Word. It's not a tightly woven philosophical argument; it's a person. The person. The answer to suffering cannot just be an abstract idea, because this isn't an abstract issue; it's a personal issue. It requires a personal response. The answer must be someone, not just something, because the issue involves someone—God, where are you?" That question almost echoed in his small office. It demanded a response. To Kreeft, there is one—a very real one. A living One. "Jesus is there, sitting beside us in the lowest places of our lives," he said. "Are we broken? He was broken, like bread, for us. Are we despised? He was despised and rejected of men. Do we cry out

that we can't take any more? He was a man of sorrows and acquainted with grief. Do people betray us? He was sold out himself.
Are our tenderest relationships broken? He too loved and was rejected. Do people turn from us? They hid their faces from him as
from a leper. "Does he descend into all of our hells? Yes, he does.
From the depths of a Nazi death camp, Corrie ten Boom wrote:
'No matter how deep our darkness, he is deeper still. 'He not only
rose from the dead, he changed the meaning of death and therefore
of all the little deaths—the sufferings that anticipate death and
make up parts of it. "He is gassed in Auschwitz. He is sneered at
in Soweto. He is mocked in Northern Ireland. He is enslaved in the
Sudan. He's the one we love to hate, yet to us he has chosen to
return love. Every tear we shed becomes his tear. He may not wipe
them away yet, but he will." (Peter Kreeft in Lee Strobel, The Case
For Faith: A Journalist Investigates The Toughest Objections To
Christianity, 45-52 (Kindle Edition); Grand Rapids, Michigan;
Zondervan)

[69]"Second, the Greek word for "dog" is not the usual word for
an unkempt street dog (Gk. kyōn), but a diminutive (Gk. kynarion),
meaning a small dog that could be kept in the house as a pet. 14 In
casting the word in the diminutive form Mark essentially empties
it of opprobrium, for one feels entirely differently of a house pet
than of an unclean street mongrel. The fact that the woman refers
to her daughter and herself with the same term in her reply to Jesus
shows that she does not take kynarion in a hostile or contemptuous
sense. Third, "dog" signifies a traditional distinction between the
Jews and the Gentiles that is important to the story. In the thought-
world of the day, the Jews considered themselves "children" of
God (Exod 4: 22; Deut 14: 1; Isa 1: 2). They differed from other
nations because of their inclusion in the covenant of Abraham
(Genesis 17) and because they possessed the Torah (Exodus 19).
The issue at stake between Jesus and the woman is whether Jesus
is sent to "the children" or "to the dogs." The woman maintains the
same distinction between "children" and "dogs" in her reply to Jesus, though with one slight change. Whereas Jesus refers to Israel
as teknōn (" biological children"), the woman refers to Israel as
paidiōn, which is more inclusive, implying both children and servants in a household. The change in terminology suggests that the

woman understands the mercies of God to extend beyond ethnic Israel. The basic issue in the repartee between Jesus and the woman is not whether Gentiles have a claim on God's mercies, but the relation of that claim to the Jewish claim. Jesus does not deny the woman's request. "First let the children eat all they want" simply establishes a priority of mission; it does not exclude other hungry mouths. In the present context it implies the messianic priority of Jesus' ministry to Israel to his ministry to the Gentiles, particularly, as we suggested earlier, with regard to teaching about the kingdom of God. But the priority of Israel in Jesus' mission does not imply the exclusion of the Gentiles. The Servant of the Lord must first "restore the tribes of Jacob," and then be "a light to the nations" (Isa 49: 6; also 42: 1; 61: 1-11). The choice of kynarion implies the dogs are house pets; that is, they belong to the household and will be fed along with the children. Indeed, the analogy of the children and dogs suggests a relationship to Jesus himself, for who might be the "father" who feeds the children —and their dogs —if not Jesus? The woman's reply to Jesus in v. 28 shows her understanding and acceptance of Israel's privilege. 15 Indeed, she appears to understand the purpose of Israel's Messiah better than Israel does. Her pluck and persistence are a testimony to her trust in the sufficiency and surplus of Jesus: his provision for the disciples and Israel will be abundant enough to provide for one such as herself. Mark provides a clue to this understanding in the Gk. chortazō (NIV, "eat all they want"). This word occurs only twice elsewhere in Mark, in the feedings of the five thousand (6: 42) and four thousand (8: 4, 8). In its present location, the word bridges Jesus' feeding of the Jews (6: 31-44) and his subsequent feeding of the Gentiles (8: 1-10). When dogs eat crumbs from the table they do not rob children of their food; they simply eat what is theirs from the surplus of the children." (James R. Edwards, *The Pillar New Testament Commentary: The Gospel According To Mark,* 4179-4205 (Kindle Edition); Grand Rapids, Michigan; William B. Eerdmans' Publishing Company)

[70]"Blinzler states, "Crucifixion was unknown in Jewish criminal law. The hanging on a gibbet, which was prescribed by Jewish law for idolaters and blasphemers who had been stoned, was not a death penalty, but an additional punishment after death designed

to brand the executed person as one accursed of God, in accordance with Deut. 21:23 (LXX): 'For he is accursed of God that hangeth on a tree.' The Jews applied these words also to one who had been crucified. If crucifixion was the most shameful and degrading death penalty even in the eyes of the pagan world, the Jews in the time of Jesus regarded a person so executed as being, over and above, accursed of God." 2/247,248 The Encyclopedia Americana records: "The history of crucifixion as a mode of punishment for crime must be studied as a part of the Roman system of jurisprudence.... The Hebrews, for example, adopted or accepted it only under Roman compulsion: under their own system, before Palestine became Roman territory, they inflicted the death penalty by stoning." 8/253 " . . . In 63 B.C., Pompey's legions cut their way into the Judean capital. Palestine became a Roman province, though nominally a puppet Jewish dynasty survived." 29/262 THUS, THE TYPE OF DEATH PICTURED IN ISAIAH 53 AND PSALMS 22 DID NOT COME INTO PRACTICE UNDER THE JEWISH SYSTEM UNTIL HUNDREDS OF YEARS AFTER THE ACCOUNT WAS WRITTEN." (Josh McDowell, Evidence that Demands a Verdict, eBook: Fast Answers for Skeptics' Questions about Jesus, 151-152 (Kindle Edition, emphasis added, M.T.); Nashville, TN; Thomas Nelson Publishers)

[71]"When Jesus said, "I thirst" (John 19: 28–30), there is no question that this was a gross underestimation. He had been deprived of liquids since His last meal, which was at the Last Supper, and suffered loss of fluids from excessive sweating, trauma to His chest (pleural effusion), hemorrhage from scourging, nailing of the hands and feet, hematidrosis, etc. Water is so basic to one's survival that individuals have reacted both inappropriately and violently when deprived of it. Individuals suffering from dehydration can lose all sense of rationality, and survival becomes the all-encompassing mental focus. The agony associated with thirst is clearly portrayed in the article by LeBec (Catholic Medical Guardian, October, 1925), who quoted an Arab scribe, el Sujuti, who in 1247 described a young Turk who was crucified in Damascus: "His worst agony was thirst. An eyewitness told me that he looked constantly from side to side imploring someone to give him a little water." McGee, an American geologist, who extensively studied

the effects of thirst on individuals suffering from extremes of water deprivation in desert areas, distinguished five stages through which one passes on the way to death (as quoted by Dr. J. R. Whittaker in a paper read in 1935 before the St. Luke's Guild in London). He suggests that in the first stage, there is a dryness of the mouth and throat accompanied by a craving for liquid. This is the common experience of normal thirst, and the condition may be alleviated, as ordinary practice shows, by a moderate quantity of water or by exciting a flow of saliva in some way. In the second stage, the saliva and the mucus in the mouth begin to dry out, and the throat becomes sticky and scanty. There is a feeling of dry deadness of the mucus membranes. Inspired air feels hot, and the tongue clings to the teeth and to the roof of the mouth. A lump seems to rise in the throat and starts endless swallowing motions in an attempt to dislodge it. According to McGee, during the last three stages "the eyelids stiffen over the eyeballs set in a sightless stare, the tongue tip hardens to a dull weight and wretched victim has illusions of limpid pools and sparkling streams.'" (Frederick T. Zugibe, The Crucifixion of Jesus, Completely Revised and Expanded: A Forensic Inquiry, 2073-2091 (Kindle Edition, emphasis added, M.T.); New York, NY; M. Evans and Company, Inc.).

[72]"Both the thirst and the action in seeking to satisfy it belong to the fulfillment of the Scripture, namely Ps 69: 22: "They gave me vinegar for my thirst." (The term [ḥomeṣ] was used of vinegar, but the Greek rendering of it ὄξος [oxos] denoted a drink, whether a watered-down vinegar or cheap wine, which was popular among soldiers.) The saying is part of the lengthy description of the desolation, isolation, and scorn experienced by the Righteous Sufferer, and in the psalm the giving of the drink appears to be part of the torment inflicted upon the sufferer." (George R. Beasley-Murray, John, Volume 36: Revised Edition (Word Biblical Commentary), 351 (Kindle Edition); Grand Rapids, Michigan; Zondervan)

[73] CROSSBAR (patibulum, Latin; gibbet, Old English). Wooden beam that forms the top of a T-shaped cross used to crucify people. A Roman linguist named Nonius Marcellus (AD 300s) described it as the long, thick board that people used in ancient times to "bar the door shut." Executioners sometimes forced the

condemned folks to carry it to the execution site. Ancient pictures and written descriptions suggest that during crucifixion, some executioners nailed or tied the arms of the victim to this beam and set the beam on top of a vertical stake. When Bible writers had to describe what most Bible experts seem to think was the crossbar that Jesus carried to his execution, they had to translate into Greek the word Romans used to describe the beam. The Roman word, written in their language of Latin, is patibulum. But for Greek, the international language of the day, Bible writers chose stauros, which people often used to describe a vertical pole or sometimes the entire cross. Bible writers wouldn't have been the only ones who used the word to describe the crossbeam. So did Roman writers such as Macrobius (AD 370–430). He said the patibulum, or crossbar, was Latin for the Greek word stauros (Macrobius 1.10, AD 395). In time, both words came to mean the entire cross. When Matthew reports that the Romans drafted Simon from Cyrene to haul a piece of execution timber for Jesus, Matthew called it a stauros, presumably referring to at least part of a cross." (Stephen M. Miller, Eyewitness to Crucifixion: The Romans, the Cross and the Sacrifice of Jesus, 257-270 (Kindle Edition); Grand Rapids, MI; Our Daily Bread Publishing)

[74]"Simply put, the cross was one of the most vicious, torturous, and effective methods of execution that human depravity has ever devised. The torment of the cross was so extreme that a word was invented to describe it: excruciating, which translates from Latin to describe a pain "from the cross.".…"There was no standard procedure for the crucifixion, as executioners were often given license to express profligate brutality. Victims were at times fixed to the cross in awkward poses, at times nailed through their groins, at times forced to watch the violation of their wives, at times made to witness the slaughter of their whole families, and at times having their slain sons hung around their necks. 13 Crucifixion was not just another means of execution, as there are much more efficient ways to kill. The cross was intended for brutality, and victims were not treated gently." (Nabeel Qureshi, No God but One: Allah or Jesus? (with Bonus Content): A Former Muslim Investigates the Evidence for Islam and Christianity, 165-166 (Kindle Edition); Grand Rapids, Michigan; Zondervan)

[75]"The Roman execution squads actually pierced the wrists—not the palms. Dr. Frederick Zugibe, a modern forensic pathologist, claimed the most likely site of the spikes 'placements was the position he named the Z area. When one touches his thumb to his little finger, the thenar furrow develops. Zugibe theorized the Romans nailed the condemned to his cross by driving the pile through this spot. He formulated his postulation by examining the Shroud of Turin, by examining victims of violent crimes using forensic science, and by his own experimentation. The pathologist claimed the palm could serve as the entry point of the stake if placed at just the right angle to enable it to exit through the wrist abutting the wood of the cross. In either case, the nail passed through the wrist to secure the crucified to his cross. Anatomists have always considered the wrist to be part of the hand. Just as modern medicine has held to this tenet, Roman and Greek scientists also regarded the wrist to be part of the hand. In this light, Plautus referred to crucifixion by nailing the arms—not the palms. Would such a placement then violate Scripture? The biblical words for hand (Hebrew: yad; Greek: cheir) included the wrist and the forearm as integral parts. As a matter of fact, the Hebrew language had a different word for the palm of the hand (kaph). When David prophesied about the pierced hands of Suffering Messiah, he used yad—not kaph. The New Testament confirmed this assertion as well. Thomas uttered his disbelief in Jesus 'resurrection until he saw the imprint of the nails in His hands (cheir). Eight days later, Jesus exhorted Thomas to place his finger into the scars of His hands (cheir). Cheir included the fingers, the palms, the wrists, and the forearms as part of the hands. The only New Testament designation of the palm (rhaphizo) in relation to Christ was when the abusers slapped Him. Thus, Scripture never pointed to pierced palms per se." (J. Shan Young, Crushed: A Physician Analyzes the Agony of Jesus, 3436-3642 (Kindle Edition); Glass Road Media)

[76]"As for Psalm 22: 16 , almost all of the standard medieval Hebrew manuscripts (known as Masoretic) read ka'ari, followed by the words "my hands and my feet." According to Rashi, the meaning is "as though they are crushed in a lion's mouth," while the commentary of Metsudat David states, "They crush my hands and my feet as the lion which crushes the bones of the prey in its

mouth." Thus, the imagery is clear: These lions are not licking the psalmist's feet! They are tearing and ripping at them. 245 Given the metaphorical language of the surrounding verses (cf. w. 12-21[13-22]), this vivid image of mauling lions graphically conveys the great physical agony of the sufferer. Would this in any way contradict the picture of a crucified victim, his bones out of joint, mockers surrounding him and jeering at him, his garments stripped off of him and divided among his enemies, his feet and hands torn with nails, and his body hung on pieces of wood? 246 "But you're avoiding something here," you argue. "Where did the King James translators come up with this idea of 'piercing 'the hands and feet? That's not what the Hebrew says." Actually, the Septuagint, the oldest existing Jewish translation of the Tanakh, was the first to translate the Hebrew as "they pierced my hands and feet" (using the verb oruxan in Greek), followed by the Syriac Peshitta version two or three centuries later (rendering with baz'u). Not only so, but the oldest Hebrew copy of the Psalms we possess (from the Dead Sea Scrolls, dating to the century before Yeshua) reads the verb in this verse as ka'aru (not ka'ari, "like a lion"), 247 a reading also found in about a dozen medieval Masoretic manuscripts—recognized as the authoritative texts in traditional Jewish thought—where instead of ka'ari (found in almost all other Masoretic manuscripts) the texts say either ka'aru or karu. 248 (Hebrew scholars believe this comes from a root meaning "to dig out" or "to bore through.") So, the oldest Jewish translation (the Septuagint) translates "they pierced"; the oldest Jewish manuscript (from the Dead Sea Scrolls) reads ka'aru, not ka'ari; and several Masoretic manuscripts read ka'aru or karu rather than ka'ari. This is not a Christian fabrication. I have copies of the manuscript evidence in front of my eyes as I write these words. 249 There is also an interesting notation made by the Masoretic scholars in the margin to Isaiah 38: 13, where the Hebrew word ka'ari, "like a lion," also occurs—the only other time in the Tanakh that ka'ari is found with the preposition k-, "like," joined to this form of the word. 250 In this instance, however, ka'ari occurs with a verb explaining the lion's activity (" break"), whereas in Psalm 22: 16 the meaning is ambiguous. As noted by Franz Delitzsch, "Perceiving this, the Masora [i.e., the marginal system of notation of the Masoretic scholars to the Hebrew biblical text] on Isaiah xxxviii. 13 observes, that k'ry in the two passages in which it occurs (Ps. xxii. 17, Isa. xxxviii. 13), occurs in two different meanings [Aramaic lyshny btry], just as the Midrash then also understands k'ry in the Psalm as a verb used of marking with conjuring, magic characters." 251 So, the Masoretes indicated that k'ry in Psalm 22 was to be understood differently than k'ry in Isaiah 38, where it certainly meant "like a lion."'" (Michael L. Brown, Answering Jewish Objections to Jesus : Volume 3: Messianic Prophecy Objections, 125-126 (Kindle Edition); Grand Rapids, Michigan; Baker Books)

[77]"See the critical apparatus of Biblica Hebraica Stuttgartensia. Rydelnik and Vanlaningham support the reading translated "they pierced" as follows: "The culminating statement of this suffering is they pierced my hands and my feet (v. 16), representing one of the most specific predictive references to Messiah's crucifixion (paralleled only by Zch 12: 10). Yet this is one of the most debated passages in the Bible. The debate centers on the key Hebrew word ka'aru, rendered they pierced, though in most (but not all) medieval Hebrew manuscripts this word is written ka'ariy, meaning 'like a lion. 'The first reading, however, is to be preferred for five reasons. First, it is supported by three of the four ancient translations (the Septuagint, the Peshitta, and the Vulgate; the fourth translation, the Targum to Psalms, was translated in the second century AD by non-Christian Jews). Second, even for Hebrew poetry, the phrase 'like a lion 'is far too elliptical and makes no sense without a verb—which supporters of this reading are forced to supply (e.g., 'like a lion they bite my hands and my feet'). Third, were the symbol of a lion intended, it would have been employed in the plural, not the singular, in order to agree with the plural subject (' evildoers') in the verse (as in Jr 50: 17 and Zph 3: 3). Fourth, one of the leading medieval Jewish scribal authorities (Jacob ben Chayyim) himself affirms that the older and better manuscripts read ka'aru ('they pierced') rather than ka'ariy ('like a lion'). Fifth, the reading ka'aru ('they pierced') is attested in earliest the manuscript of this psalm (5/ 6 HevPs) from the Dead Sea Scrolls, which predates the medieval manuscripts by approximately one thousand years" (" Psalms" in The Moody Bible Commentary ed. Michael Rydelnik and Michael G. Vanlaningham [Chicago:

Moody Publishers, 2014], 779–80).” (Robert L. Cole, “Psalm 22: The Suffering Of The Messianic King,” in Michael Rydelnik & Edwin Blum, The Moody Handbook of Messianic Prophecy: Studies and Expositions of the Messiah in the Old Testament, 541-542 Footnote 30 (Kindle Edition); Chicago; Moody Press)

[78]“Once a person is hanging in the vertical position,” he replied, “crucifixion is essentially an agonizingly slow death by asphyxiation. “The reason is that the stresses on the muscles and diaphragm put the chest into the inhaled position; basically, in order to exhale, the individual must push up on his feet so the tension on the muscles would be eased for a moment. In doing so, the nail would tear through the foot, eventually locking up against the tarsal bones. “After managing to exhale, the person would then be able to relax down and take another breath in. Again he’d have to push himself up to exhale, scraping his bloodied back against the coarse wood of the cross. This would go on and on until complete exhaustion would take over, and the person wouldn’t be able to push up and breathe anymore. “As the person slows down his breathing, he goes into what is called respiratory acidosis—the carbon dioxide in the blood is dissolved as carbonic acid, causing the acidity of the blood to increase. This eventually leads to an irregular heartbeat. In fact, with his heart beating erratically, Jesus would have known that he was at the moment of death, which is when he was able to say, ‘Lord, into your hands I commit my spirit. ’And then he died of cardiac arrest.” (Alexander Metherell, “The Medical Evidence: Was Jesus’ Death A Sham And His Resurrection A Hoax?” In Lee Strobel, The Case For Christ: Solving The Biggest Mystery Of All Time, 215 (Kindle Edition); Grand Rapids, Michigan; Zondervan)

[79]“This prophecy from Psalms 22:14, describes the Messiah’s heart melting like wax within Him. Finally, when dehydration and exhaustion ended their efforts to raise their body up to breathe, the torture achieved its intended goal; being deprived of oxygen, the heart begins to accelerate its rate to over 300 beats per minute, called: “Tachardia.” In one final massive failure, the heart bursts due to the stress placed upon it and the crucified dies immediately. The testimony of those who were present at the time that Jesus was

crucified—describes a Roman soldier who pierced Jesus side to ensure that He was dead. As the lance pierced Jesus flesh—blood and water came from the wound. John 19:34 " But one of the soldiers pierced His side with a spear, and immediately blood and water came out. " Medical science describes the process of intense stress on the heart when under the suffering of crucifixion: The outer lining of the heart will often fill with fluid. As the heart races to try and carry the limited availability of oxygen to the lungs, the stress becomes so great that the heart ruptures. The presence of blood and water from the wound as described by the Apostle John, is an indication that Jesus heart had ruptured due to "Pericardial Effusion." Literally, Jesus heart melted within Him and He died of a broken heart. The horror of crucifixion is the topic of Psalm 22. Unquestionably, David was not describing anything that he had personally experienced. He was never placed on a cross—nor had anyone in Israel ever heard of this brutal form of death before. The specific details written by David which graphically describe a man being pierced in His hands and feet, his ribs protruding due to his outstretched arms, and ruptured heart from the intense suffering of the cross—were written one thousand years before this horrific form of death was invented. David's description in Psalm 22, was clearly intended as a prophetic prediction for the coming Messiah." (Robert Clifton Robinson, The Suffering Servant: The Messiah of Isaiah 53 and Psalms 22, 336-337 (Kindle Edition, emphasis added, M.T.); Scottsdale, Arizona; Teach The Word Ministries, Inc.)

[80]"In the prophecy of Psalm 22, we read that the soldiers will divide His garments among them, And for His clothing they cast lots. Before Jesus was raised upon the cross, His executioners removed all of His garments. We notice that John records the soldiers dividing the clothing into four parts: the loin cloth, the shorts, the shirt and the outer robe. Each of the three soldiers took one garment; the fourth, they determined ownership by drawing straws. Every aspect of crucifixion was designed to disgrace and humiliate the condemned. As if it were not enough to be nailed to a cross before the whole world, the victim was also displayed completely naked. Those who were crucified were stripped of all of their clothing, exposing their genitals and allowing the watching

crowd to witness the condemned relieving themselves by urination or defecation. 148 The results of this horrific display brought insects which further tormented the dying and added to their shame before the watchful eyes of those who often hated and despised the condemned criminal." (Robert Clifton Robinson, The Suffering Servant: The Messiah of Isaiah 53 and Psalms 22, 352 (Kindle Edition, emphasis added, M.T.); Scottsdale, Arizona; Teach The Word Ministries Inc.)

[81]"The Romans humiliated the scourged in many ways to shame them to the most extreme manner possible. Unless it was the chosen method of execution, the lictors (executioners trained in torture) halted their assaults just short of death—distinguishing it as the halfway death. The Roman scourge was unlimited in the number of thrashes given. The judge determined the severity and the number, and these components varied in individual cases. PRIES ESTIMATED SOME LICTORS INFLICTED AS MANY AS SEVEN HUNDRED TWENTY-FOUR STRIPES. They marred the whole body with lashes. The Romans embarrassed the flogged to deter similar crimes against Rome by others. Thus, the Roman scourge differed from the Jewish flagellation in purpose, in technique, and in severity. ..."Nude and tightly secured, the criminal was helpless. He was unable to protect his extended body or his face from the flogging. His public nakedness wreaked more embarrassment on one already ashamed. In Oriental culture, himas possessed a defiled connotation, and the whole process debased those who suffered it. After stretching out the victim, the lictors flayed him with full force. ONE TO SIX LICTORS TYPICALLY PARTICIPATED IN THE SCOURGE—WITH EACH WHIPPING UNTIL THEY TIRED. The assailants used different directions to subject as much of the doomed man's body to the torture as was possible. THEY ROTATED THE VICTIM TO INFLICT THE TORMENT ON EVERY PART OF THE BODY. The degree and the form of the punishment varied from region to region, from lictor to lictor, from judge to judge, and from crime to crime. Thusly, not all the scourges were the same...."Even though the severity of the flogging varied, the Romans intended "to weaken the victim to a state just short of collapse or death." The lictor would test the pulse of the wounded if he fainted to insure he had not

endured too much. Fainting protected the body from further knowledge of pain. The Romans prevented this escape to disallow any reprieve from the intense suffering. If the victim's pulse was still strong, the officer revived the doomed—only to inflict more stripes. To awaken the unconscious victim, they kicked the sufferer, or they doused the scourged with cold water. THE SHOCK OF THE COLD WATER ON THE FRESH WOUNDS CAUSED GREAT DISCOMFORT, FOR THE SEVERED NERVE ENDINGS WERE HYPERSENSITIVE. They repeated this process until they determined the abused was at a fatal end. Thus, the populace named the Roman flagellation, the half-way death. Jesus used this same manner of language to describe the wounded man who was left for dead after his beating in "The Parable of the Good Samaritan.""..."To scourge the victims, the Romans utilized the flagrum—a whip with multiple leather straps attached to a handle. The number of leather thongs varied, but there were sometimes as high as nine straps attached (the infamous cat-o'-nine-tails). The length of the thongs varied, with some extending six feet or more. These leather straps had metal balls, metal pellets, jagged shards of glass and sharp animal bones embedded at variable distances from the ends, which magnified the destruction these instruments of torture inflicted on the human body. The Romans even thrashed the condemned with metal chains at times. EACH BLOW CAUSED EXTENSIVE DAMAGE, BLEEDING AND PAIN BEYOND OUR COMPREHENSION. The metal balls bruised the skin deeply to soften it. The leather straps sliced through the skin and underlying tissues—cutting into the dermis of the skin and beyond. The metal pellets, jagged shards of glass, and razor-sharp animal bones lacerated the deeper tissues, muscles, nerves, and blood vessels. As these sharply incisive objects embedded into the underlying tissues, they ripped these tissues apart as the lictors withdrew the lash—causing deep lacerations well below the skin's surface." (J. Shan Young, Crushed: A Physician Analyzes the Agony of Jesus, 2154-2312 (Kindle Edition, emphasis added, M.T.); Glass Road Media)

[82]"For the scourge, the soldiers stripped the prisoner. Matthew employed a Greek term (ekduo), which meant: to forcefully unclothe. New Testament usage of ekduo implied complete removal

of garments. Jesus 'nudity before those who judged Him mirrored Adam's shameful nakedness before His Judge.". Luke affirmed the forceful stripping of prisoners prior to flogging when he reported on the whipping of Paul and Silas in first century Philippi. "The soldiers rent their clothes from them—implying a violent show of force. The assailants then bound their victims to a post or beam with arms extended. Scripture reiterated this when the authorities stretched out (Greek: proteino) Paul for the lash on another occasion. Proteino made the body taut, which worsened the effects on the skin of those scourged. Combined with the Greek word for lash (himas), the phrase portrayed the officials strapping Paul in a vulnerable, outspread position. Nude and tightly secured, the criminal was helpless. He was unable to protect his extended body or his face from the flogging. His public nakedness wreaked more embarrassment on one already ashamed. In Oriental culture, himas possessed a defiled connotation, and the whole process debased those who suffered it". (J. Sham Young, Crushed: A Physician Analyzes the Agony of Jesus, 2178-2195 (Kindle Edition, emphasis added, M.T.); Glass Road Media)

[83]" Basalinda was a game the Roman soldiers often played, mocking their dying victims. This Latin term meant king, and the executioners tormented the doomed in barbaric ways before they finally put them to death. Instead of having a chess piece they designated as the king, these barbarians exploited human beings as their pawns in their cruel contests by sarcastically calling them kings. Their amusement was all about altering the methods whereby they tortured the condemned to avoid boredom with their sardonic duties. Basalinda allowed them the luxury of a pastime entertainment while they sadistically fulfilled their duties on the Roman death squads. They afflicted the torments of basalinda to the extremes in every way their vile imaginations allowed them to torture their prisoners physically, mentally, emotionally, and socially." (J. Shan Young, Crushed: A Physician Analyzes the Agony of Jesus, 2787-2794 (Kindle Edition); Glass Road Media)

[84]"To explore this question further, it is helpful to distinguish between sexual abuse that involves only sexual humiliation (such as enforced nudity, sexual mockery and sexual insults) and sexual

abuse that extends to sexual assault (which involves forced sexual contact, and ranges from molestation to penetration, injury or mutilation). The Gospels clearly indicate that sexual humiliation was a prominent trait in the mistreatment of Jesus and that sexual humiliation was an important aspect of crucifixion. If this is the case, the possibility of sexual assaults against Jesus will also need to be considered. In the absence of clear evidence to decide this one way or another, I will suggest that what has proved so common in recent torture practices cannot be entirely ruled out in the treatment of Jesus. Crucifixion in the ancient world appears to have carried a strongly sexual element and should be understood as a form of sexual abuse that involved sexual humiliation and sometimes sexual assault. Crucifixion was intended to be more than the ending of life; prior to actual death it sought to reduce the victim to something less than human in the eyes of society. Victims were crucified naked in what amounted to a ritualized form of public sexual humiliation. In a patriarchal society, where men competed against each other to display virility in terms of sexual power over others, the public display of the naked victim by the 'victors 'in front of onlookers and passers-by carried the message of sexual domination. The cross held up the victim for display as someone who had been–at least metaphorically–emasculated. 17 Depending on the position in which the victim was crucified, the display of the genitals could be specially emphasized. Both Josephus and the Roman historian Seneca the Younger attest to the Romans 'enthusiasm for experimentation with different positions of crucifixion. 18 Furthermore, Seneca's description suggests that the sexual violence against the victim was sometimes taken to the most brutal extreme with crosses that impaled the genitals of the victim. This practice might never have been the case in Palestine–and there is no evidence that suggests it happened to Jesus–but at the very least it suggests the highly sexualized context of violence in which Roman crucifixions sometimes took place. The sexual element in Roman practices was part of their message of terror. Anyone who opposed the Romans would not only lose their life but also be stripped of all personal honour and human dignity. It is therefore not surprising that the Gospels themselves indicate that there was a high level of sexual humiliation in the way that Jesus was flogged, insulted and then crucified. From evidence of the ancient world it seems that flogging the victim in public while naked was routine. Mark, Matthew and John all imply that this was also the case with the flogging of Jesus. 19 Likewise, as noted above, crucifixion usually took place while the victim was naked and there is little reason to think that Jesus or other Jews would have been an exception to this. 20 If the purpose was to humiliate the victim, full nakedness would have been particularly shameful in the Jewish context. 21 Furthermore, prior to crucifixion, Jesus was handed over to a cohort of Roman soldiers to be further humiliated (Mark 15.16–20; Matt. 27.27–31; John 19.1–5). 22 All the Gospels apart from Luke report that the Roman soldiers mocked Jesus by placing a crown of thorns on his head (Mark 15.17; Matt. 27.29; John 19.2) and clothing him in a purple (Mark 15.17; John 19.2) or scarlet garment (Matt. 27.28). 23 The texts also mention that the soldiers spat at Jesus (Mark 15.19; Matt. 27.30), struck him with a reed (Mark 15.19; Matt. 27.30), and mocked him with verbal taunts (calling him king: Mark 15.18; Matt. 27.29; John 19.3) and symbolic homage (kneeling before him, Mark 15.19; Matt. 27.29). 24 Based on what the Gospel texts themselves indicate, the sexual element in the abuse is unavoidable. An adult man was stripped naked for flogging, then dressed in an insulting way to be mocked, struck and spat at by a multitude of soldiers before being stripped again (at least in Mark 15.20 and Matt. 27.31) and reclothed for his journey through the city–already too weak to carry his own cross–only to be stripped again (a third time) and displayed to a mocking crowd to die while naked. When the textual presentation is stated like this, the sexual element of the abuse becomes clear: the assertion is controversial only in so far as it seems startling in view of usual presentations." (Jayme R. Reavers, David Tombs, and Rocio Figueroa, When Did We See You Naked? Jesus As A Victim Of Sexual Abuse, 576-612 (Kindle Edition); London, England; SCM Press)

[85]"Trexler, Sex and Conquest, p. 20. According to Trexler, 'in the Ancient Greek world … the premier sign of male dependence was to be anally or orally penetrated by another male without, at least fictively, being able to resist', p. 33; he continues, 'Seneca … declared that "bad army officers and wicked tyrants are the main sources of rapes of young men"', p. 34. In this context even the

widely held assumption that the soldiers forced Jesus to wear scarlet/ purple clothing for solely political mockery might be reconsidered. Dressing a male victim in bright clothing might also have been a prelude to sexual assault. See also Trexler, Sex and Conquest, p. 34." (Jayme R. Reavers, David Tombs, and Rocio Figueroa, When Did We See You Naked? Jesus As A Victim Of Sexual Abuse, 836-840 (Kindle Edition); London, England; SCM Press)

[86]"Clearly, the weight of the historical and medical evidence indicates that Jesus was dead before the wound to his side was inflicted. . . . Accordingly, interpretations based on the assumption that Jesus did not die on the cross appear to be at odds with modern medical knowledge." (William D. Edwards et al., "On the Physical Death of Jesus Christ," Journal of the American Medical Association (March 21, 1986), 1455–63).

[87]"Tradition implied the wound was on the right side. The Ethiopic version of John's Gospel and the Acts of Pilate (B recension 11:2) depicted the right side as the one pierced. Early church fathers such as St. Augustine also agreed with this tradition. There were some reasonable facts lending credence to this tradition of the piercing the heart through the right side. First, the fencing schools of the Roman army taught this fatal theist— puncturing the heart to produce immediate death. The right side was usually unprotected in combat because shields protected the left side. Renowned French surgeon Dr. Pierre Barbet recalled Caesar's use of the expression, " latus apertum the side being opened," to denote classically the right side. A legionnaire delivered this joust with deadly accuracy. "The ancient sculpture The Dying Gaul immortalized this wound, for it depicted the death of an enemy warrior struck just beneath his right breast in battle. This particular sculpture dated to Pergamum between 240 and 200 BC, demonstrating the deadly thrust's usage even prior to the maneuver being taught in the Roman military academies. "Medical science has demonstrated more blood flows with perforation of the distended, thinner- walled right atrium and ventricle than from any other body part. Blood normally would not spill easily from the dead unless

the lance perforated the right atrium, for blood pooled in this chamber with death after the heart stopped pumping. In an erect corpse (for example, on a cross), gravity drains the blood above the heart to the right atrium without clotting. ..."The question of "how" still remained until physicians investigated it. Barbet performed experiments on autopsies by inserting a syringe beneath the fifth intercostals space (between the fifth and the sixth ribs) toward the heart. He first noticed serum (watery fluid). In cases of excess fluid such as heart failure, the fluid was more diluted and thus clearer. As the surgeon inserted the needle further, Barbet then noticed blood when he penetrated the right side of the heart. Barbet followed these experiments by the use of a knife instead of a syringe with the same results. If he vigorously thrust the knife into the side, the clear, serous fluid of the lungs and pericardial sac flowed along the edges of the blood from the right atrium. "American surgeon Dr. Harold Blanton reported similar findings in studies performed by a pathologist in Birmingham, Alabama. A pericardiocentesis (aspiration of the pericardial sac surrounding the heart) followed by a cardiocentesis (aspiration of the heart) then confirmed scientifically what John saw was indeed plausible. For these reasons, forensic scientists believed the flow of water was excess pericardial fluid and excess fluid in the lungs from pulmonary edema. In a case of "an exceptionally painful death- agony, as was that of the Savior, this hydropericardium would have been particularly abundant." "In Jesus 'case, the severe loss of blood and the other portions of His Passion caused His heart to fail. Congestive heart failure resulted from His agony, and this condition caused the building up of excess fluid not only around the heart, but also in the lungs with pulmonary edema. Because the heart failure worked like a dam, the excess fluid seeped from the vessels to pool in the lungs and chest. This burden of excess fluid made it easier to identify with the piercing of Jesus 'side. It proved Jesus died an agonizing death— even one causing His internal organs to fail." (J. Shan Young, M.D., Crushed: A Physician Analyzes The Agony Of Jesus, 4577-4614 (Kindle Edition); Glass Road Media)

[88]"Why has the composer of Ps 22 delayed the overt and explicit confirmation of his demise to the conclusion of the psalm? A statement of that sort at v. 21 would possibly seem to have been more

appropriate. However, its deferral to the end can be understood in view of what follows. Psalm 23 contains a similar construction using the same noun "(my) life." The traditional rendering along the lines of, "he restores my soul" (HCSB "renews my life") of Ps 23: 3 should be understood as a direct response to Ps 22: 29 which states literally, "he brought my life back." The delay of an explicit death reference to the end of Ps 22 situates it closely to the answer in Ps 23: 3, where the same messianic king is resurrected from the dead. Not only are there matching nouns between Ps 22: 29 and 23: 3—nephesh (" life"; HCSB "soul"), but also analogous verbal patterns of Piel and Polel. 37 Death in Ps 22 is defeated in Ps 23, and likewise the distance of Ps 22 is dissolved in Ps 23. A closely parallel use of language in Ps 30: 3 to Ps 22: 29 convincingly confirms that it is the messianic king who was not kept alive." (Robert L. Cole, "Psalm 22: The Suffering Of The Messianic King," in Michael Rydelnik & Edwin Blum, The Moody Handbook of Messianic Prophecy: Studies and Expositions of the Messiah in the Old Testament, 537 (Kindle Edition); Chicago; Moody Publishers).

[89]"In verses 19-21 Messiah offers a prayer for help. Then verses 22-31 records the vindication of Messiah. Verse 22b reads, "in the midst of the congregation I will praise you." How can Messiah praise God in the midst of the assembly if he died? Only by resurrection." (Massimo Lorenzini, The Promise of Messiah: A Survey of the Major Messianic Prophecies, 52 (Kindle Edition); Frontline Ministries)

[90]"However, there is significant and considerable evidence from the original Hebrew language of the book itself that proves that it is not a haphazard collection. Evidence of repeated words or expressions from one psalm to another indicates every chapter should be understood in the light of those around it. Psalms are chained together with unique vocabulary, and these are signposts from the author that they belong together and should be read accordingly. They also shed light on the message intended by the order. The immediate context of Ps 23 is its location between Pss 22 and 24, although the larger context including Pss 20 and 21 is important for its interpretation as well. Between Pss 23 and the previous Pss 20-22, there are matching and also deliberately contrasted terms

that create a meaningful sequence and message...."If the gospel writers read Ps 22 as prophecy, there is a good chance that they read the following Ps 23 likewise. There is also evidence from ancient times that both Christian and Jewish interpreters read it as messianic prophecy. The repeated language and concepts between Pss 20 and 21, and also between Pss 21 and 22, indicates they were intentionally placed together. Both speak repeatedly of the messianic king who is granted salvation out of trouble (Ps 20: 5 , 6 , 9 , and Ps 21: 1 , 5). Ps 20: 5 Let us rejoice in your salvation Ps 20: 6a ...the Lord has saved his anointed/ messiah Ps 20: 6b by the strength of the salvation of his right hand Ps 20: 9 Lord save the king Ps 21: 1 the king... how he will exceedingly exult in your salvation Ps 21: 5 his glory is great through your salvation It is no coincidence that it is only Ps 20 's final half and Ps 21 's first half that repeat the particular word "salvation." The deliberate linking of the two psalms is explicit and there are more examples. Psalm 20: 6 refers to him as "his anointed one (messiah)" and then in verse 9 as "the king." Immediately following in Ps 21: 1 he is mentioned again as "the king," as well as in verse seven. Remarkably, it is the last verse of Ps 20 that matches the word "king," found in the first verse of Ps 21. This is further proof of a deliberate juxtaposition of the two psalms. Ps 20: 6 his anointed one Ps 20: 9 the king Ps 21: 1 the king Ps 21: 7 the king It is the same king messiah whom God saves or delivers in each psalm. In all the above examples of Pss 20-21 the salvation is certain. By contrast, Ps 22: 1 quotes the same king complaining over the fact that his salvation or rescue is absent and distant from him. Instead of salvation he is experiencing terrible suffering. Psalm 22 portrays that suffering at length, and then not only speaks of answers to it in verses 22-31[22-32], but also describes his restoration. Psalm 23 explains his restoration as resurrection from the dead. These psalms describe the same king presented at the book's introductory Pss 1-2 and in the intervening Pss 3-19. As noted above, Ps 20: 6 calls him the "Lord's anointed," which is the same title Ps 2: 2 gives him. Undoubtedly it is the same messianic king described in both. " (Robert Cole, Why Psalm 23 Is Not About You, 33-82 (Kindle Edition))

[91]"Psalms 22, 23, and 24 are sometimes viewed as a trilogy, with Psalm 22 speaking of Christ as our suffering Savior, Psalm

23 representing Him as our daily Lord, and Psalm 24 as our coming King. Psalm 22 and 23 have been discussed previously, as messianic psalms. Psalm 24 also features Christ, but now as victorious over death and sin, preparing to complete His purpose in creation and to establish His eternal kingdom." (Henry M. Morris with Henry M. Morris III, Treasures In The Psalms, 187 (Kindle Edition); Green Forest, AR; Master Books)

[92] Speaking of the odds of just thirty of these prophecies coming to pass randomly in one person, former atheist Ralph Muncaster notes:

"The cumulative probability of all these prophecies randomly coming true in one person would be 1 chance in 10^{110}. This would be like winning about 16 lotteries in a row. Even if a skeptic were to substantially reduce some of the above estimates, the result would still be deemed impossible. For example, let's very conservatively assume the above estimates are off by a factor of a trillion trillion! This would still result in the "impossible odds" of all prophecies coming true in one man-Jesus-of one chance in 10^{86}! How remote are these odds? They would still be like taking all of the matter in the entire universe (that is, one billion billion stars and solar systems) and breaking it all down into subatomic particles, and randomly selecting one marked electron! Truly the prophecies made about Jesus in the Old Testament alone verify the Bible's claims about him, and his claims about himself." (Ralph Muncaster, *Examine The Evidence: Exploring The Case For Christianity*, 355; Eugene Oregon; Harvest House Publishers)

[93] "Professor Emeritus of Science at Westmont College, Peter Stoner, has calculated the probability of one man fulfilling the major prophecies made concerning the Messiah. The estimates were worked out by twelve different classes of 600 college students. The students carefully weighed all the factors, discussed each prophecy at length, and examined the various circumstances which might indicate that men had conspired together to fulfill a particular prophecy. They made their estimates conservative enough so that there was finally unanimous agreement even among the most skeptical students. But then Professor Stoner took their estimates and made them even more conservative. He also encouraged other

skeptics or scientists to make their own estimates to see if his conclusions were more than fair. Finally, he submitted his figures for review to a Committee of the American Scientific Affiliation. Upon examination, they verified that his calculations were dependable and accurate in regard to the scientific material presented. (19: 4) For example, concerning Micah 5: 2, where it states the Messiah would be born in Bethlehem Ephrathah, Stoner and his students determined the average population of Bethlehem from the time of Micah to the present; then they divided it by the average population of the earth during the same period. They concluded that the chance of one man being born in Bethlehem was one in 2.8 x 105—or rounded, one in 300,000. After examining eight different prophecies, they conservatively estimated that the chance of one man fulfilling all eight prophecies was one in 1017. To illustrate how large the number 1017 is (a figure with 17 zeros), Stoner gave this illustration. Imagine covering the entire state of Texas with silver dollars to a level of two feet deep. The total number of silver dollars needed to cover the whole state would be 1017. Now, choose just one of those silver dollars, mark it and drop it from an airplane. Then thoroughly stir all the silver dollars all over the state. When that has been done, blindfold one man, then tell him he can travel wherever he wishes in the state of Texas. But some time he must stop, reach down into the two feet of silver dollars and try to pull up that one specific silver dollar that has been marked. Now, the chance of his finding that one silver dollar in the state of Texas would be the chance the prophets had for eight of their prophecies coming true in any one man in the future. In financial terms, is there anyone who would not invest in a financial venture if the chance of failure were only one in 1017? This is the kind of sure investment we are offered by God for belief in His Messiah. Professor Stoner concluded: "The fulfillment of these eight prophecies alone proves that God inspired the writing of those prophecies to a definiteness which lacks only one chance in 1017 of being absolute." (19: 107) Another way of saying this is that any person who minimizes or ignores the significance of the biblical identifying signs concerning the Messiah would be foolish. But, of course, there are many more than eight prophecies….Remember, this number represents the chance of only 48

prophecies coming true in one person. It illustrates why it is absolutely impossible for anyone to have fulfilled all the Messianic
prophecies by chance. In fact, a leading authority on probability
theory, Emile Borel, states in his book Probabilities and Life, that
once we go past one chance in 1050, the probabilities are so small
it's impossible to think they will ever occur. (34) Here is one last
illustration of the immensity of the number 10157 and why the science of probability shows we are dealing with the miraculous. Imagine one ant traveling at the speed of only one inch every 15 billion years. If he could only carry one atom at a time, how many
atoms could he move in 10157 years? He could, even at that incredibly slow speed, be able to move all the atoms in 600,000 trillion, trillion, trillion, trillion universes the size of our universe, a
distance of 30 billion light years!(50: 120) Again, all of this means
it is impossible for 48 prophecies to be fulfilled by chance. It is
proof that there must be a God who supernaturally gave this information." (John Weldon, John Ankerberg, Walter C. Kaiser, Jr.,
The Case for Jesus the Messiah, 12-15 (Kindle Edition); ATRI
Publishing)

[94] "The term archaeology is a compound word (from the Greek
archaios and logos) meaning the "study of ancient things...In modern times, when we speak of archaeology, in general we are referring to the discipline typically within the field of anthropology and
history that draws upon an investigation of current material human
remains in order to understand past customs, cultures, and civilizations.. These remains include pottery, graves, buildings, coins,
tools, weapons, clothing, jewelry, literature, inscriptions, and
more. "Archaeology of the Bible" exists as a specific field of inquiry within this discipline; its primary goal is the excavation of
areas associated with the Bible and its societies and cultures, such
as Jerusalem,, Sodom, Jericho, Egypt, Israel, the Levant as a
whole, and Mesopotamia." (Joseph M. Holden & Norman Geisler,
*The Popular Handbook Of Archaeology And The Bible: Discover-
ies That Confirm The Reliability Of Scripture,* 2023-2031 (Kindle
Edition); Eugene, Oregon; Harvest House Publishers)

[95] "It may be stated categorically that no archaeological discovery has ever controverted a Biblical reference. Scores of archaeological findings have been made which confirm in clear outline or in exact detail historical statements in the Bible. And by the same token, proper evaluation of Biblical descriptions has often led to amazing discoveries. They form tesserae in the vast mosaic of the Bible's almost incredibly correct historical memory." (Nelson Glueck, Rivers in the Desert: A History of the Negev (New York: Farrar, Straus and Cudahy, 1959), 31)

"Of the hundreds of thousands of artifacts found by the archeologists, not one has ever been discovered that contradicts or denies one word, phrase, clause, or sentence of the Bible, but always confirms and verifies the facts of the biblical record." (Quotation from J. O. Kinnaman found at www.geocities.com/Heartland/7234/quotes.html (accessed October 26, 2009).

[96] "There are several lines of evidence to indicate that Moses, the great lawgiver and deliverer of Israel who wrote the other four books of the Law, was the author of Genesis. (1) The earliest and continual tradition of the Jewish people, as recorded in the Talmud, attributes this book to Moses. (2) Moses is the only person we know of from this early time period who had the ability to write this book. The rest of the Israelites were a nation of uneducated slaves, whereas Moses was a highly educated son of the king (Acts 7:22). (3) Moses was the only one who had both the interest and information to write Genesis. Being Jewish Moses would have had access to the family records of his ancestors (cf. Gen. 5:1; 10:1; 25:19; etc.) which were no doubt brought down to Egypt by Jacob (Gen. 46). Since Moses was bent on delivering his people from Egypt, it is natural to assume that he was familiar with the promises of God passed down by his forefathers that God would indeed deliver them (cf. Gen. 46:3-4; Exod. 2:24). (4) Citations from Genesis show that the rest of the Old Testament regards it as part of the Law of Moses (Deut. 1:8; II Kings 13:23; I Chron. 1:1ff.). Since Moses was the author of the other "books of Moses," as we will see later, it is reasonable to attribute the first book of Moses to him as well. (5) Jesus and the New Testament writers clearly regard Moses as the author of an essential part of Scripture (cf.

Matt. 19:8; Luke 16:29; 24:27). We can conclude that Moses, using the family records which had been passed on to him, compiled the Book of Genesis." (Norman Geisler, *A Popular Survey Of The Old Testament,* 610-623 (Kindle Edition); Grand Rapids, Michigan; Baker Books)

"1B. R.H. Rfeiffer writes: 'There is no reason to doubt that the Pentateuch was considered the divine revelation to Moses when it was canonized about 400 B.C.' (Pfeiffer, JOT, 133) 1C. Ecclesiasticus, one of the books of the Apocrypha, written about 180 B.C., gives this witness: 'All this is the covenant book of God Most High, the law which Moses enacted to be the heritage of the assemblies of Jacob' (Ecclesiasticus 24:23 NEB). 2C. The Talmud (*Baby Bathra,* 146), a Jewish commentary on the Law (*Torah*) dating from 200 B.C., and the Mishnah (*Pirqe Aboth,* I, 1), a rabbinic interpretation and legislating dating from 100 B.C., both attribute the *Torah* to Moses. 3C. Likewise, Philo, the Jewish philosopher theologian born approximately A.D. 20, held Mosaic authorship: 'But I will...tell the story of Moses as I have learned it, both from the sacred books, the wonderful monuments of his wisdom which he has left behind him and from some of the elders of the nation.' (Philo, WP, 279) 4C. The first century A.D. Jewish historian Flavius Josephus writes in his *Josephus Against Apion* (11:18): 'For we have not an innumerable multitude of books among us, disagreeing from and contradicting one another (as the Greeks have) but only 22 books (our present 39), which are justly believed to be divine; and of them, five belong to Moses, which contain his laws, and the traditions of the origin of mankind till his death.' (Josephus, WFJ, 609)" (Josh McDowell, *The New Evidence That Demands A Verdict,* 458-459; Nashville, TN; Thomas Nelson Publishers).

[97] "These Old Testament verses record that the Torah or "the Law," was from Moses: Joshua 8:32 speaks of "the Law of Moses, which he had written." (The verses marked by an asterisk refer to an actual written "Law of Moses," not simply an oral tradition): Joshua 1:7,8*; 8:31*,34*; 23:6* 1 Kings 2:3* 2 Kings 14:6*; 23:25 1 Chronicles 22:13 2 Chronicles 5:10; 23:18*; 25:4*; 30:16; 33:8; 34:14; 35:12* Ezra 3:2; 6:18*; 7:6 Nehemiah 1:7,8; 8:1*,14*; 9:14; 10:29; 13:1* Daniel 9:11,13* Malachi 4:4 WITNESS OF

THE NEW TESTAMENT The New Testament held that the Torah or "law" came from Moses: The apostles believed that "Moses wrote for us a law" (Mark 12:19). John was confident that "the Law was given through Moses" (John 1:17). Paul, speaking of a Pentateuchal passage, asserts "Moses writes" (Romans 10:5). Other passages which insist on this include: Luke 2:22; 20:28 John 1:45; 8:5; 9:29 Acts 3:22; 6:14; 13:39; 15:1,21; 26:22; 28:23 1 Corinthians 9:9 2 Corinthians 3:15 Hebrews 9:19 Revelation 15:3 Jesus believed the Torah to be from Moses: Mark 7:10; 10:3-5; 12:26 Luke 5:14; 16:29-31; 24:27,44 John 7:19,23 Notice especially John 5:45-47: Do not think that I will accuse you before the Father; the one who accuses you is Moses, in whom you have set your hope. For if you believed Moses, you would believe Me; for he wrote of Me. But if you do not believe his writings, how will you believe My words? Eissfeldt states: The name used in the New Testament clearly with reference to the whole Pentateuch—the Book of Moses—is certainly to be understood as meaning that Moses was the compiler of the Pentateuch. 27/158" (Josh McDowell & Bill Wilson, *The Best Of Josh McDowell: A Ready Defense:* 148-149 (Kindle Edition); Nashvillee, TN; Thomas Nelson Publishers)

[98]"Critics have also suggested that Moses could not have written his account in the fifteenth century before Christ because, they claim, writing had not yet been invented. However, the discovery of numerous ancient written inscriptions, including the famous black stele containing the laws of Hammurabi written before 2000 B.C., prove that writing was widespread for many centuries before the time of Moses." (Grant Jeffrey, *The Signature Of God,* 42 (Kindle Edition); Waterbrook Press @ Books)

[99]"Perhaps the massive accumulation of inscriptions on stone, clay, and papyrus that have been exhumed in Mesopotamia and Egypt might have been questioned as necessarily proving the extensive use of writing in Palestine itself—until the 1887 discovery of the archive of Palestinian clay tablets in Tell el-Amarna, Egypt, dating from about 1420 to 1380 B.C. (the age of Moses and Joshua). This archive contained hundreds of tablets composed in

Babylonian cuneiform (at that time the language of diplomatic correspondence in the Near East), which were communications to the Egyptian court from Palestinian officials and kings. Many of these letters contain reports of invasions and attacks by the Ha-bi-ru and the so-called SA.GAZ (the oral pronunciation of this logogram may well have been Habiru also) against the city-states of Canaan. Wellhausen himself chose to ignore this evidence almost completely after the earliest publication of these Amarna Tablets came out in the 1890s. He refused to come to terms with the implications of the now-established fact that Canaan even before the Israelite conquest was completed contained a highly literate civilization (even though they wrote in Babylonian rather than their own native tongue). The later proponents of the Documentary Hypothesis have been equally closed-minded toward the implications of these discoveries. The most serious blow of all, however, came with the deciphering of the alphabetic inscriptions from Serabit el-Khadim in the region of Sinai turquoise mines operated by the Egyptians during the second millennium B.C. These consisted of a new set of alphabetic symbols resembling Egyptian hieroglyphs but written in a dialect of Canaanite closely resembling Hebrew. They contained records of mining quotas and dedicatory inscriptions to the Phoenician goddess Baalat (who was apparently equated with the Egyptian Hathor). The irregular style of execution precludes all possibility of attributing these writings to a select group of professional scribes. There is only one possible conclusion to draw from this body of inscriptions (published by W.F. Albright in The Proto-Sinaitic Inscriptions and Their Decipherment [Cambridge: Harvard University, 1966]): Already back in the seventeenth or sixteenth centuries B.C., even the lowest social strata of the Canaanite population, slave-miners who labored under Egyptian foremen, were well able to read and write in their own language." (Gleason L. Archer Jr., New International Encyclopedia of Bible Difficulties, 98-100 (Kindle Edition); Grand Rapids, Michigan; Zondervan)

[100] "These higher critics maintained that some of Genesis, especially the material in the first eleven chapters, had been derived from myths of the ancient Babylonians...Today it is beyond question that writing was practiced widely, and in many forms, long

before the time of Moses...Similarly, archaeologists now recognize that the cultural indications in Genesis, at least from the time of Abraham onward, are exactly what would be expected of eyewitness records from those times....In similar fashion, linguistic studies by numerous first-rate Biblical scholars have repeatedly shown that there is no real substance to the claims of the higher critics that the language of Genesis was much later than the time of Moses." (Henry Morris, *The Genesis Record: A Scientific & Devotional Commentary On The Book Of Beginnings,* 7-8 (Kindle Edition); Grand Rapids, Michigan; Baker Books).

[101]"Besides this, there are several reasons why conservative scholars do not believe Moses was dependent upon these earlier creation myths. First, the critical scholars' overemphasis on similarities has blinded their eyes to the many differences that set the accounts apart as unique. Unlike the mythic stories, the Genesis account offers one monotheistic God as the creator of all things. The Mesopotamian tamian epic speaks of a pantheon of gods involved in creation. Genesis offers a loving and all-powerful Lord as creator, unlike the Enuma Elish, which portrays the gods as conspiring, vengeful monsters who are seeking ill for one another. In the Enuma Elish, human beings are created from the blood of a rebel god and are seen as lowly slaves created to serve and feed the gods. This is in stark opposition to the Genesis account, which records that man was made in the image of God and meant to be like His creator-the highest of His creation. Moreover, in the epic, creation was made out of something evil (Tiamat's body) and pre-existing (that is, ex deo or ex materia), whereas Genesis describes a creation from a good source (that is, God) and out of nothing (ex nihilo). Second, the similarities may be accounted for by the fact that different groups were writing about the same original historical event (creation). If the creation of the world actually occurred, and various civilizations later reinterpreted the story within the contexts texts of their polytheistic religions and purposes, it would account for the basic similarities in content. Moses would have received his monotheistic creation account directly from God or from oral tradition that was passed down through Noah and his descendants. Third, we now know the Genesis account is not dependent on or identified with any earlier Mesopotamian, Egyptian,

or Assyrian creation tradition because of the recognized direction of myth. Near-Eastern scholar D.J.Wiseman and others familiar with myth literature (for example, C.S.Lewis) have understood that an early myth can become even more mythical over time, and that earlier historical events can become embellished with myth over time. But never do we see earlier myth traditions (such as these Mesopotamian and Egyptian creation accounts) become more historical-sounding, believable, and simpler over time. The Genesis record is more simple, historical, natural,, and believable than these early myth traditions, and therefore it cannot possibly be dependent on them or classified as just another Near-Eastern creation account. The mythical tone is obvious in the Enuma Elish, but it is absent in the Genesis account. The epic tells of Marduk killing Tiamat and splitting her in two parts like a "shellfish" and creating the sky from her body. However, Genesis simply opens with the statement: "In the beginning, God created the heavens and the earth" (Genesis 1:1). It continues with the simple and natural formula, "Then God said, `Let there be.....' (Genesis 1:3,6,11,14). Fourth, some critical scholars forget that early creation myths are not necessarily concerned with creation per se; rather, they are attempts to justify or elevate the standing ing of particular deities or cities in the eyes of the people. For example, creation is not the main story of Enuma Elish; it is the relatively unknown Babylonian god Marduk. It appears now that the story is an effort by its author to elevate Marduk as the chief god of Babylon, though prior to this story he was not given prominence among the multitude of other deities. In the above example of the Egyptian account, most scholars recognize that the creation elements present are not the main theme, but the raising of the city of Memphis and its god (Ptah) to prominence in order to justify Memphis as the location of the capital city of Egypt. For these reasons, we must consider the Genesis account as an independent historical tradition, without dependency on the earlier Mesopotamian or Egyptian myth literature." (Joseph M. Holden & Norman Geisler, The Popular Handbook of Archaeology and the Bible: Discoveries That Confirm the Reliability of Scripture, 2314-2355 (Kindle Edition); Eugene, Oregon; Harvest House Publishers)

[102]"In some cases, however, the early Babylonian seals, which contained devices taken from these legends, more closely approached the Genesis story. One striking and important specimen of early type in the British Museum collection has two figures sitting one on each side of a tree, holding out their hands to the fruit, while at the back of one is stretched a serpent. We know well that in these early sculptures none of these figures were chance devices, but all represented events or supposed events, and figures in their legends; thus it is evident that a form of the story of the Fall, similar to that of Genesis, was known in early times in Babylonia." (George Smith, *The Chaldean Account Of Genesis: Containing The Description Of The Creation, The Fall Of Man, The Deluge, The Tower Of Babel, The Times Of The Patriarchs , And Nimrod; Babylonian Fables And Legends Of The Gods, From The Cuneiform Inscriptions,* 1364-1368 (Kindle Edition); Global Grey)

[103] " My personal study into the history of the written Chinese language through various treatises in English found in Harvard's Chinese-Japanese Yenching Library gave its approximate time of origin as 2500 B.C. This dating is provocative, for it coincides quite closely with the time (2218 B.C.) of the great dispersion of races from the tower of Babel, as calculated from the Biblical genealogies in a recent chronological study...When the Chinese, very early in their history as a separate people, found a need to communicate with a written language, a system of word-pictures was invented in keeping with the characteristic calligraphy of the ancient world. True to all primitive written languages, these so-called pictographs were satisfactory for representing objects but carried limitations in expressing abstract concepts. The early graphic symbols, therefore, were combined in meaningful ways to convey ideas, called ideograms, and these "picture stories" of necessity had to contain common knowledge in order to be understood. It would have been only natural to use as a basis for some of the ideograms the history of the ancient beginnings of humanity with which all were familiar by oral tradition. Consequently, the written Chinese language is composed of characters uniquely adapted to the possibility of containing the stories of Genesis." (C.H.Kang & Ethel R. Nelson, *The Discovery Of Genesis: How The Truths Of Genesis Were Found Hidden In The Chinese Language,* 844-181

(Kindle Edition); St. Louis, Missouri; Concordia Publishing House)

"From the Chinese writing, we learn that in the beginning (B)1 (), there were just two persons on earth. Furthermore, another bronzeware rendition of beginning (B)2 reveals that the original couple had sinless characters. They were reflectors of God, heaven ()....The man was named Adam, meaning "the ground," from which he had been created by God. We learned that the Chinese radicals for ground, earth (B), , , (O) () all have reference to Adam (review p. 36). And we learned that "Adam called his wife's name Eve, because she was the mother of all living....Thus we find a record of the first two ancestors , (O)4 (). Comparing and above, representing Adam arising from the earth, we find not only Adam, but two persons, he and his wife, Eve, "the mother of all living." The ancestors are found with the God radical , indicating that ShangTi is, of course, the ultimate ancestor in whose image Adam and Eve had been created. This character denotes not only ancestor, but also the founder, prototype, original, beginning." (Ethel Nelson & Richard Broadberry, *Genesis And The Mystery Confucius Couldn't Solve,* 665-684 (Kindle Edition); Saint Louis, Missouri; Concordia Publishing House)

[104]"Let us once more take some time to bridge some of the Mysteries and background of this mythical antediluvian period, concerning those legendary heroes of renown. The word Nephilim derives from the Hebrew language, and specifically the Hebrew word nopelim or nepelim. The root word for nopelim is npl, meaning "fall." The suffix im translates as "the ones." 1 Therefore, by piecing these two words together alongside their literal translation, we find the definition of nopelim as "fallen ones," just as Josephus described the infamous ones, the fallen angels, those who procreated with the daughters of men. Additionally, Nephilim is also the root Aramaic word for Nephila, for the "Orion" constellation suggesting to me that Nephilim are somehow directly connected to Orion. 2 In legend, Orion is the constellation where the fallen angel Shemyaza/ Azazel is believed to be hung; therefore suggesting Nephilim somehow derive from Shemyaza/ Azazel. Remember, Nephilim were considered giant demigods, the unnatural offspring of

the daughters of men and fallen angels, violating God's natural order of creation." (Gary Wayne, The Genesis 6 Conspiracy: How Secret Societies and the Descendants of Giants Plan to Enslave Humankind, 1749-1760 (Kindle Edition); Deep River Books)

[105]"One of the great debates over Genesis 6:1–4 is the meaning of the word nephilim . We've seen from the Mesopotamian context that the apkallus were divine, mated with human women, and produced giant offspring. We've also seen that Jewish thinkers in the Second Temple period viewed the offspring of Genesis 6:1–4 in the same way—as giants. Any analysis of the term nephilim must account for, not ignore or violate, these contexts. Interpretation of the term nephilim must also account for another Jewish phenomenon between the testaments—translation of the Old Testament into Greek. I speak here of the Septuagint. The word nephilim occurs twice in the Hebrew Bible (Gen 6:4 ; Num 13:33). In both cases the Septuagint translated the term with gigas ("giant"). 15 Given the backdrop we've covered, it would seem obvious that nephilim ought to be understood as "giants." But many commentators resist the rendering, arguing that it should be read as "fallen ones" or "those who fall upon" (a battle expression). These options are based on the idea that the word derives from the Hebrew verb n-p-l (naphal , "to fall"). More importantly, those who argue that nephilim should be translated with one of these expressions rather than "giants" do so to avoid the quasi-divine nature of the Nephilim. That in turn makes it easier for them to argue that the sons of God were human. In reality, it doesn't matter whether "fallen ones" is the translation. In both the Mesopotamian context and the context of later Second Temple Jewish thought, their fathers are divine and the nephilim (however translated) are still described as giants . 16 Consequently, insisting that the name means "fallen" produces no argument to counter a supernatural interpretation." (Michael S. Heiser, The Unseen Realm: Recovering the Supernatural Worldview of the Bible, 1942-1965 (Kindle Edition); Bellingham, WA; Lexham Press)

[106]"Jewish targums (Aramaic translations of the Old Testament) flirt with the human view but do not completely move away from a supernatural view until roughly the same time period as the

Christian departure (the third century AD). Newman writes in this regard: "It is difficult to know where to place the targumim. These Aramaic translations of Scripture (often paraphrases or even commentaries) have an oral background in the synagogue services of pre-Christian times, but their extant written forms seem to be much later. Among these, the Targum Pseudo-Jonathan [Tg. Ps.-J .] presents at least a partially supernatural interpretation. Although in its extant form this targum is later than the rise of Islam in the 7th century A.D., early materials also appear in it.... [Its translation] 'sons of the great ones 'may reflect a non-supernatural interpretation, but the reference to Shamhazai and Azael falling from heaven certainly does not. The names given are close to those in 1 Enoch , considering that the latter has gone through two translations to reach its extant Ethiopic version. Notice also that the Nephilim are here identified with the angels rather than their offspring as in Enoch , Jub ., and Josephus.... Targum Neofiti [Targ. Neof .] is the only complete extant MS of the Palestinian Targum to the Pentateuch. The MS is from the 16th century, but its text has been variously dated from the 1st to the 4th centuries A.D. In place of the Hebrew בני האלהים is the Aramaic דייניא בני , 'sons of the judges, 'using a cognate noun to the verb ידון appearing in the MT of Gen 6:3. Nephilim is rendered by גיבריה , 'warriors. 'The text of the targum seems to reflect a nonsupernatural interpretation, unless we press the last sentence of 6:4—'these are the warriors that (were there) from the beginning of the world, warriors of wondrous renown'—so as to exclude human beings. However, the MS has many marginal notes, which presumably represent one or more other MSS of the Palestinian Targum. One such note occurs at 6:4 and reads: 'There were warriors dwelling on earth in those days, and also afterwards, after the sons of the angels had joined (in wedlock) the daughters of the sons. 'Thus the text of Targ. Neof . seems to be nonsupernatural while a marginal note is clearly supernatural.... The Targum of Onqelos [Tg. Onq .] became the official targum to the Pentateuch for Judaism. According to the Babylonian Talmud [Bab. Talm .] (Meg. 3a) it was composed early in the 2nd century A.D., but this seems to be a confusion with the Greek translation of Aquila. Although the relations between the

various targumim are complicated by mutual influence in trans-
mission, Onq . was probably completed before A.D. 400 in Babylonia using Palestinian materials as a basis. In our passage Onq .
reads רברביא בני , 'sons of the great ones, 'probably referring to rul-
ers." See Newman, "The Ancient Jewish Exegesis of Genesis 6:2,
4," 21 , 23–24 . It should be noted that the first-century writer Philo
reflects both views. Newman also notes: "In his treatise On the Giants , the Alexandrian Jewish philosopher Philo (20 B.C.–A.D. 50)
quotes the Old Greek version of this passage with the readings
ἄγγελοι τοῦ θεοῦ and γίγαντες . Unfortunately Philo is not always
a clear writer. Apparently he takes the literal meaning of the verses
to refer to angels and women since, immediately after quoting Gen
6:2, he says: 'It is Moses 'custom to give the name of angels to
those whom other philosophers call demons [or spirits], souls that
is which fly and hover in the air. And let no one suppose that what
is here said is a myth. 'After a lengthy discussion arguing for the
existence of non-corporeal spirits, however, Philo proceeds to al-
legorize the passage: 'So, then, it is no myth at all of giants that he
[Moses] sets before us; rather he wishes to show you that some
men are earth-born, some heaven-born, and some God-born.' " See
Newman, "Ancient Jewish Exegesis," 19 ." (Michael S. Heiser,
Demons: What the Bible Really Says About the Powers of Darkness, 9900-9935 (Kindle Edition); Bellingham, WA; Lexham
Press)

[107]"The "angel" view of this classic Genesis text is well documented in both ancient Jewish rabbinical literature and Early
Church writings. In addition to the Septuagint translation, the ven-
erated (although non-canonical) Book of Enoch, the Syriac Version of the Old Testament, as well as the Testimony of the 12 Pa-
triarchs234 and the Little Genesis, 235 confirm the lexicological
usage and the extant beliefs of ancient Jewish scholars. Clearly the
learned Philo Judaeus understood the passage as relating to angels.
236 Josephus Flavius also represents this view: "They made God
their enemy; for many angels of God accompanied with women,
and begat sons that proved unjust, and despisers of all that was
good, on account of the confidence they had in their own strength,
for the tradition is that these men did what resembled the acts of
those whom the Grecians call giants." 237 In accordance with the

ancient interpretation, the Early Church fathers understood the expression "sons of God" as designating angels. These included Justin Martyr, 238 Irenaeus, 239 Athenagoras, 240 Pseudo-Clementine, 241 Clement of Alexandria, 242 Tertullian, 243 Commodianus, 244 and Lactantius, 245 to list a few. This interpretation was also espoused by Luther and many more modern exegetes including Koppen, Twesten, Dreschler, Hofmann, Baumgarten, Delitzsch, W Kelly, A. C. Gaebelein, and others." (Chuck Missler and Mark Eastman, Alien Encounters, 207-208 (Kindle Edition); Coburn d'Alene, ID; Koinonia House)

[108] "A mountain of the island of Crete having been burst asunder by the action of an earthquake, a body was found there standing upright, forty-six cubits in height; by some persons it is supposed to have been that of Orion; while others again are of opinion that it was that of Otus. It is generally believed, from what is stated in ancient records, that the body of Orestes, which was disinterred by command of an oracle, was seven cubits in height. It is now nearly one thousand years ago, that that divine poet Homer was unceasingly complaining, that men were of less stature in his day than they had formerly been. Our Annals do not inform us what was the height of Nævius Pollio; but we learn from them that he nearly lost his life from the rush of the people to see him, and that he was looked upon as a prodigy. The tallest man that has been seen in our times, was one Gabbaras by name, who was brought from Arabia by the Emperor Claudius; his height was nine feet and as many inches. In the reign of Augustus, there were two persons, Posio and Secundilla by name, who were half a foot taller than him; their bodies have been preserved as objects of curiosity in the museum of the Sallustian family." (Pliny The Elder, Translated by John Bostock and Henry Thomas Riley, Complete Works of Pliny the Elder, 6064-6075 (Kindle Edition); Hastings, East Sussex; Delphi Classics)

"The body of Orestes which Pliny mentions, was measured at seven cubits, which equals some 12 feet in our terms; 6 whilst those of Pusio and Secundilla were some 10 feet 3 inches in height. It is a great pity that Pliny did not discuss them at greater length, though it is worth mentioning that the Romans were very exact in measuring things. If they tell us that Gabbara stood at 9 feet 9 inches, and Pusio and Secundilla at 10 feet 3, then we can rely on the exactness of those measurements. The Romans were not fools, and Pliny treasured his own reputation as a scholar too much to be caught out in a lie. After all, when he wrote his account, there were many hundreds in Rome still living who would have seen and spoken with these giants -and many rival scholars (Pollio and Livy among them) who would have delighted in exposing Pliny as a fraud or a fool had he got his facts wrong. The fact that that never happened should tell us something.". (Bill Cooper, The Authenticity Of The Book Of Judges, 694-700 (Kindle Edition)).

[109] "For many angels of God accompanied with women, and begat sons that proved unjust, and despisers of all that was good, on account of the confidence they had in their own strength; for the tradition is, that these men did what resembled the acts of those whom the Grecians call giants. But Noah was very uneasy at what they did; and being displeased at their conduct, persuaded them to change their dispositions and their acts for the better: but seeing they did not yield to him, but were slaves to their wicked pleasures, he was afraid they would kill him, together with his wife and children, and those they had married; so he departed out of that land." (The Complete Works Of Flavius Josephus, One of the best known translations of Josephus's work, translated by William Whiston in 1737 Formatted by E.C. Marsh 2010, 1103-1108 (Kindle Edition); ecmarsh.com)

"For which reason they removed their camp to Hebron; and when they had taken it, they slew all the inhabitants. There were till then left the race of giants, who had bodies so large, and countenances so entirely different from other men, that they were surprising to the sight, and terrible to the hearing. The bones of these men are still shown to this very day, unlike to any credible relations of other men." (Flavius Josephus, The Complete Works Of Flavius Josephus, translated by William Whiston in 1737 Formatted by E.C. Marsh 2010, 4571 (Kindle Edition); ecmarsh.com)

[110] The testimony of the ancient Egyptians is equally incredible. In describing the warrior campaigns against the Canaanites, we read:

"23,5 ones to look. Their eyes are good, thy hand grows weak(?)". 25: T\' Q "^ /Q3 rn2«*'. Thou makest the name of every Maher, officers of the land of Egypt". Thy name becomes like (that of) K-dr-d-y ^ the chief of *I-s-r ^* ^ when the hyena" found him in the balsam-tree'*. —The(r) narrow defile'* is infested (?) with Shosu concealed beneath the bushes; some of them are of four cubits or of five cubits, from head(??) to foot(?)'", fierce of face, their heart is not mild, and they hearken not to coaxing. Thou art alone, there is no helper(?)" with thee, no army"". (Alan henderson Gardiner, Egyptian Hieratic Texts, 1068-1086 (Kindle Edition))

The Egyptians here record their battles against the Shosu, who were a race of giants that lived in the land of Canaan. The cubit mentioned here is an Egyptian royal cubit of 20.62 inches, which means that the Shosu were anywhere from 7-10 feet tall!

[111] "For as there were at that time dealings under truce with the men of Tegea, he had come to a forge there and was looking at iron being wrought; and he was in wonder as he saw that which was being done. The smith therefore, perceiving that he marvelled at it, ceased from his work and said: "Surely, thou stranger of Lacedemon, if thou hadst seen that which I once saw, thou wouldst have marvelled much, since now it falls out that thou dost marvel so greatly at the working of this iron; for I, desiring in this enclosure to make a well, lighted in my digging upon a coffin of seven cubits in length; and not believing that ever there had been men larger than those of the present day, I opened it, and I saw that the dead body was equal in length to the coffin: then after I had measured it, I filled in the earth over it again."". (Herodotus, The Histories, 527-537 (Kindle Edition); Start Publishing LLC)

[112] "But why should we be surprised at these things? Like dragons -like the Great Flood itself -giants are known to every culture under the sun. Virtually every nation on earth remembers a time when they were neighbours to, or lived amongst giant populations, and the Israelites were no exception. Giant peoples were known to them under various names: The Nephilim, the Rephaim, the Tzuzim, the Anakim, to name a few, all of whom were noted by the Israelites for their great stature; and even amongst later scholars and writers of the classical world we find mention of similar

gigantic peoples. Homer, Lucretius, Virgil, Juvenal, Pliny, and even po-faced Augustine of Hippo all write of them. Whether they were writing truth or fable, however, may be judged by the mention of gigantic peoples which have appeared in more modern times, and which have been written about and lectured upon by 'establishment 'anthropologists and archaeologists. Note the following report which appeared in The Princeton Union, on October 11th 1894: "In a prehistoric cemetery recently uncovered at Montpellier, France, while workmen were excavating a waterworks reservoir, human skulls were found measuring 28, 31 and 32 inches in circumference. The bones which were found with the skulls were also of gigantic proportions. These relics were sent to the Paris academy, and a learned 'savant 'who lectured on the find says that they belonged to a race of men between ten and fifteen feet in height." 10 The 'learned savant 'of the article was Dr Georges Vacher de Lapouge (1854-1936), and his findings were corroborated in full by Dr Paul Valéry, a colleague of his at the University of Montpellier between 1886 -1891.11 Would these men -these revered figures of the establishment –have willingly thrown away their careers and reputations for a stupid hoax? It seems not, for six months later, this same report appeared again in another journal, there having been plenty of time for the facts to be checked. 12 And then, out of Castelnau in France appeared this report: "In the year 1890, some human bones of enormous size, double the ordinary in fact, were found in the tumulus of Castelnau (Herault) [France], and have since been carefully examined by Prof. Kiener, who, while admitting that the bones are those of a very tall race, nevertheless finds them abnormal in dimensions and apparently of morbid growth. They undoubtedly re-open the question of 'giants 'of antiquity, but do not furnish sufficient evidence to decide it." 13...The photo taken of the bones at the time of their discovery (see Fig. 19 above) shows clearly the immense difference in size between them and the 'normal 'modern human femur placed between them. Kiener's staid and learned paper on the remains may be read to this day, 14 and it is notable that neither in the case of the Montpellier remains, nor yet those of Castelnau, has any serious attempt been made by anthropologists or archaeologists to dispute the simple facts of the case. In other words, the facts are unarguable. These are indeed the bones of gigantic human beings who stood up to 15 feet in height. As for the most famous giant in all history -Goliath -what can we say of him other than this? -his name has been discovered inscribed on a potsherd in the ruins of his hometown of Gath (Tel es-Safi, Israel) dating to within 70 years of his slaying by David, i.e. to about 950 BC (see Fig. 20 below). 15 Interesting, isn't it, when we consider what the critics have been saying all these years.". (Bill Cooper, *The Authenticity Of The Book Of Judges,* 751-776 (Kindle Edition))

[113]"Rarely do we hear why the Creator destroyed the earth with water. I turned my attention back to PipeCarrier, whose war scarred face was showered with moonlight as it cascaded down his back as if tracing the length of his long black hair and asked him, "What do you know of the star people?" PipeCarrier focused his gaze beyond the moon into the deep evening sky full of shining stars. He pointed to The Warrior constellation's belt and said. "They fell from the heavens in the ancient times. They took our women. They were not washte [good]." PipeCarrier confirmed what I have heard from many other tribal elders. My father told me that there was a great battle in the Sky World where good spirit and bad spirits were fighting one another. The bad spirits were thrown from the heavens down to the earth below where they made themselves out to be gods. These star people took our women by force and the resulting children became the race of giants that we read about in historical accounts from cultures around the world, including the Bible. Interestingly enough, the repeating similarity is these beings came from the sky, took the human women, and produced a race of giants....When I served in the U.S. Army, I met a traditional Navajo woman whose family was of the Bitter Water and Towering House Clans. We were on guard duty together one evening when we were deployed out in the desert, and we began talking about the star people. The most famous of the Southwestern star people is Kokopelli. This figure is well-known in pan-Indian Native American art and even common art that can be found in national retail stores although its origin is in Southwest United States. Kokopelli is one of the star people who fell from the heavens to the desert region of the Southwest, according to native tradition. He quickly made himself out to be a god of rain and fertility

demanding worship and tribute of a young woman in exchange for bringing the rains to the fields or fertility to women by playing his flute. In the older renditions of him, he is often depicted with a hunched back, four protrusions sticking out of his back and two arms holding a flute which he would play to lure women to himself. Sometimes in more modern depictions, the four protrusions are what look like four crazy dreadlocks poking out from the top and back of his head. There are even many of the ancient drawings that depict him with an erect phallus, alluding to the sexual nature and focus of this false god. His portraits are not just found in the Southwest; there is even a petroglyph carving of Kokopelli on the island of Puerto Rico where he visited the Taino Native Americans. The stories of Kokopelli are vast across many Native cultures. It is strange to me that this seducing spirit could have grown in such popularity across the country. It is crucial that we know the origins of the things that we have or decide to pass along to another generation. For some time as a child, my wife lived on the Navajo reservation in Shonto, Arizona where an old song is occasionally sung: "Fathers, hide your daughters; Kokopelli is coming!" Kokopelli is just one of many "star people" that fell to the earth and made themselves out to be "gods." There are numerous accounts of giant tribes that sprung forth as a direct result of these fallen ones mixing with the human women. The common thread in the many cross-cultural stories across the globe is that these beings taking human women and breeding a race of giants. It is found throughout the world; so many cultures have stories that have been passed down for thousands of generations centering on these giants." (Chief Joseph RiverWind Assisted by Laralyn RiverWind, That's What The Old Ones Say: Pre-Colonial Revelations Of God, 122-129 (Kindle Edition); Marble, NC; Word Branch Publishing)

[114]"On the upper terrace, within the corporate limits of Monongahela City, are situated the garden and greenhouse of Mr. I.S. Crall. Two ravines on the east and west sides open directly south into Pigeon Creek, and their erosion has lowered the ground until it is surrounded by higher land on every side except along the bluff next to the creek. ...In excavating for foundation walls and other purposes, Mr. Crall has, at different times, unearthed skeletons of large size: the ground is strewn with mussel shells, flint chips etc.

On the eastern side of this levee, near the break of the ravine, and close to a never-failing spring, stands the largest mound above the one at McKee's rocks, measuring 9 feet in height and 60 feet in diameter... at the center a hole measuring 3 feet across the top and 2 feet into the original soil. In this were fragments of human bones too soft to be preserved. They indicated an adult of large size. The gray clay was unbroken over this hole. Directly over this, above the clay and resting upon it, were portions of another large skeleton, with which was found part of an unburned clay tube or pipe." (The Wichita Daily Eagle - November 17, 1891)

"There has just been received at the Maryland Academy of Sciences, the skeleton of an Indian seven feet tall. It was discovered near Antietam. There are now skeletons of three powerful Indians at the Academy who at one time in their wildness roamed over the state of Maryland armed with such instruments as nature gave them or that their limited skill taught them to make. Two of these skeletons belonged to individuals evidently of gigantic size. The vertebrae and bones of the legs are nearly as thick as those of a horse and the length of the long bones exceptional. The skulls are of fine proportions, ample and with walls of moderate thickness and of great strength and stiffened beyond with a powerful occipital ridge. The curves of the forehead are moderate and not retreating, suggesting intelligence and connected with jaws of moderate development.". (BALTIMORE AMERICAN, NOVEMBER 15, 1897)

"The skeleton of a giant Indian, maybe seven or more feet in height, who died and was buried about the time Christ was born, has been unearthed from prehistoric burial grounds along the Potomac River near Point of Rocks recently. Nicholas Yinger, who has been excavating at this and other sites of early Indian villages along the Potomac River in recent years, discovered the skeleton of the giant Indian, along with the other artifacts buried with the body, on Saturday, April 28, just a few weeks ago." (MORNING HERALD, MAY 14, 1956)

"Along the Susquehanna River in Indiana County, Pennsylvania a major Indian burial site was uncovered. All together, forty-nine skeletons were exhumed, the tallest being eight feet tall. These skeletons were reportedly taken to the Harrisburg Museum for re-assembly and then shipped to the Smithsonian for further study. However, the Smithsonian denies any knowledge of them. On the site of the William H. Rhea farm (circa 1871–1880) in Conemaugh Township just west of the mouth of Black Legs Creek, skeletons of men, probably Indians, were found. Noted local historian Clarence Stephenson says, "One of the skeletons is of a giant nearly eight feet tall. The giant's skeleton measured 89 inches from the top of the skull to the phalanges of the feet. It was covered with small stones, lay on the back, and measured 26 inches across the chest."". (CHARLEROI MAIL, MAY 7, 1953)

"On July 13, Professor Skinner of the American Indian Museum, excavating the mound at Tioga Point, near Sayre, Pennsylvania, uncovered the bones of 68 men, which he estimates had been buried at least seven or eight hundred years. The average height indicated by the skeletons was seven feet, but many were taller. Evidence of the gigantic size of these men was seen in huge axes found beside the bones." (CHARLESTON DAILY MAIL, SEPTEMBER 20, 1916)

[115] "In my opinion it becomes clear that those at the helm of the Smithsonian were engaged in the deliberate obfuscation of evidence that would offer another paradigm than the accepted Darwinian one that then and now permeate all of science and academia. The question is why would men of science deliberately engage in this? And, I believe I have an answer. If these skeletons exist, and by all of the overwhelming evidence both from the written record found in newspapers and accounts from scientists, as well as the oral traditions from Native Americans, they pose a direct threat to the pervading world view, Darwinism.". (L.A. Marzulli, On The Trail Of The Nephilim-Volume One-Giant Skeletons & Ancient Megalithic Structures,1341-1350 (Kindle Edition); Spiral Of Life Publishing)

[116] "The following is a brief list of documented findings, all recorded in the Annual Report of the Board of Regents of the Smithsonian Institution Showing the Operations, Expenditures, and Condition of the Institution for the Year […] series (each book title

ending with the year the discovery was made): · One skull measuring "36 inches in circumference." Anna, Illinois, 1873. (The average circumference measurement for the human skull is between twenty-one and twenty-three inches, depending on varying factors such as sex, ethnicity, etc.) · One full skeleton with double rows of teeth, buried alongside a gigantic axe, referred to in the report as a "gigantic savage." The skeleton—with a colossal skull—fell apart after exhumation, so an exact height/ head circumference was not reported, but the record states that "its height must have been quite [meaning "at least"] seven feet." Amelia Island, Florida, 1875. · Giant axes and "skinning stones." One weighed over fifteen pounds, had an ornately carved handle, and was of such mass that it was documented: "Only a giant could have wielded this." Kishwaukee Mounds, Illinois, 1877. · One jawbone that easily slipped around the entire face of a large man on the research team; one thigh bone measuring "four inches longer than that of a man six feet two inches high"; one "huge skeleton, much taller than the current race of men." Kishwaukee Mounds, Illinois, 1877. According to the Fifth Annual Report of the Bureau of Ethnology to the Secretary of the Smithsonian Institution 1883–1884, shortly following the discoveries in this bullet list, the Smithsonian team found ten more skeletons in mounds and burial sites in Wisconsin, Illinois, West Virginia, North Carolina, and Georgia. Not every one of them was measured for height, but each was documented as much larger than the skeletons of our current race; those that were measured ranged between seven to seven and a half feet long. Similarly, in the Twelfth Annual Report of the Bureau of Ethnology to the Secretary of the Smithsonian Institution 1894, two enormous skulls, several baffling femur bones, and seventeen full skeletons also measuring between seven to seven and a half feet long (one in East Dubuque, Illinois, measured almost eight feet) were unearthed in Illinois, Mississippi, Georgia, North Carolina, Tennessee, Ohio, Pennsylvania, and West Virginia. The West Virginia dig report contains an additional claim of "many large skeletons," generically. From these reports listed, more than forty thousand artifacts were found, including weapons, tools, jewelry, and various utensils that could not have feasibly been used by regular-sized humans." (Stephen Quayle & Dr.Thomas R. Horn, Unearthing the

Lost World of the Cloudeaters: Compelling Evidence of the Incursion of Giants, Their Extraordinary Technology, and Imminent Return, 4911-4937 (Kindle Edition); Defender Publishing)

[117]1 Enoch 15:8-12—My judgment for the giants is that since they are born from flesh they will be called evil spirits and will remain on the earth. 9 Because they were created from above, from the holy Watchers, at death their spirits will come forth from their bodies and dwell on the earth. They will be called evil spirits. 10 The heavenly spirits will dwell in heaven, but the terrestrial spirits who were born on earth will dwell on earth. 11 The evil spirits of the giants will be like clouds. They will afflict, corrupt, tempt, battle, work destruction on the earth, and do evil ; they will not eat nor drink, but be invisible . 12 They will rise up against the children of men and against the women, because they have proceeded from them.

Jubilees 10:1-6 (emphasis added, M.T.) -1. And in the third week of this jubilee the unclean demons began to lead astray the children of the sons of Noah; and to make to err and destroy them. 2. And the sons of Noah came to Noah their father, and they told him concerning the demons which were, leading astray and blinding and slaying his sons' sons. 3. And he prayed before the Lord his God, and said: God of the spirits of all flesh, who hast shown mercy unto me, And hast saved me and my sons from the waters of the flood, And hast not caused me to perish as Thou didst the sons of perdition; For Thy grace hath been great towards me, And great hath been Thy mercy to my soul; Let Thy grace be lift up upon my sons, And let not wicked spirits rule over them Lest they should destroy them from the earth. 4. But do Thou bless me and my sons, that we may increase and multiply and replenish the earth. 5. And Thou knowest how THY WATCHERS, THE FATHERS OF THESE SPIRITS, acted in my day: and as for these spirits which are living, imprison them and hold them fast in the place of condemnation, and let them not bring destruction on the sons of thy servant, my God; for these are malignant, and created in order to destroy. 6. And let them not rule over the spirits of the living; for Thou alone canst exercise dominion over them. And let

them not have power over the sons of the righteous from hence-
forth and for evermore."

[118] "The story of Nimrod in the book of Genesis may illustrate
how this could happen through genetic engineering or a retrovirus
of demonic design that integrates with a host's genome and re-
writes the living specimen's DNA, thus making it a "fit extension"
or host for infection by the entity. Note what Genesis 10: 8 says
about Nimrod: And Cush begat Nimrod: he began to be a mighty
one in the earth. Three sections in this unprecedented verse indicate something very peculiar happened to Nimrod. First, note
where the text says, "he began to be." In Hebrew, this is chalal,
which means "to become profaned, defiled, polluted, or desecrated
ritually, sexually or genetically." Second, this verse tells us exactly
what Nimrod began to be as he changed genetically—" a mighty
one" (gibbowr, gibborim), one of the offspring of Nephilim. As
Annette Yoshiko Reed says in the Cambridge University book,
Fallen Angels and the History of Judaism and Christianity, "The
Nephilim of Genesis 6: 4 are always… grouped together with the
gibborim as the progeny of the Watchers and human women." And
the third part of this text says the change to Nimrod started while
he was on "earth." Therefore, in modern language, this text could
accurately be translated to say: "And Nimrod began to change genetically, becoming a gibborim, the offspring of watchers on
earth." Bible commentator Adam Clarke seems to agree with Dr.
Horn's conclusions by quoting the Syraic Targum regarding Nimrod: "The Syriac calls him a warlike giant." Then Clarke continues
to share about Nimrod and the building of the Tower of Babel and
its connection to giants: On this point Bochart observes that these
things are taken from the Chaldeans, who preserve many remains
of ancient facts; and though they often add circumstances, yet they
are, in general, in some sort dependent on the text. 1. They say
Babel was built by the giants, because Nimrod, one of the builders,
is called in the Hebrew text גבור gibbor, a mighty man; or, as the
Septuagint, γιγας, a giant. 2. These giants, they say, sprang from
the earth, because, in Genesis 10: 11, it is said, He went,
מהארץההוא min haarets hahiv, out of that earth; but this is rather
spoken of Asshur, who was another of the Babel builders. 3. These
giants are said to have waged war with the gods, because it is said

of Nimrod, Genesis 10: 9, He was a mighty hunter before the Lord; or, as others have rendered it, a warrior and a rebel against the Lord. See Jarchi in loco. 4. These giants are said to have raised a tower up to heaven, as if they had intended to have ascended thither. Nimrod achieved something that only the Watchers of old had accomplished, yet he took it to a whole new level. In fact, no one has been able to reproduce this highly revered occult achievement. This cutting-edge breakthrough of Nimrod has been the goal of all secret societies, alchemists, wizards, sorcerers, warlocks, and Illuminati elite throughout the millennia. You see, he was a fully grown man who was able to become a gibborim (another type of Nephilim)—he was not born that way. It would appear that Nimrod took the arcane knowledge of his family line and pushed it beyond what the Watchers themselves could do: He was able to alter his DNA and become a Nephilim. This transmogrification must have thrilled the kingdom of darkness. The fallen angels of Genesis 6 required the use of women in their genetic breeding program. Nimrod accomplished this alchemical feat without the use of a woman's womb. This is important to note, because the Word of God in Daniel gives us a hint that the Antichrist will be able to reproduce the dark magic of Nimrod. Neither shall he regard the God of his fathers, nor the desire of women, nor regard any god: for he shall magnify himself above all. (Daniel 11: 37) Some have speculated that this refers to the Antichrist being a homosexual. Although it is true that most within the occult are bisexual (for use in ritual magic), I believe this is a prophetic clue linking the coming man of sin with Nimrod. This powerful working of dark magic and esoteric wisdom will be reproduced one more time in human history." (Michael Lake & Thomas Horn, The Shinar Directive: Preparing the Way for the Son of Perdition's Return, 1446-1482 (Kindle Edition); Crane, MO; Defender)

[119] "Jubilees 10.1-12 informs us that after the flood evil spirits began afflicting many of Noah's descendants. Noah prayed to God to bind all of the demons away from men. God bound nine-tenths of the demons, leaving only one-tenth to tempt and torment man. Revelation 9 tells that the other nine-tenths will be released during the Great Tribulation. If the angels are bound, and the Nephilim are disembodied spirits, where did the giants after the flood come

from? A third rebellion? No. The story continues: Genesis tells us that after the flood Noah divided the planet among his three sons. Ham was given what we call Africa and Shem, the middle east. Canaan, Ham's son, left his territory and ventured North along the Mediterranean Sea. Why did Canaan travel all the way up the cost to found Sidon, his first city, in an area he knew was not his territory, then quickly settle another city (Tyre)? The map at the right shows that those two locations are the closest he could get to mount an expedition to Mount Hermon. He wanted to find information about the pre-flood giants! And Canaan grew, and his father taught him writing, and he went to seek for himself a place where he might seize for himself a city. And he found a writing which former (generations) had carved on the rock, and he read what was thereon, and he transcribed it and sinned owing to it; for it contained the teaching of the Watchers in accordance with which they used to observe the omens of the sun and moon and stars in all the signs of heaven. And he wrote it down and said nothing regarding it; for he was afraid to speak to Noah about it lest he should be angry with him on account of it. Jubilees 8.1-5 After finding the writing containing the science of the Watchers, Canaan sought to create a race of warrior giants using the same type of genetic tampering which was done before the flood. This explains how the giants came to be, but with a few problems. Second Samuel 21: 20 describes giants with six fingers on each hand and six toes on each foot. Moses led the children of Israel into battle with Og, the king of Bashan, who being a true giant, stood at least twelve feet tall (Deuteronomy 3: 11). Bashan was anciently called the Land of the Giants. Og actually reigned from Mt. Hermon (Joshua 12: 4-5), the place where the angels descended. Even up to King David's time, Goliath remained (1 Samuel 17: 4). He was one-quarter giant and three-quarters Philistine and reached only nine feet, nine inches tall. Another race of giants were the Anakim (Numbers 13: 21-33). Some of the Amorites were as tall as a cedar tree (Amos 2: 9), probably referring to the sons of Anak. Other giant races found in the Old Testament included the Emim (Deuteronomy 2: 9-11), and the Zamzummim (Deuteronomy 2: 20-21). The Anakim, Emim, and the Zamzaummim were all equally tall. The valley of Hinnom was anciently called the Valley of Giants (Joshua 15: 8; 18: 16).

Joshua destroyed all the Anakim except for a giant that escaped to Gaza (Joshua 11: 21-22), the later home of Goliath. David's men killed Goliath's brother and one other son of the giant (2 Samuel 21: 20-21). In four hundred years time the giant out bred, so that Goliath and his brothers were only nine feet tall instead of thirteen feet tall. The Genesis 6 word for giants (Nephilim) occurs in only one other place: Numbers 13: 33. These same post-flood giants who are called Nephilim in Numbers, are referred to as Rephaim in Deuteronomy 2: 11 and Genesis 14: 5. These passages show that the post-flood giants were a special kind of Nephilim called Raphaim. This means they were not the procreation of another angelic rebellion, but a genetic tampering by man in a similar fashion as the angels did in the pre-flood world." (Ken Johnson, Ancient Book of Enoch, 182-184 (Kindle Edition)).

[120] "The Hebrew prophet Ezekiel made an important statement about "magic bands" (kesatot), which were cryptically used to dispel (magically eject) the souls of men in order to replace those spirits with resurrected ones from the dead (as in the Rephaim or dead Nephilim). Will ye hunt the souls of my people, and will ye save [Hebrew, chayah, "restore to life"] the souls alive that come unto you… to slay the souls that should not die, and to save [restore to life] the souls alive that should not live…? Wherefore thus saith the Lord God; Behold, I am against your [Kesatot, "magic bands" used for binding and loosing souls], wherewith ye there hunt the souls to make them fly [Parach, "to fly away," or alternatively "to sprout up from out of the ground"] and I will tear them from your arms, and will let the souls go, even the souls that ye hunt to make them fly (Ez[ekiel] 13: 18b–20). (emphasis added) The kesatot was a magic arm band used in connection with a container called the kiste. Wherever the kiste is inscribed on sarcophagi, it is depicted as a sacred vessel (a spirit prison?) with a snake peering through an open lid. How the magic worked and in what way a spirit was ejected and replaced with a spirit from the dead is a mystery (unless, again, modern occultists have these demonic incantations in their possession today). Pan, the half-man/ half-goat god that guarded the entrance to the "gates of hell" at the base of Mount Hermon—beyond which the Rephaim (dead Nephilim) were imprisoned—is sometimes pictured kicking the lid open and letting

the snake (spirit?) out. Such loose snakes were then depicted as being enslaved around the limbs and bound in the hair of the Bacchae women, the servants of the demonic god Dionysus. Whatever this imagery of Pan, the serpents, the imprisoned spirits, and the magic kesatot and kiste actually represented, a noteworthy verification of the magical properties represented by them is discussed in the scholarly book Scripture and Other Artifacts by Phillip King and Michael David: In the closing verses of Ezekiel 13 the prophet turns his attention to magic practices whose details remain obscure. Two key terms are kesatot and mispabot.... The kesatot are worn on the arms, while the mispabot are made "on the head of every height" (?), which has been understood to mean "on the heads of persons of every height" [including those of great height; giants, offspring of the Watchers].... In modern times archaeological discoveries and texts from Babylonia in particular have shed further light on what might be involved: G. A. Cooke cited Hellenistic figurines from Tell Sandahannah (Mareshah) in Palestine with wire twisted around their arms and ankles... and a magical text from Babylonia that speaks of white and black wool being bound to a person or to someone's bed.... J. Herrmann [notes] that both words can be related to Akkadian verbs, kasu and sapabu, which mean respectively "to bind" and "to loose." Herrmann also drew attention to texts in which these verbs were used in a specifically magical sense.... This indicates that, whatever the objects were, their function was to act as "binders" and "loosers" in a magical sense, in other words as means of attack and defense [of spirits] in sorcery. ". (Thomas R. Horn & Josh Peck, Abaddon Ascending: The Ancient Conspiracy at the Center of CERN'S Most Secretive Mission, 118-120 (Kindle Edition))

[121]" Many such Jewish and Christian apocalypses have been studied for millennia, but it was not until the first half of the nineteenth century that this literature was authoritatively identified as a distinct group of writings. 12 This advancement coincided with the discoveries of several ancient Jewish manuscripts and the publication of their critical editions, especially of 1 Enoch and the Ascension of Isaiah. The bulk of these and other works—including some that do not take the form of an apocalypse yet still can be described as apocalyptic because they share constitutive traits of

the genre13—were studied and made accessible in English around the turn of the twentieth century by British scholar R. H. Charles, who drew heavily on them in his own scholarship on Revelation. Charles maintained that these sources offer such valuable contextual insight for exegesis that "the New Testament Apocalypse cannot be understood apart from Jewish Apocalyptic literature." 14 In fact, Charles credited much of his newfound respect for the theological profundity of Revelation to his contextual studies. "The first ground for such a revolution in my attitude to the Book," Charles explained, "was due to an exhaustive study of Jewish Apocalyptic. The knowledge thereby acquired helped to solve many problems, which could only prove to be hopeless enigmas to scholars unacquainted with this literature." 15 Charles is not alone in his appreciation for this body of texts and its significance for unlocking Revelation. 16 In the decades that have followed, his contention has come to be shared by many others, including Bauckham, who remarks, "The tradition of apocalyptic literature is the living literary tradition to whose forms and content [John of Patmos] is most indebted."" (Ben C. Blackwell, John K. Goodrich, & Jason Maston, Reading Revelation in Context: John's Apocalypse and Second Temple Judaism 22-23 (Kindle Edition); Grand Rapids, Michigan; Zondervan Academic)

[122]Jasher 4:20-20 And all men who walked in the ways of the Lord, died in those days, before the Lord brought the evil upon man which he had declared, for this was from the Lord, that they should not see the evil which the Lord spoke of concerning the sons of men.

Jasher 5:5—And all who followed the Lord died in those days, before they saw the evil which God declared to do upon earth.

Jasher 5:21—And all the sons of men who knew the Lord, died in that year before the Lord brought evil upon them; for the Lord willed them to die, so as not to behold the evil that God would bring upon their brothers and relatives, as he had so declared to do.

[123]Unless otherwise noted, the following historical accounts are from: Henri Nissen (translated from Danish by Tracy Jay Skondin, Bruce Steuer, Dorthe Orbesen and Irene Kjaedegaard), Noah's

Ark-Ancient Accounts And New Discoveries; Copenhagen, Denmark; Scandinavia Publishing House)

[124] "Along with American composer George Gershwin, many people find it difficult to believe that Methuselah lived to be 969 years old. Nevertheless, the Bible teaches quite plainly that the early patriarchs often lived to be nearly 1,000 years old and even had children when they were several hundred years old! Similar claims of long life spans are found in the secular literature of several ancient cultures (including the Babylonians, Greeks, Romans, Indians, and Chinese). But even a life span of nearly 1,000 years is sadly abbreviated when we consider that God initially created us to live forever." (Dr. David Menton & Dr. Georgia Purdon, 'Did People Like Adam And Noah Really Live Over 900 Years Of Age?' in Ken Ham, *The New Answers Book 2; Over Thirty Questions On Creation/Evolution & The Bible,* 2812-2819 (Kindle Edition); Green Forest, AR; Master Books)

"The Sumerian King List is of interest to students of the Bible for at least two reasons: its mention of a major flood and the incredibly long reigns attributed to the kings. The brief mention of the flood in the Sumerian King List is reminiscent of the biblical flood story involving Noah (Genesis 6). Admittedly, the Sumerian King List gives no details of the flood, but the Sumerian flood, like the biblical flood, was viewed as an event of tremendous proportions, covering the land. The flood serves as a dividing line: the institution of kingship had to be reinstated after the flood, and kings are listed as being prior to the flood or after the flood...At most, one can say that the idea of a massive, ancient flood was widespread spread in antiquity...The other connection between the Sumerian King List and the Bible is the listing of the reigns of the kings, comparable to the genealogies in Genesis 5 and n. In both the Sumerian and biblical lists, approximately ten generations are listed prior to the flood. In both, the reigns or life spans are exceptionally long...In both traditions the time spans decline and generally are longer before the flood than after." (Clyde E. Fant & Mitchell D. Reddish, *Lost Treasures Of The Bible: Understanding The Bible Through Archaeological Artifacts In World Museums,*

490-502 (Kindle Edition); Grand Rapids, Michigan; William B. Eerdmans Publishing Company)

[125]"Because Noah and his family were the only human survivors of the Flood approximately 4,500 years ago, all people today are descended from them. This is consistent with population statistics. Indeed, starting with Noah's family and calculating the population growth using a generation span of 40 years and an average of 2.5 children per family, the present world population of more than six billion people would be obtained in those 4,500 years. Since the parameters used are conservative, this would allow for even more people to have lived and then died early in wars or of disease." (Andrew Snelling, 'The Geological Evidence For Creation' in John Ashton & Michael Westacott, *The Big Argument: Does God Exist? Twenty-Four Scholars Explore How Science, Archaeology And Philosophy Haven't Disproved God*, 2172-2179 (Kindle Edition); Green Forest, AR; Master Books)

"One of the strongest arguments for a young Earth comes from the field of human population statistics. According to historical records, the human population on Earth doubles approximately every 35 years. If you break down that figure, it represents an annual increase of 20,000 people per every million. Let's suppose that humankind started with just two individuals (we will call them Adam and Eve for the sake of our argument). And suppose that they lived on the Earth one million years ago (some evolutionists suggest that man, in one form or another, has been on the Earth 2-3 million years). Suppose, further, that an average generation was 42 years, and that each family had an average of 2.4 children. (They probably had many more than that, but we will use a conservative estimate that would allow for at least some population growth; if a family unit had only two children, there would be zero population growth, since each parent simply would replace himself or herself, providing no net increase.) Allowing for wars, famine, diseases, and other devastation, there would be approximately 1 x 10 5000 people on the Earth today! That number is a 1 followed by 5,000 zeroes. But the entire Universe (at an estimated size of 20 billion light- years in diameter) would hold only 1 x 10 100 people. Evolutionary time scales simply cannot account for the present, relatively small human population. However, using young- Earth figures (of eight people having survived the Noahic Flood), the current world population would be around 6-8 billion people. The question is—which of the two figures is almost right on target, and which could not possibly be correct?" (Eric Lyons & Kyle Butt, *The Dinosaur Delusion: Dismantling Evolution's Most Cherished Icon*, 1917-1927 (Kindle Edition); Montgomery, Alabama; Apologetics Press)

[126] "Sixteen thousand clay tablets from the third millennium B.C. were discovered at Ebla in modern Syria, beginning in 1974. Biovanni Pettinato dates them 2580–2450 B.C. and Paolo Matthiae suggests 2400–2250 B.C. Either period predates any other written material by hundreds of years. Apologetic Importance of the Tablets. The importance of the Ebla tablets is that they parallel and confirm early chapters of Genesis. Although clouded by subsequent political pressure and denials, the published reports in reputable journals offer several possible lines of support for the biblical record (see ARCHAEOLOGY, OLD TESTAMENT). Tablets reportedly contain names of the cities Ur, Sodom and Gomorrah, and such pagan gods mentioned in the Bible as Baal (see Ostling, 76–77). The Ebla tablets reportedly contain references to names found in the book of Genesis, including Adam, Eve, and Noah (Dahood, 55–56). Of great importance is discovery of the oldest known creation accounts outside the Bible. Ebla's version predates the Babylonian account by some 600 years. The creation tablet is strikingly close to that of Genesis, speaking of one being who created the heavens, moon, stars, and earth. Parallels show that the Bible contains the older, less embellished version of the story and transmits the facts without the corruption of the mythological renderings. The tablets report belief in creation from nothing, declaring: "Lord of heaven and earth: the earth was not, you created it, the light of day was not, you created it, the morning light you had not [yet] made exist" (Ebla Archives, 259). There are significant implications in the Ebla archives for Christian apologetics. They destroy the critical belief in the evolution of monotheism (see MONOTHEISM, PRIMITIVE) from supposed earlier polytheism and henotheism. This evolution of religion hypothesis has been popu-

lar from the time of Charles Darwin (1809–1882) and Julius Well-hausen (1844–1918). Now monotheism is known to be earlier. Also, the force of the Ebla evidence supports the view that the earliest chapters of Genesis are history, not mythology." (Norman Geisler, Baker Encyclopedia Of Christian Apologetics, 208 (Kindle Edition); Grand Rapids, Michigan; Baker Books)

[127]"In spite of its limitations and shortcomings, this book has attempted to present a true narrative representation of the discovery of Sodom, in a manner that reflects the true narrative representational nature of the source of the site's history, the Bible. The existence of a significant Middle Bronze Age city at Tall el- Hammam is now confirmed beyond any doubt. In terms of the biblical Sodom criteria, it's in the right place, at the right time, with all the right stuff." (Dr. Steven Collins & Dr. Latayne C. Scott, Discovering The City Of Sodom: The Fascinating True Account Of The Discovery Of The Old Testament's Most Infamous City, 3440-3442 (Kindle Edition); Nashville, TN; Howard Books)

"Collins has identified Sodom's location as Tall el-Hammam, which is situated on the eastern edge of the Jordan disk, eight miles northeast of the mouth of the Jordan (hayarden). It is the largest tell in the southern Levant, measuring 1,000 meters long and containing within its walls 85 acres, a much smaller area than the general occupational spread beyond the walls of 240 acres....After eight seasons of excavation at the site, Collins has discovered several key indicators that confirm the city as Sodom. First, an abrupt occupational gap of several centuries immediately after the Middle Bronze Age II (1800-1550 BC) offers a perfect fit for the timing of the destruction of Sodom....Second, Tall el-Hammam contains a massive destruction and ash layer (one meter thick in some areas) distributed at various locations of the Middle Bronze Age layer of the city. The site reveals extensive destruction by fire of architectural features such as roofs, dwellings, walls, fortification barriers, as well as personal items such as jewelry, tools, and pottery. In addition to these, one of the most sobering and striking features involves human remains that depict catastrophic destruction. It appears that many of the inhabitants' bones are charred and distorted, like those pictured, and are situated in a way that indicates a violent high-heat heat flash event that may have thrown inhabitants to the western side of their dwellings, showing that the destruction could have originated from the east....Third, in addition to the architectural destruction, distorted human remains, and pottery environmental analysis of the site has revealed high-heat indicators that are consistent with the biblical description of Sodom's fiery destruction. For example, one sample of Middle Bronze Age pottery had its surface transformed into glass. After visual and scientific testing of the shard, its transformation could only be explained by an extreme high-heat flash event; only a temperature of thousands of degrees Fahrenheit (much hotter than kilns of that day could heat pottery) could achieve such a process. Related to this, samples of area soil and sand have been examined. These samples give evidence of a high-heat event that was hot enough to turn desert sand into "desert glass," a phenomenon more associated with lightning, airbursts, or atomic explosions in the deserts of New Mexico than the once fertile tile Jordan River valley....In support of these archaeological finds are the many geographical reasons why Tall el-Hammam fits the biblical account of Sodom. As mentioned, Dr. Steven Collins has compiled a massive assortment of geographical data, some of which is adapted in the chart below." (Joseph M. Holden & Geisler, The Popular Handbook Of Archaeology And The Bible: Discoveries That Confirm The Reliability Of Scripture, 2473-2515 (Kindle Edition); Eugene, Oregon; Harvest House Publishers)

[128] This is seen especially in God's command in Genesis 1:1:28 for mankind to "subdue the earth." Henry Morris points out:

"The command to "subdue the earth," although couched in military terminology, should be understood to mean bringing all earth's systems and processes into a state of optimum productivity and utility, offering the greatest glory to God and benefit to mankind. Thus, the primeval commission authorizes—in fact, commands—those human enterprises that we now denote as science and technology, or research and development. First we are to learn to understand the full nature of earth's processes, and then we are to organize them in useful and beautiful systems and products."

(Henry M. Morris, The Biblical Basis for Modern Science - A Biblical Defense of Creation Science, 482-486 (Kindle Edition); Green Forest, AR; Master Books)

[129]"In previous years, textbooks correctly taught students the Law of Biogenesis: that life comes only from other life. This law of science was established after empirical evidence demonstrated that life cannot spontaneously arise from non-life in nature. This is not a theory or hypothesis, but rather, a scientific law that has never been observed to be incorrect. Current textbooks however, have dropped the Law of Biogenesis in favor of abiogenesis—a theory that teaches students the possibility that life can arise from non-life under "suitable circumstances." Do we have any scientific data to back up this new theory of abiogensis? Absolutely not—but at least it doesn't contradict the evolutionary theory. Have we lost the ability to reason? How logical is it to replace a scientific law with an unproven theory?" (Brad Harrub Ph.D, Convicted: A Scientist Examines the Evidence for Christianity, 3723-3732 (Kindle Edition); Brentwood, TN: Focus Press)

[130]"The writer became interested in the passage quoted above in connection with experimental research he and his assistants have conducted on the effects of drugs and toxins on living plant protoplasm...The material examined was serum obtained from blood specimens drawn from 'come-back' patients of the Lying-In Department of the Women's Clinic, John Hopkins Hospital. In this clinic, as a routine procedure, every maternity case is required to return for a complete examination six weeks after the birth of the child. The author endeavored to obtain specimens from as many of such 'come-back' patients in good health as possible. A total number of 223 blood specimens from as many patients were examined...What is of greater interest in the present connection is the fact that there was a distinct difference in the toxicity of puerperal blood specimens obtained from six weeks after delivery in respect to sex of the offspring. The average of all readings obtained from blood specimens procured after female births revealed that these were more toxic than those obtained after male births. These results are not altogether surprising. It is quite possible that blood obtained after childbirth may show differences dependent on the

sex of the offspring. Within the last few years it has been demonstrated by the Russian investigator Manoiloff, and by others repeating and extending his work, that certain chemical differences between the blood of male and female animals and, indeed, between the extracts of male and female plants, can be detected by suitable methods. It is therefore possible that blood obtained from women who have given birth to male children may show chemical and biological differences from blood obtained from mothers bearing female offspring. The present findings certainly speak in favor of such a view and throw an interesting light on the Biblical passage which is the subject of the present paper. It seems entirely possible that observation of the relative danger involved for the male in the resumption of intercourse, danger inherent in the relative toxicity of the post-puerperal blood conditions in the female, is responsible for the distinction between the duration of a woman's impurity after the birth of male and female children. Moreover, it is interesting to note that this scientific basis for the Biblical distinction between the two sexes after childbirth is in complete agreement with the most orthodox Hebrew commentators on the Bible." (David I. Macho, 'A Scientific Appreciation Of Leviticus 12:1-5,' in *The Journal Of Biblical Literature* (Volume 52; Number 4—December, 1933); 2-9).

[131]"When a woman had a male child she was excluded from the sanctuary for 33 days and for a female child 66 days. Was this an arbitrary ruling by God? Before we get into that, let's look at childbirth in general. Back in the days the Torah was written, infant mortality rates were much higher than they are today (and they still remain high in some parts of the world). The mother's immune system is depressed at childbirth from the stress of the birth and hormonal changes, and needs some time to recover and build up immunity. The last thing she needs is to go into an environment where they are slaughtering animals and there is a buildup of infectious organisms. The baby's immune system is also suppressed. The reason for this is that babies are born with more or less sterile intestinal tracts. Growing the correct intestinal flora is critical for proper digestion, immune function, etc. A short list of what the gut flora accomplishes is as follows: Help kill harmful microbes that get into your intestine through eating contaminated food. Stimulate

lymphoid tissue to make antibodies to pathogens. Decrease allergies by increasing oral tolerance to certain foods. Help in the synthesis of certain B vitamins, as well as magnesium, calcium and iron. Help regulate body weight and prevent obesity. Metabolize ingested carcinogens. Increases the body's absorption of water. Helps proper carbohydrate digestion and fermentation. If the baby's immune system was very active it would attack the colonizing intestinal bacteria and the baby would not colonize the right microbes that are fostered by nursing. It takes approximately 5-6 weeks for this process to occur. This discovery has only been solidified in science since 2013. God knew way before that and protected mother and baby by keeping them isolated. But why do they stay away for twice as long if they have a female child? Since 1979, scientists have been aware of a phenomena called fetomaternal microchimerism. What this term means is that after childbirth they still find some Y chromosomes (females have two X chromosomes while males have an X and a Y) still in the mother. Some theories suggest that the mother's body treats them as a foreign invader and ramps up the immune system to try to deal with them. That being the case, a mother's immunity will recover quicker if she has a male child, as opposed to having a female child, and she can return to normal functions sooner without putting her or her baby's health at risk. God thus protects the mother with this commandment by giving her the correct amount of time to "recover"." (Dr. Michael Lebowitz, God's Preventative Medicine: New Scientific Discoveries Validate Biblical Instructions, 108-109 (Kindle Edition); MZBooks)

[132]"This prescription comes from the famous Ebers Papyrus, a medical book from 1500 B.C. Of course this treatment was useless and dangerous. But if the pinkeye did not get better fast, the poor woman probably had to explain herself. The Ebers Papyrus gives us a picture of medicine in ancient Egypt, that day's most advanced civilization. To cure baldness, doctors applied "a mixture of six fats... [from] the horse, the hippopotamus, the crocodile, the cat, the snake, and the [wild goat]." 1 All that grease grew few hairs, but at least it shined the hairless dome. The Ebers Papyrus lists hundreds of prescriptions, with an amazing array of ingredients: statue dust, beetle shells, mouse tails, cat hair, pig eyes, dog toes,

breast milk, human semen, eel eyes, and goose guts. The best one can say about these medications is that at least they were "100 percent natural." Good and Laudable Pus To splinters, the ancient Egyptian doctors applied a salve of worm blood and donkey dung. Since dung is loaded with tetanus spores, a simple splinter often resulted in a gruesome death from lockjaw. Until the late 1800s, however, most doctors thought pus promoted healing. Thus doctors infected wounds to get them to produce pus. They agreed with the Ebers Papyrus: "It is good for a wound to rot a little.... Therefore, put something in the wound that will [make it produce pus]." 2 A modern doctor comments on the Ebers Papyrus: [This is] the first known statement of the dirtiest, messiest, most pernicious, and most persistent mistake in the history of surgery: getting the badness out of a wound.... It has been among the catchiest concepts in the history of medicine.... Rivers of pus flowed for another 3,500 years, and the dreadful doctrine of good and laudable pus... has only recently faded. 3 In the ancient world, well-meaning doctors killed millions by deliberately infecting their wounds." (S. I. MD McMillen, David E. MD Stern, None of These Diseases: The Bible's Health Secrets for the 21st Century, 202-219 (Kindle Edition); Grand Rapids, MI; Revel a division of Baker Publishing Group)

[133]"A mixture of animal fats and ashes sounds neither clean nor pleasant, but that is how soap was made for most of human history. clay cylinders dating from about 2800 B.C., discovered during excavations in Babylon, contain a soapy substance, and the writing on the cylinders confirms that fat and ashes were boiled together to produce it. What actually got washed with soap is less clear. The Egyptians, whose soap contained milder vegetable oils as well as animal fats, used it for washing their bodies. The Greeks and Romans did not: they preferred coating themselves with sand and oil and scraping it off with a strigil. Although soap, probably made with olive oil, was a regular part of the turkish bath, or hamam, that aspect of washing did not travel to europe when the bath returned in the middle ages. Europeans were still boiling animal fats and ashes together to make a soap that was used to wash clothes and floors but was too harsh for bodies. Toilet soap, made from olive oil, was manufactured in small batches in pioneering soap

businesses in Marseilles, Italy and Spain (where the soap made in Castile was so prized that eventually all fine white soap made with olive oil was called Castile soap), but it was a luxury and beyond the budgets of most people in the Middle Ages. They made do with plain water, to which they sometimes added herbs believed to have cleansing or medicinal qualities." (Katherine Ashenburg, The Dirt on Clean: An Unsanitized History 32 (Kindle Edition); New York, N.Y.; North Point Press)